PART ONE

YOU CAN SKETCH & DRAW IN COLOR

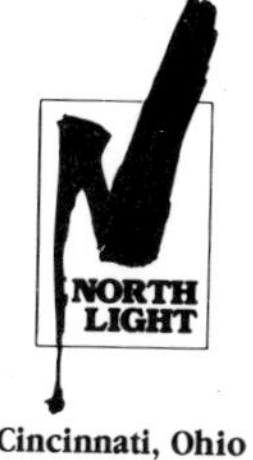

Cincinnati, Ohio

CONTENTS

HOW TO USE THIS BOOK

Here are step-by-step demonstrations of a range of subjects in different drawing media, designed specially to show you how to draw from a wide range of subjects. To get the most out of these exercises, study each one first and then either re-draw it yourself or, using the same medium, apply the techniques to your own subject.

Copying. Don't be concerned about the fact that you are copying these exercises — many famous artists have used other artists' ideas and techniques to develop their own unique style. And copying the exercises will make learning the techniques easier for you as you won't have to worry about finding a subject, composition or design.

Stay loose. It is best to attack each subject vigorously, and aim to make a strong drawing. Don't worry about making mistakes along the way — the more you practise and experiment, the quicker and more dramatic will be your improvement in drawing.

Experiment. By working boldly and taking risks with lines, colour, shapes and values, you will avoid the risk of your pictures looking tight and overworked. When you are making broad, generous strokes, don't hold your pencil or brush too near the point or your lines will look tentative. Only when working on detail should you hold the pen or pencil close to the point — and keep your details to a minimum when beginning a drawing. Usually they are best left for the finishing touches.

Keep it simple. Select simple subjects and compositions to start with. If you are using colour, restrict it to a limited range.Take care not to overwork and smudge the colours, especially if you are using a soft medium such as pastel or charcoal.

If you observe these basic points, you will quickly produce surprisingly good pictures and then you can really start to experiment with bolder compositions, more vibrant or subtle colour schemes, and develop your unique drawing style. *Happy painting*!

A QUINTET BOOK

First published in North America by
North Light, an imprint of Writer's Digest Books
9933 Alliance Road
Cincinnati, Ohio 45242

ISBN 0 89134 138 2

This book was designed and produced by
Quintet Publishing Limited
6 Blundell Street, London N7

Typeset in Great Britain by
Facsimile Graphics Limited, Essex
Colour origination in Hong Kong
Printed in Hong Kong by Leefung-Asco
Printers Limited

DRAWING MATERIALS

To many the word 'drawing' suggests a work executed in pencil, but a great variety of tools has always been available and the selection is increasing all the time. Today you have a very wide range of materials to choose from. The pencil (from the Latin word pecillus meaning 'little tail') is the most common instrument used for drawing, but coloured pencils, charcoal, pen and ink, rapidograph and felt nibs are all popular alternatives. As you gain expertise and experience, the materials you choose will vary according to your personal style and the nature of the subject.

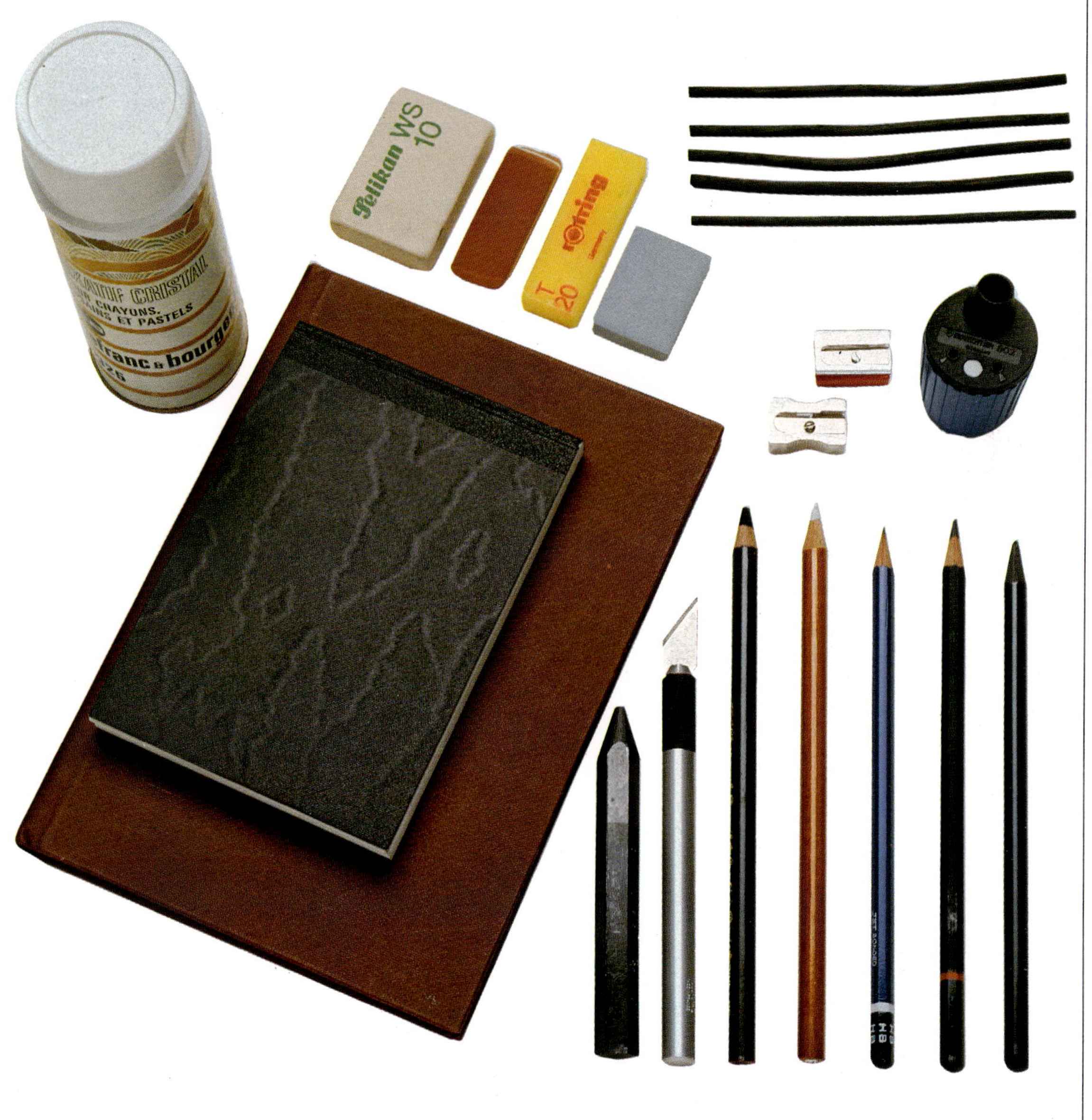

CHARCOAL AND PENCIL

The traditional pencil is a comparatively new medium in the long history of graphic art, and it was not until 1662 that the first graphite pencil was made. Graphite was discovered in Bavaria in 1400, but its potential for the artist was unexploited until 1504 when pure graphite was found at Borrowdale in England. At first the deposit was thought to be lead and pencils are still sometimes referred to as 'lead' pencils. Until the development of the graphite pencil most sketching and preliminary designs for painting were carried out with a charcoal, or with silverpoint, a silver stylus which required a special ground.

Drawing pencils come in 15 degrees of hardness. The hardest range are the H pencils: 8H is the hardest, H the least hard. F pencils are hard-medium, and HB soft-medium. The softer pencils are the Bs. B is the least soft and 7B the softest. Most artists use pencils that fall somewhere in the range 6H–6B. HB pencils are the most popular pencils for everyday use. Soft pencils have thicker leads than hard pencils, and should be sharpened with a knife or sandpaper rather than a sharpener.

Nowadays refillable pencils are available. The plastic or metal containers hold the lead rods which come in all the degrees of hardness. Replacement leads can be bought separately.

For bolder work, charcoal is still one of the most popular drawing materials. It has a long and distinguished history, and was used by prehistoric cave artists. Charcoal is a carbonized wood made from the peeled twigs of lime and willow trees. The twigs are burned in an oxygen-starved atmosphere until they are completely black and carbonized, but not burnt.

For the artist, charcoal provides a subtle range of tones, including a deep, intense black and it can also be used successfully for drawing in line and tone. It can be a rather messy material to work with and dusts off easily. The best results are achieved on textured paper — charcoal slides over smooth surfaces. All work drawings done in charcoal should be sprayed with fixative to prevent smudging and to preserve the image.

Conté crayons in black, red or sepia are an alternative to charcoal. Made in different grades from medium to extra soft, they lack the crisp freshness of charcoal but they do not dust off and adhere to most types of paper.

Charcoal **(below)**. *Compressed charcoal pencils are available in soft, medium and hard grades. Charcoal sticks can be bought in various widths — thick, medium and thin. Powder charcoal is used to produce areas of tone.*

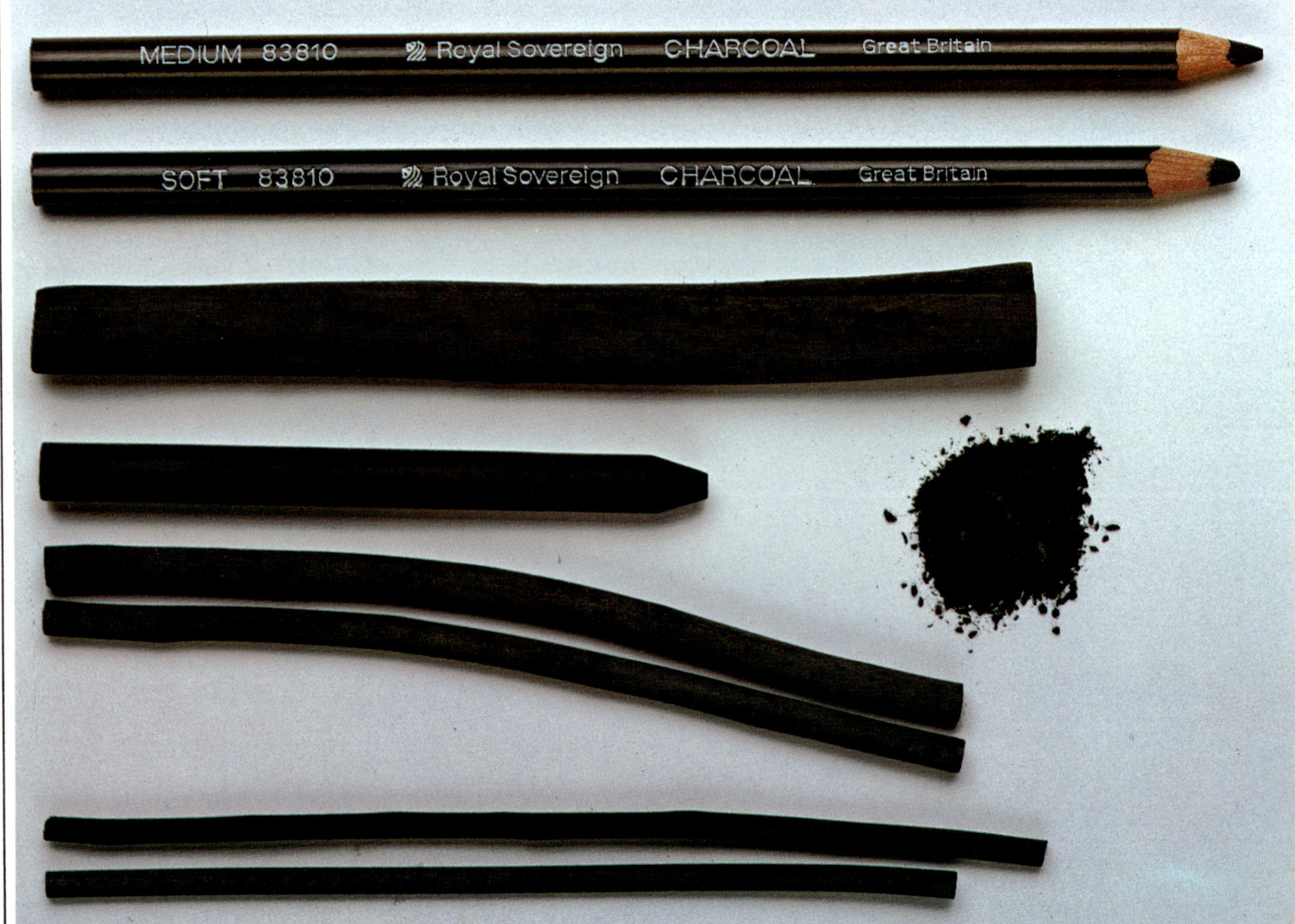

Pencils (right). *The range of drawing pencils available to the artist includes the common lead, or graphite, pencils. These range from 7B, the softest, through 6B, 5B, 4B, 3B, 2B, B, H, 2H, 3H, 4H, 5H, 6H, 7H, and 8H, the hardest. Other possibilities are propelling pencils, wax pencils for drawing on acetate, and several series of coloured pencils.*

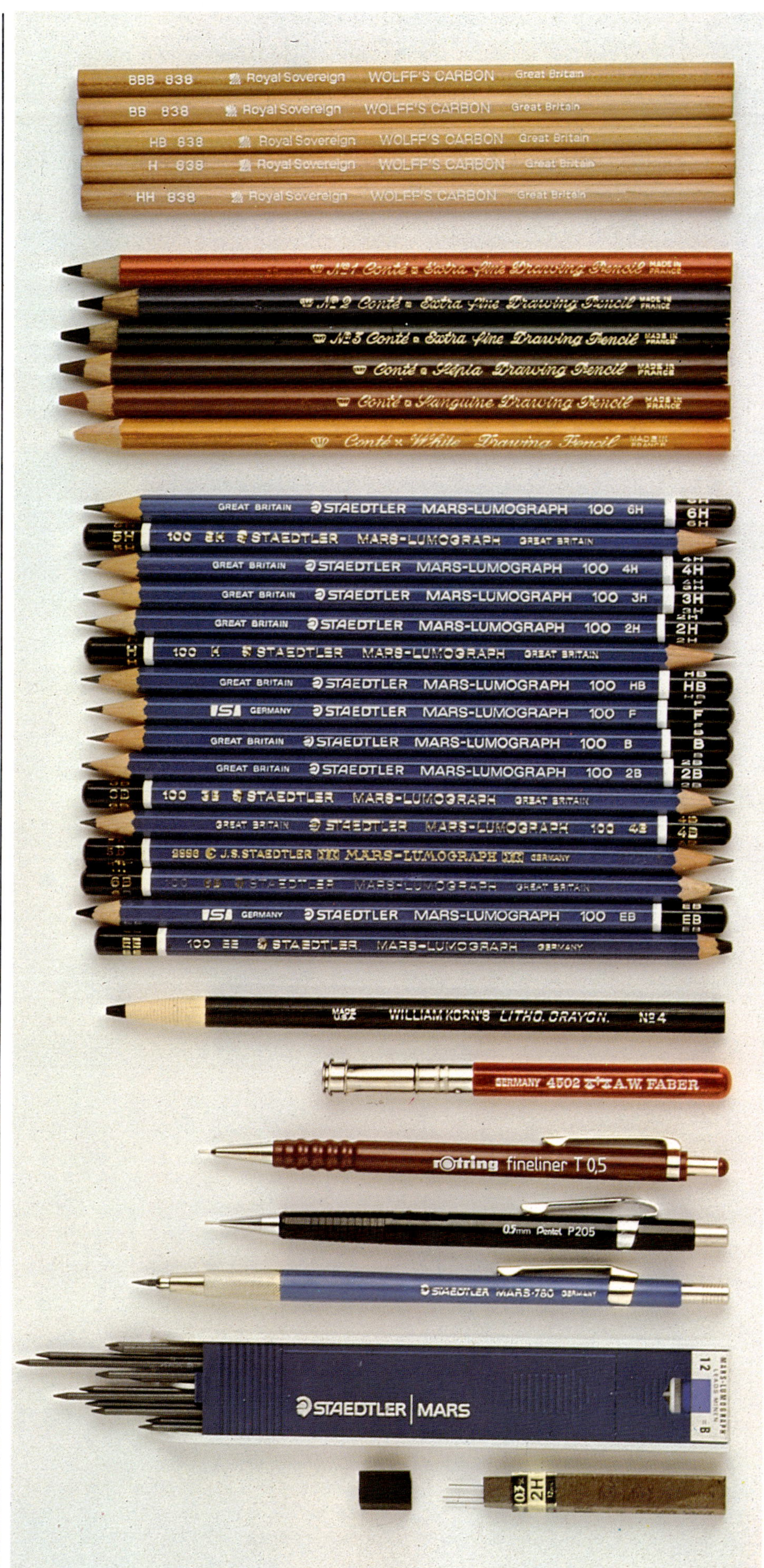

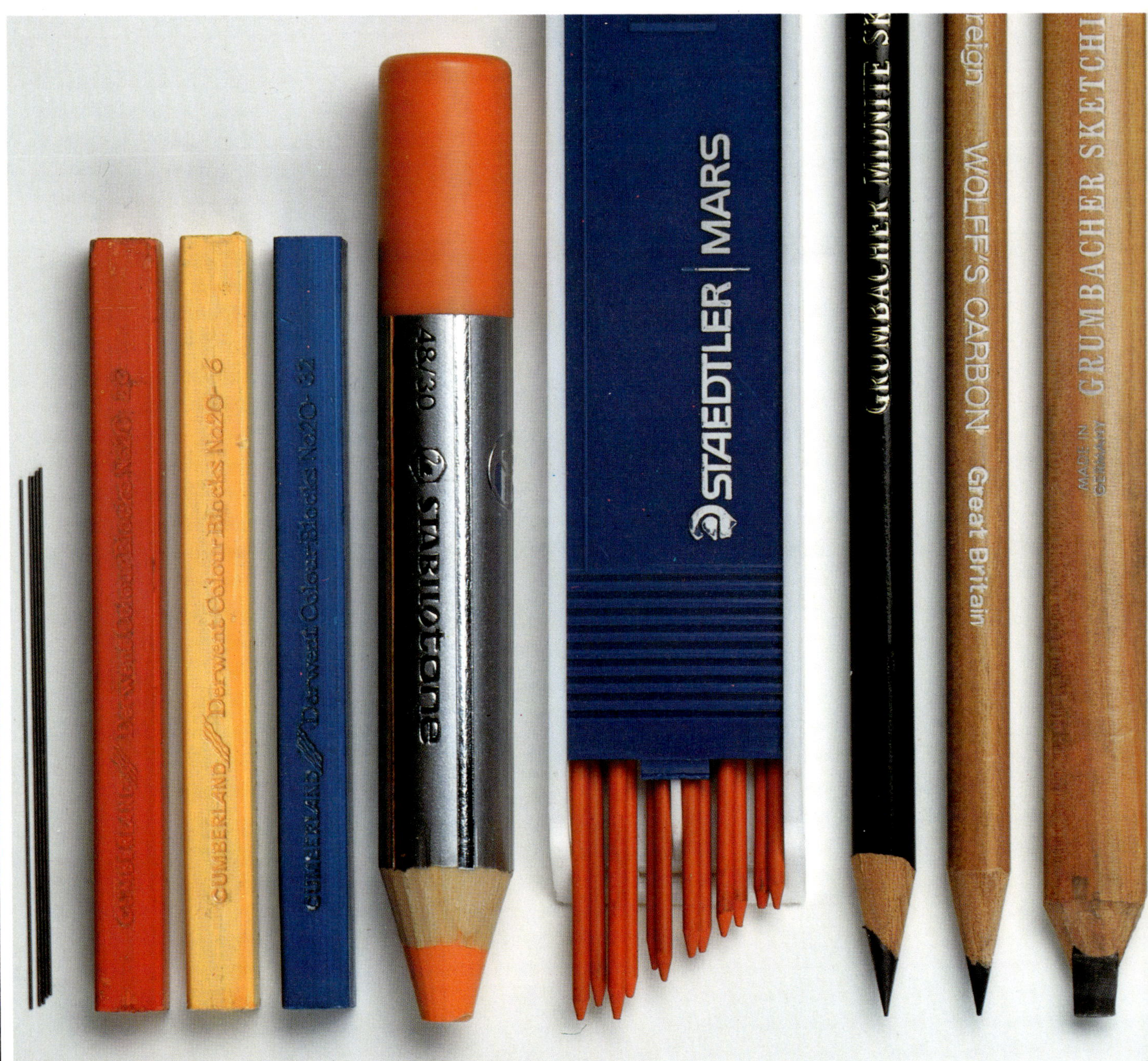

Coloured Pencils **(above)**. *The wide range of pencils available to the artist includes* **(from left to right)** *propelling pencil lead, three Derwent colour blocks, Stabilotone wax pencil, clutch pencil leads, Grumbacher midnight sketching pencil, Wolff carbon pencil, Grumbacher flat sketching pencil, 3 Derwent colour pencils, 3 Caran d'Ache Prismal pencils, 3 Carb Othello coloured pencils, All-Stabilo, K and E Audiovisual Projection and Staedtler Mars Omnichrom pencils for film.*

COLOURED PENCILS

The vast range of coloured pencils now available offers exciting prospects to the modern draughtsman. Not only has the range of colours increased, but manufacturing methods have also been developed to provide products which offer a wide choice of texture and finish. Traditionally, coloured pencils have been popular for making quick sketches and preliminary colour sketches for paintings, but modern artists are increasingly using coloured pencils and felt nib pens in their own right — often to add touches of local colour to an otherwise monochromatic drawing.

Some types of coloured pencil have special properties and can be exploited in different ways. Several brands have leads which are water-soluble, thus allowing you to create areas of flat wash-like colour by simply spreading the pencil marks with clean water. This simple technique

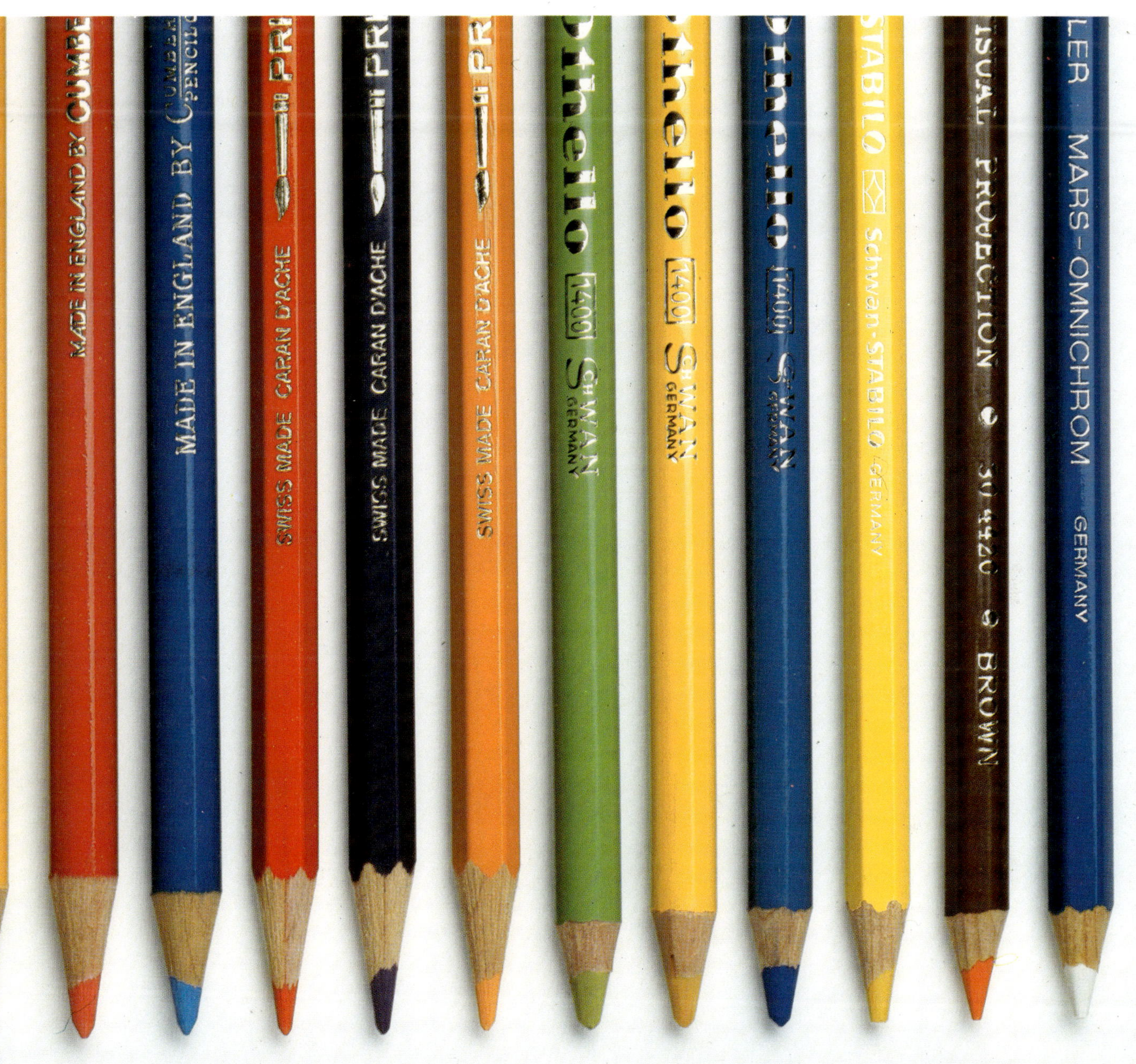

combines the qualities of water colour painting with the delicate, linear effects of coloured pencil. Coloured pencils are easier to control than water colour paint and for this reason may be particularly useful for the artist who prefers to use line but occasionally likes to introduce areas of wash and flat colour effects.

Felt-nib pens — the 'modern' coloured pencils — consist of either water or spirit-based colours soaked into strips of felt or other synthetic material. They are particularly popular in the field of illustration and graphic design where their strong colours and highly contrasting tones make them particularly suitable for print reproduction.

Although some painters feel this very brashness and commercial association makes felt nib pens unsuitable for fine art work, the medium is well worth investigating for its directness and dramatic potential. It is, however, difficult to create subtle colours and finely modulated tonal effects with felt nib pens and the medium should be reserved for bold, colourful effects.

NUDE IN A SUN HAT

Raw graphite can be bought in powder as well as the more familiar stick form. Used in the powdered state graphite can produce drawings with the soft, grey effects of lead pencil but, in place of the typical linear quality of pencil, you can produce a soft impressionistic effect.

In this drawing the spontaneous qualities of the powder allow the artist to work quickly, describing the basic tones and shapes of the subject, using the fingers to render the contours of the figure with strong directional strokes which both follow and shape the form. It is this particular aspect of the medium, drawing in tone rather than line, which gives graphite powder its unique softness and subtlety. However, pure graphite powder has a slippery quality and because it is so easily applied to the surface the artist must avoid losing control of the drawing. But if mistakes are made they can easily be rubbed out with a rag and turpentine. Because it can be a messy substance to work with, tip a small quantity of powder into a bowl before you start work.

When used with turpentine a range of tones can be created from very pale greys to bold and intense blacks. Coupled with the use of a clean pencil line, the tones of the graphite will lend a soft atmospheric mood regardless of subject matter. Use pencil with the graphite to strengthen the shadows and contours — rubbing harder will darken the tones.

Use a heavyweight cartridge paper or some highly textured support which will allow the powder to grip. Highlighted areas can be achieved by allowing the white of the paper to show through. Alternatively, the graphite can quite easily be rubbed off with a soft eraser.

Graphite dust is rubbed into the paper with the fingers to give a dense black surface and gradated grey tones. Using graphite dust can be quite messy, so shake a little into a small container before starting work. Start by rubbing a small amount of dust into the paper with your fingers to suggest the darker tones on the subject; mask the drawing with paper to get a straight edge **(below left)**. *Establish the main shadows with the graphite dust* **(below)**, *before drawing the outlines with a soft pencil* **(bottom).**

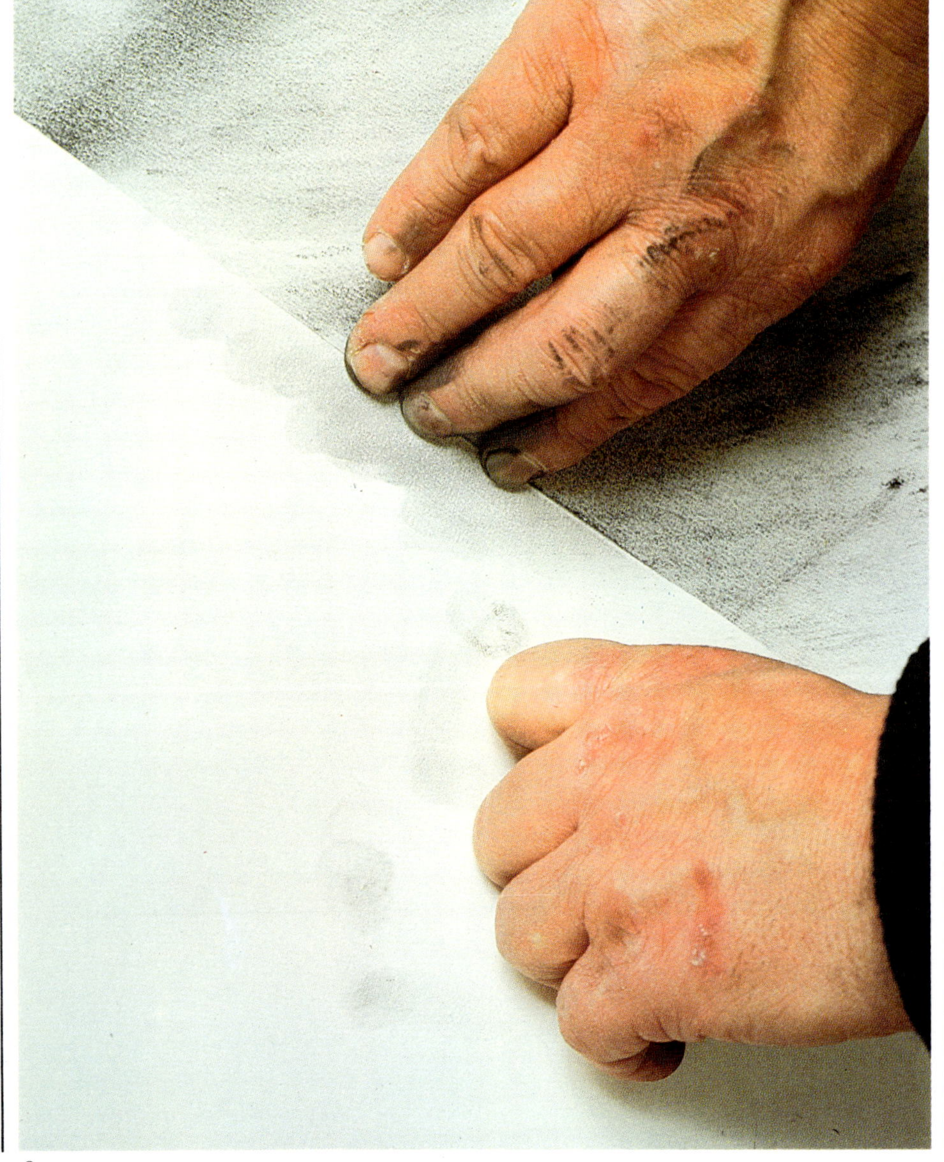

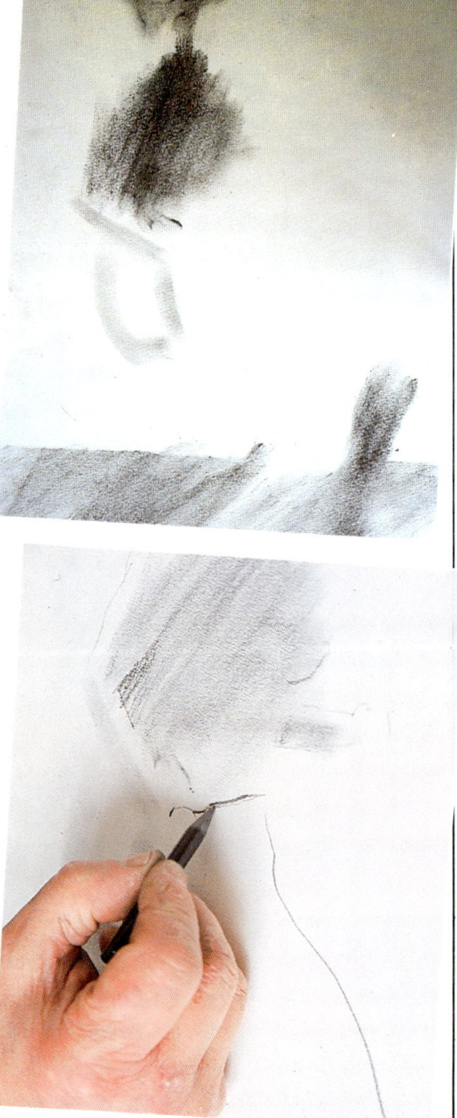

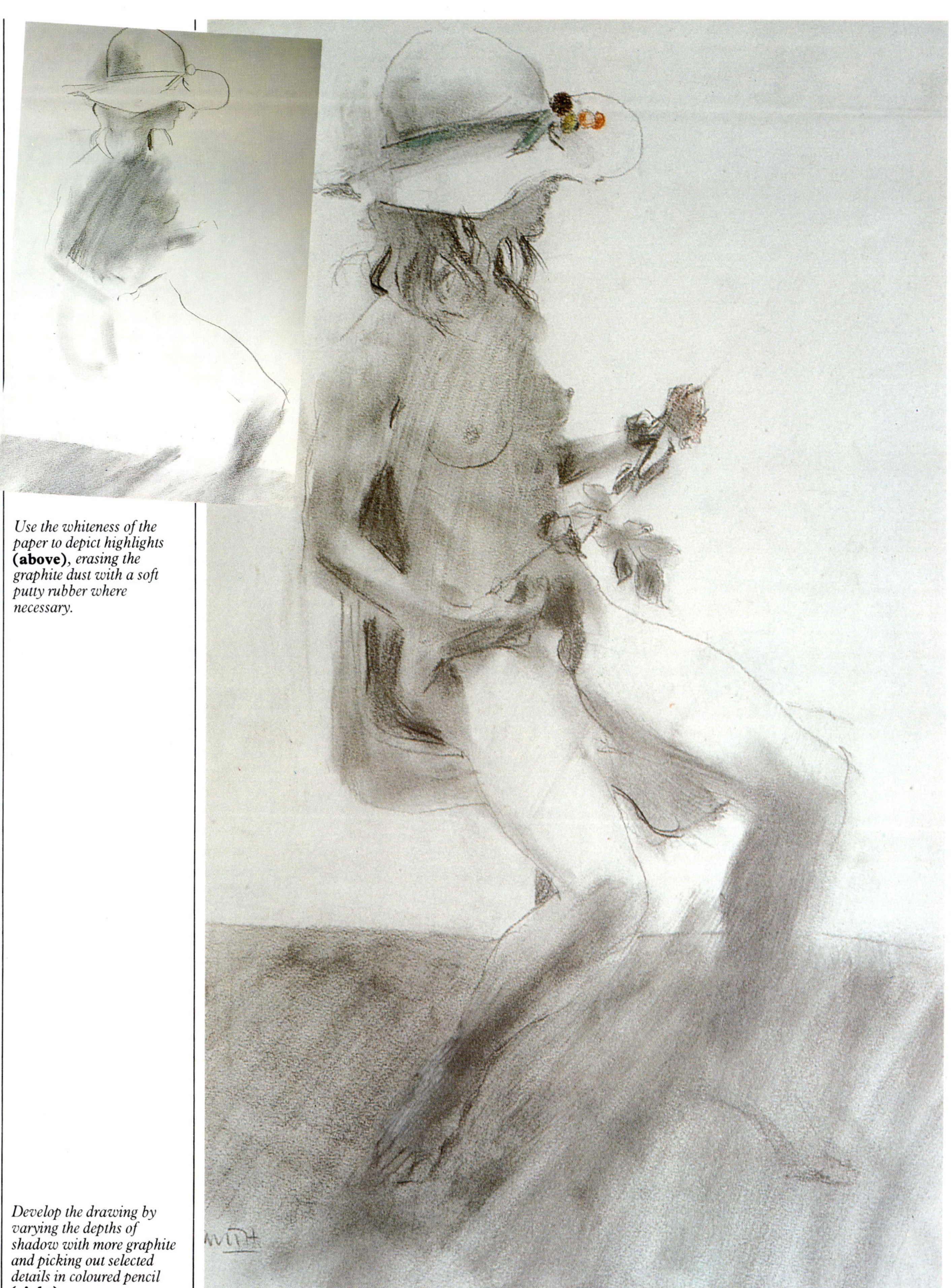

Use the whiteness of the paper to depict highlights **(above)**, *erasing the graphite dust with a soft putty rubber where necessary.*

Develop the drawing by varying the depths of shadow with more graphite and picking out selected details in coloured pencil **(right)**.

THISTLE

Pen and ink is especially suitable for tight, detailed work and densely cross-hatched

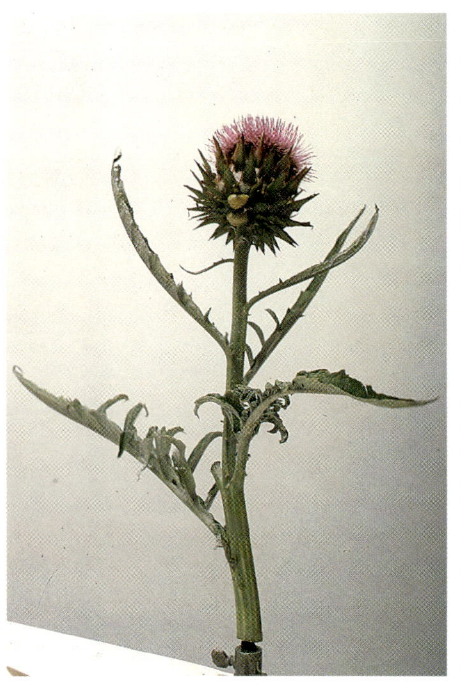

drawing — although it can also be used for loose informal work. When 'mistakes' such as running and smudging are incorporated into the technique a pen and ink drawing can become very exciting.

In this drawing the artist has taken full advantage of the unexpected without losing the strength of the drawing or the character of the subject. Little attempt has been made to control the line of the pen — something many artists struggle to achieve — but, instead, the artist has let the nib catch and jump across the page without interference.

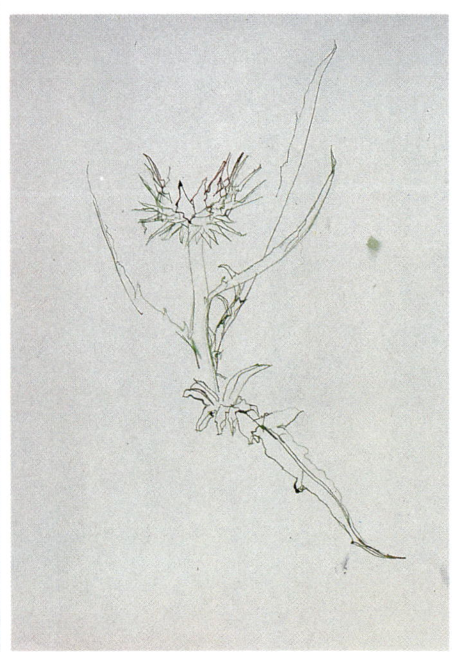

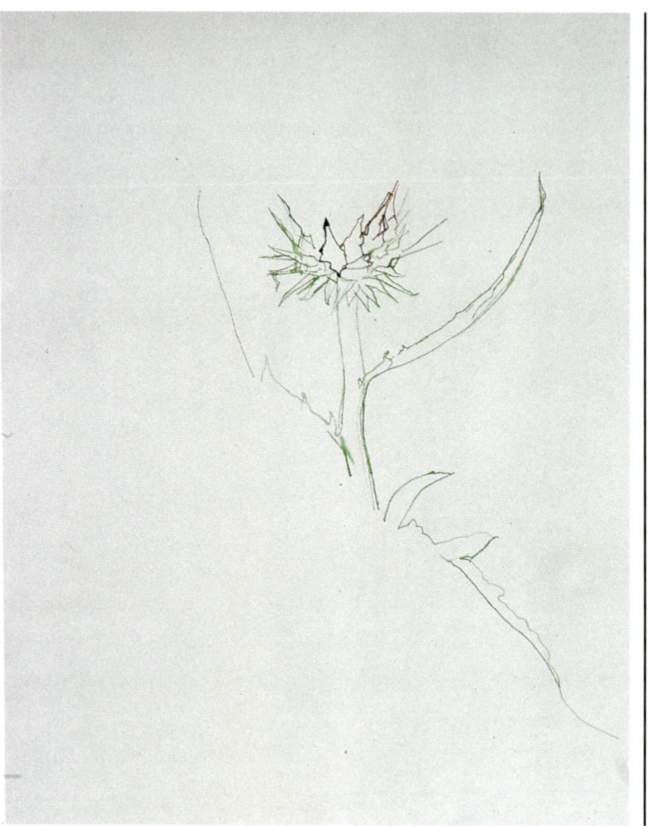

Use pen and ink to capture the jagged detail and spidery quality of the thistle **(far left)**. *Dilute the colour by dipping the pen in water and then into green ink. Start to draw the general outline of the subject* **(left)**. *Move down the thistle with green ink, holding the pen lightly to create a rough outline* **(bottom left)**. *Repeat this with red, black and blue ink for the remainder of the outline. Do not attempt to create a tightly controlled drawing, but let the pen drag loosely across the paper. Vary the thickness of the line by turning the pen on its side and pulling it across the surface* **(below)**.

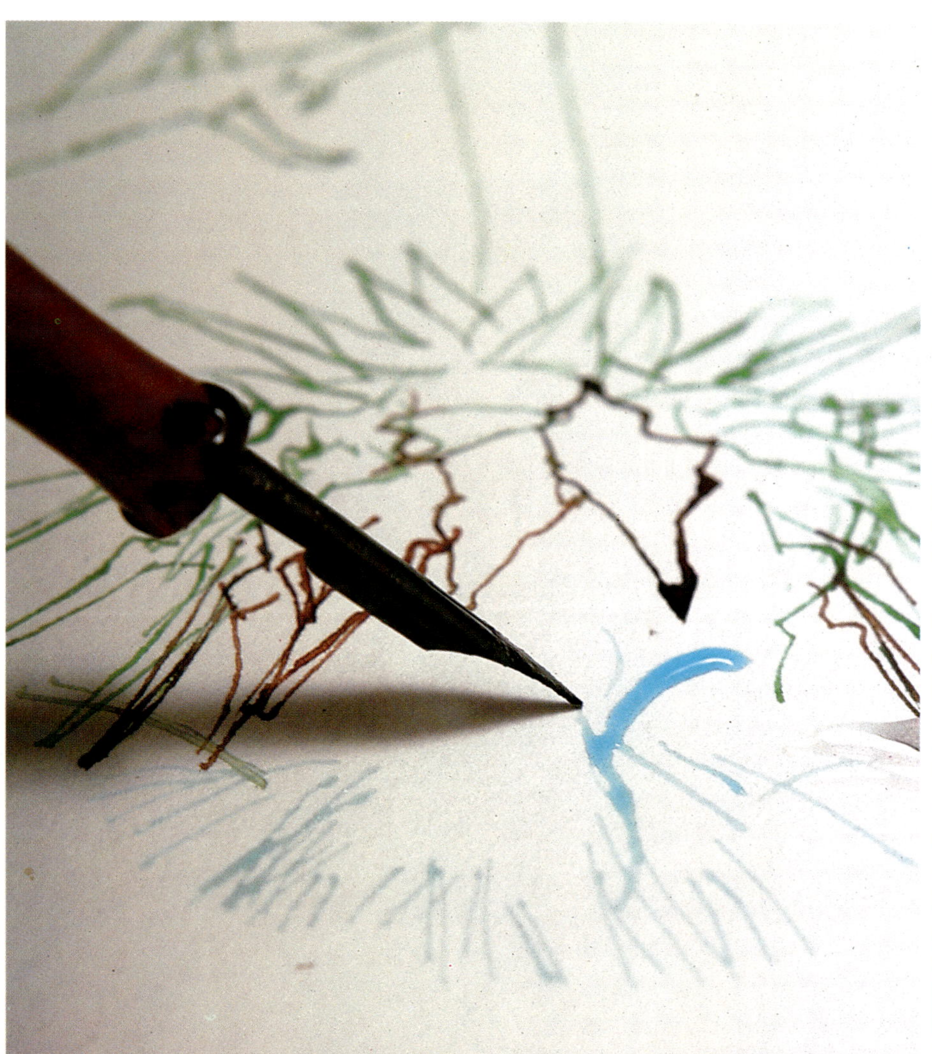

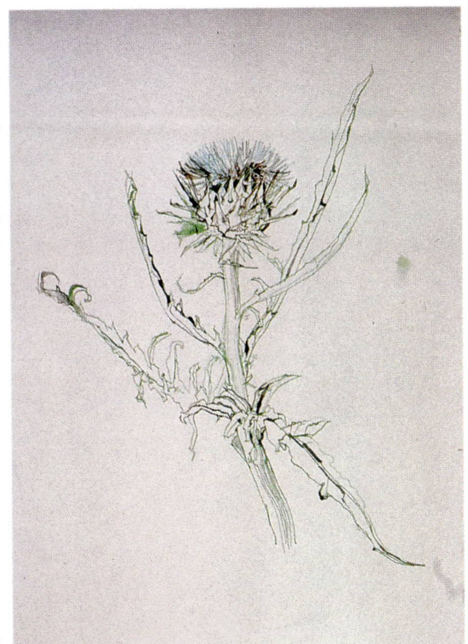

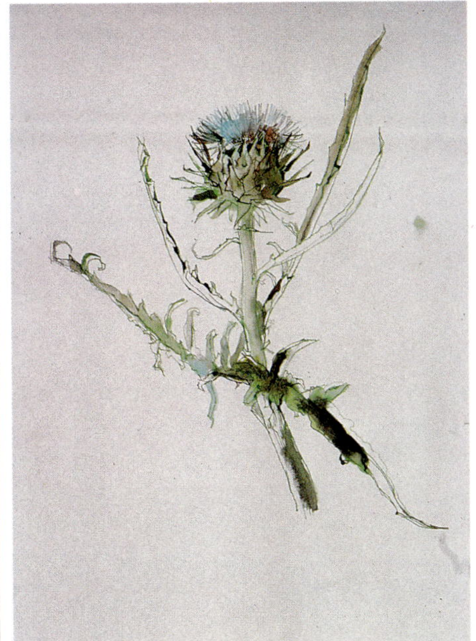

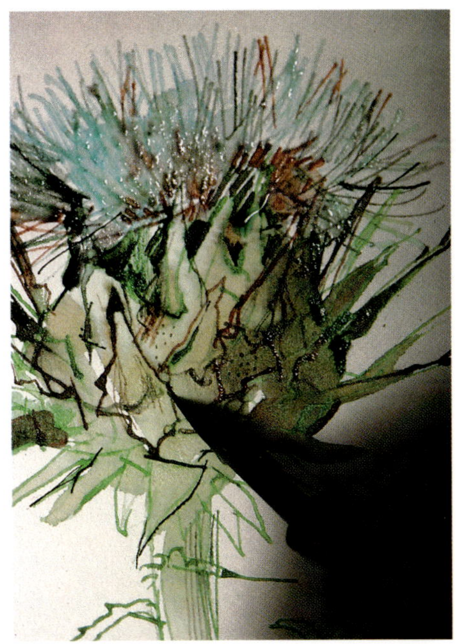

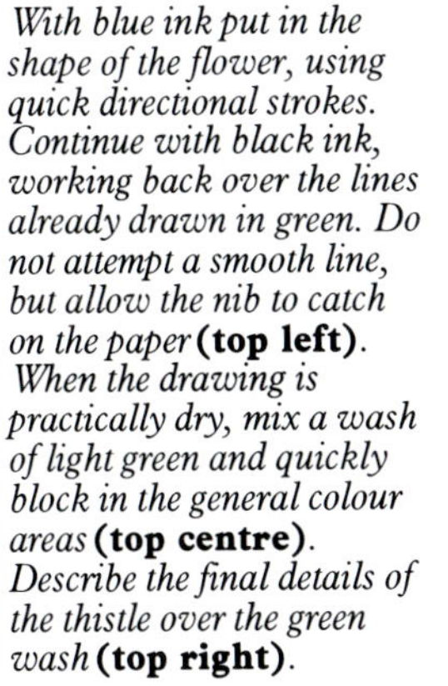

With blue ink put in the shape of the flower, using quick directional strokes. Continue with black ink, working back over the lines already drawn in green. Do not attempt a smooth line, but allow the nib to catch on the paper **(top left)**. *When the drawing is practically dry, mix a wash of light green and quickly block in the general colour areas* **(top centre)**. *Describe the final details of the thistle over the green wash* **(top right)**.

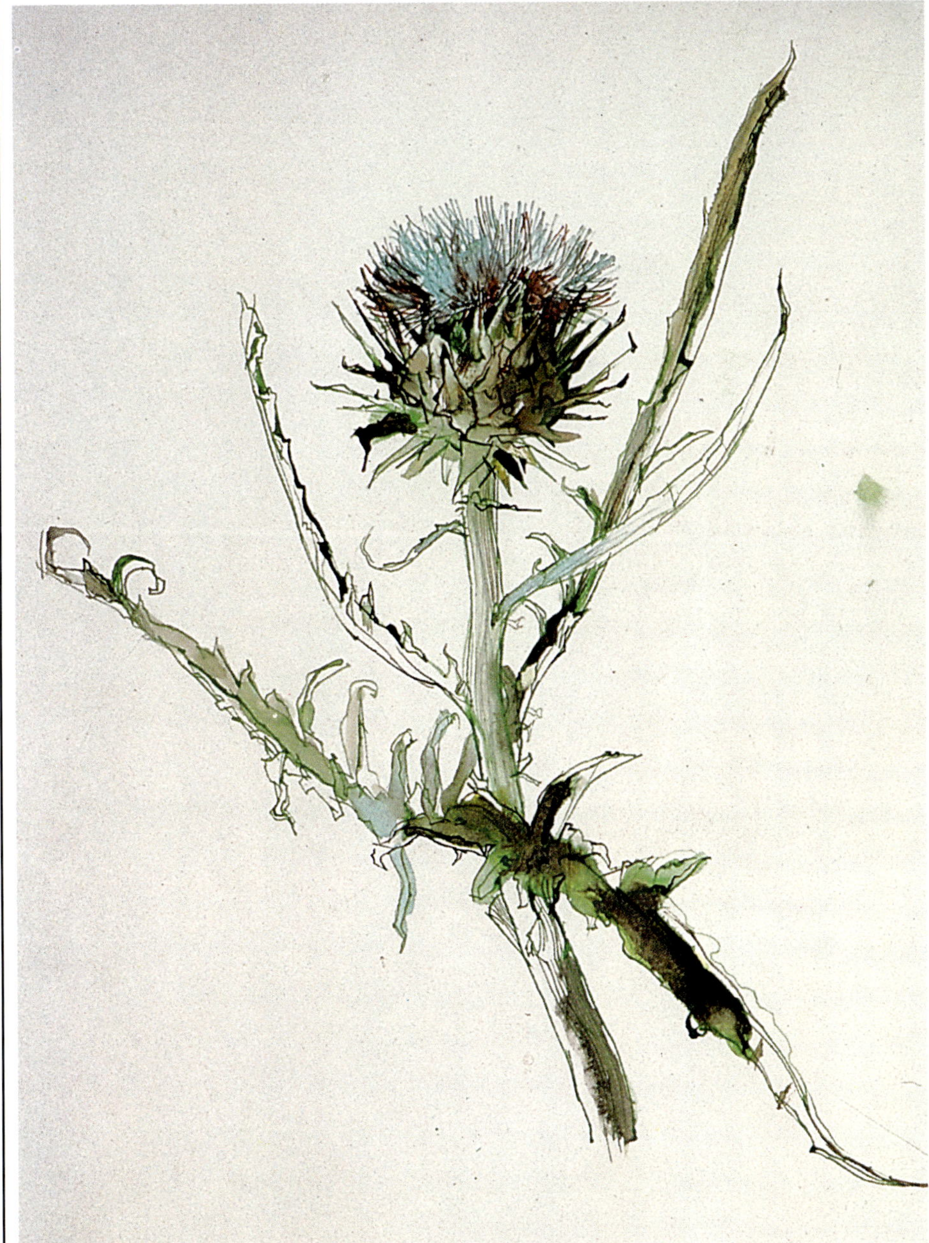

Complete the drawing by working diluted blue shadows into the flower and by adding leaf shapes in clear, undiluted colour **(right)**.

RIVER SCENE WITH BRIDGE

Complex subjects such as this bridge demand a careful analytical approach on the part of the artist. A bridge is large with strong vertical and horizontal stresses and this sense of size and architectural space must be faithfully conveyed if the structure is to have conviction. It is essential to establish the correct scale and for the uprights to be parallel if the bridge is to look strong enough to carry the weight of vehicles or people.

There are two ways of effectively achieving these ends. Firstly, a grasp of simple perspective helps, and a relentlessly analytical eye is essential. The second approach is to draw what you 'see', not what you 'know' to be there — or rather what you think you know. Here the artist has used a combination of both to achieve a solid and structured drawing.

These pens make a fairly sharp and regular line, but with practice you will be able to achieve a wide variety of marks and textures. The nib is often rigid and stiff when new, but does wear down and soften with use. This particular artist uses several pens, using new ones when a sharp clear line is required, and saving the old one for laying softer, textured areas or for producing softer, less regular lines.

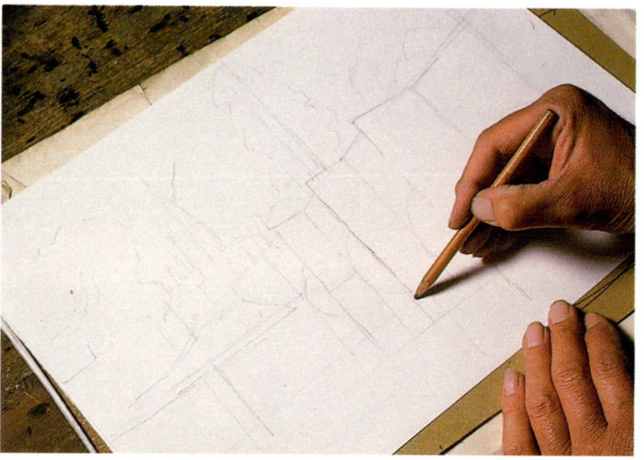

When drawing a complicated structure such as a bridge, your first consideration should be to make the subject look convincing. Concentrate on the accurate positioning of the main structural lines, pencilling them in lightly to begin with **(left)**.

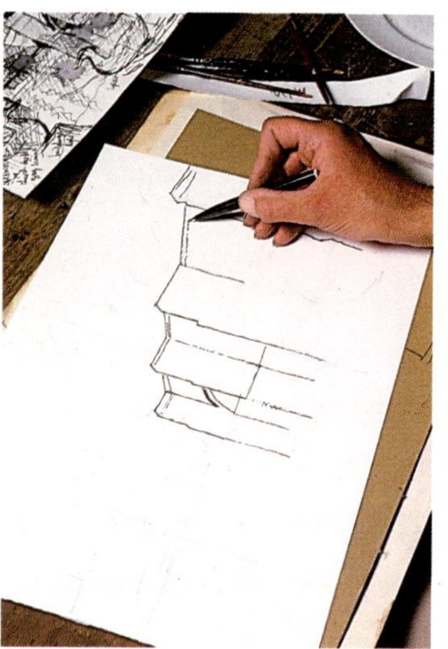

Start to draw over the light structural guidelines with a felt nib pen, keeping the lines firm and simple **(left)**.

Add areas of shadow where this helps the form and character of the subject **(below)**. *Very dark shadows can also be suggested to help establish the main areas of the composition.*

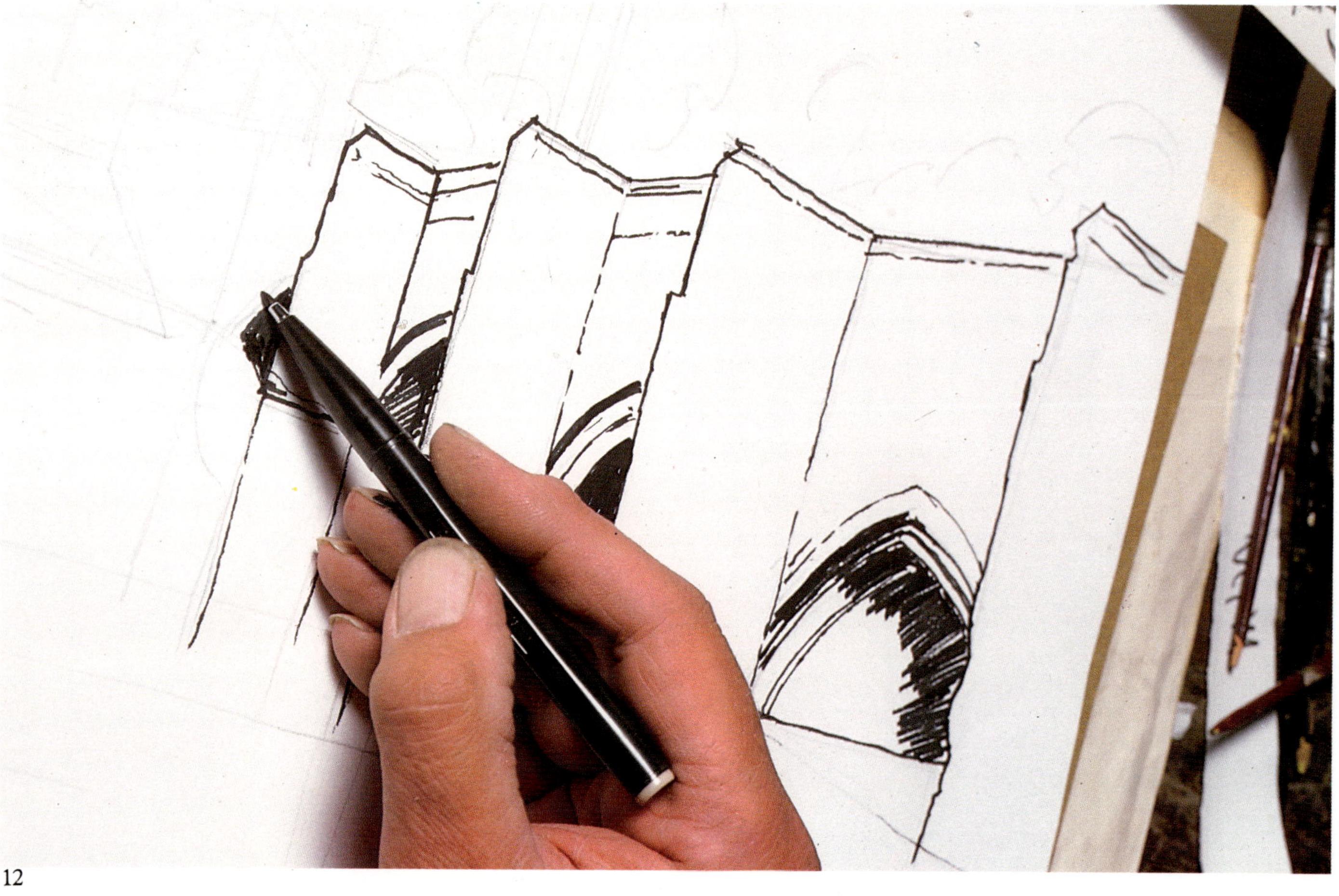

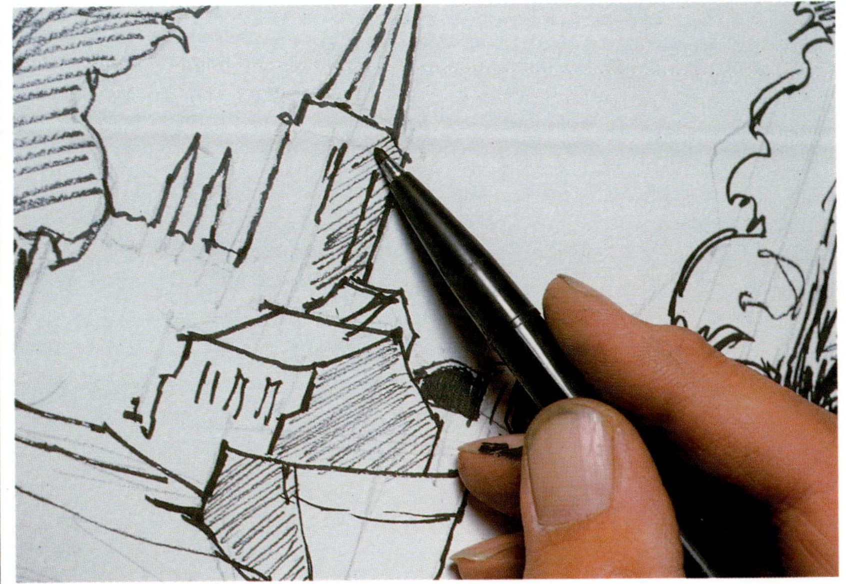

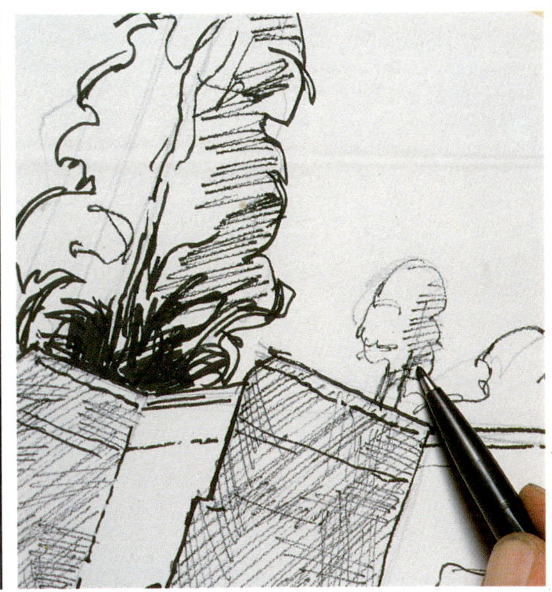

Sketch in the outline of the background shapes, using a regular hatching stroke to describe shade **(above)**.

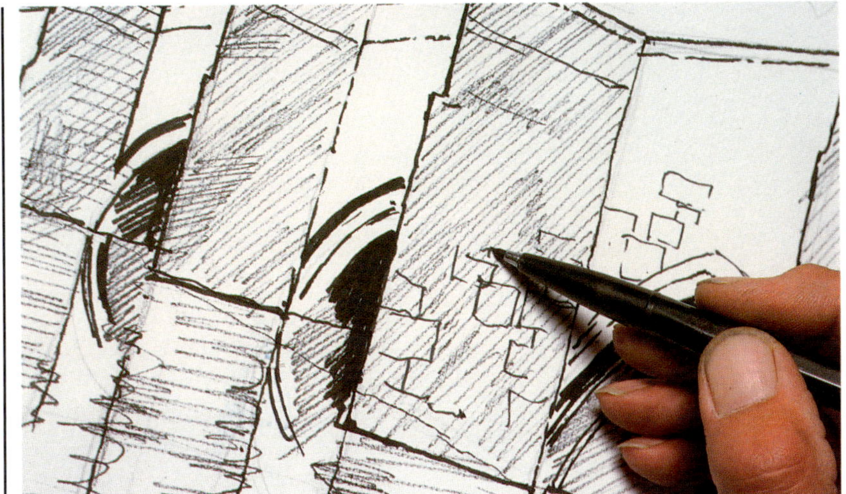

Develop the tones in the drawing by working into the shadow areas. Use cross-hatching to define very dark shadows, working over this several times if necessary to obtain the required depth **(above and left)**.

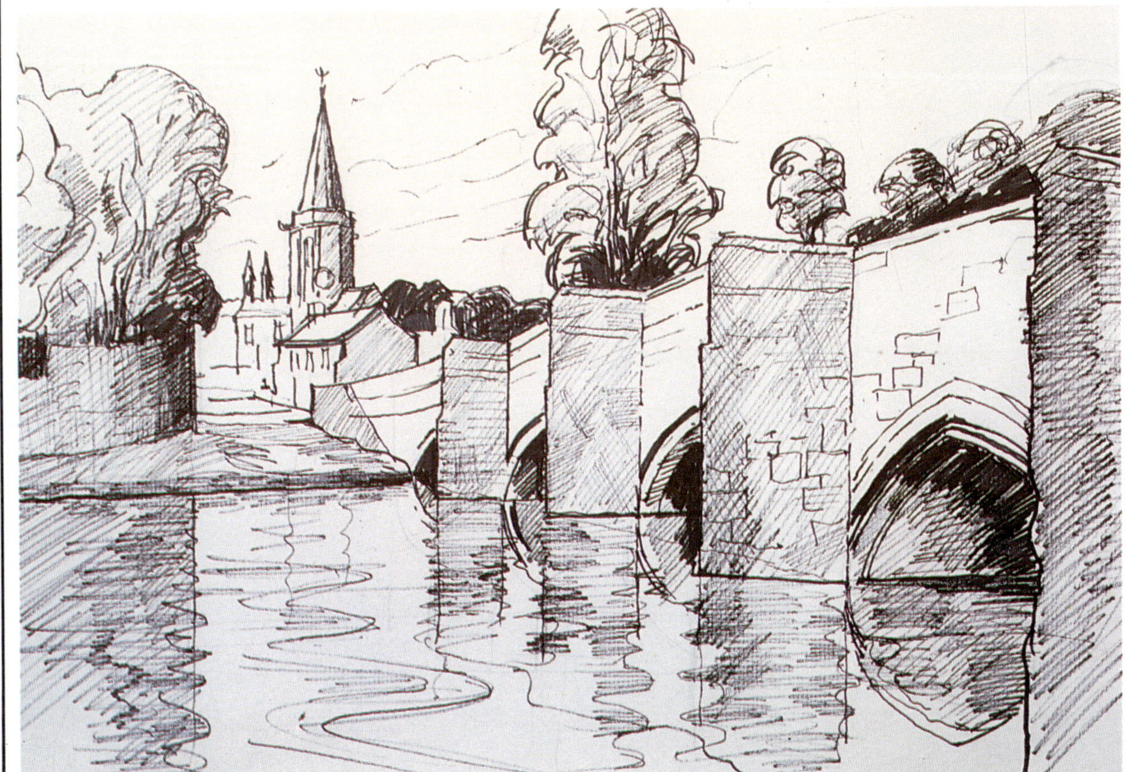

Tackle large areas of stonework by drawing selected areas rather than attempting to fill in every single stone, and complete the drawing by adding strong reflections on the water surface **(left)**.

WOMAN SITTING

In this drawing the artist used a rapidograph rather than traditional pen and ink, preferring the more consistent, regular line which rapidograph produces. This enabled areas of fine cross-hatching to be developed without fear of the ink dripping or blotting. The white paper has been allowed to stand for the highlight areas. Areas of shade are described with cross-hatching.

Rapidographs can be demanding tools. You need a light touch and must hold the pen upright to keep the ink flowing. Use a good quality cartridge paper or paper with a smooth art surface, otherwise paper fibres will clog the nib. If you are unfamiliar with this type of pen practise making a series of marks to see how you can create different textural effects. Do not try to imitate the line created by an ordinary pen — you will not succeed, nor will you get the full benefit of the inherent qualities of the rapidograph. The artist has used a variety of outlines and shaded areas, creating a strong graphic effect which is particularly appropriate to this particular medium.

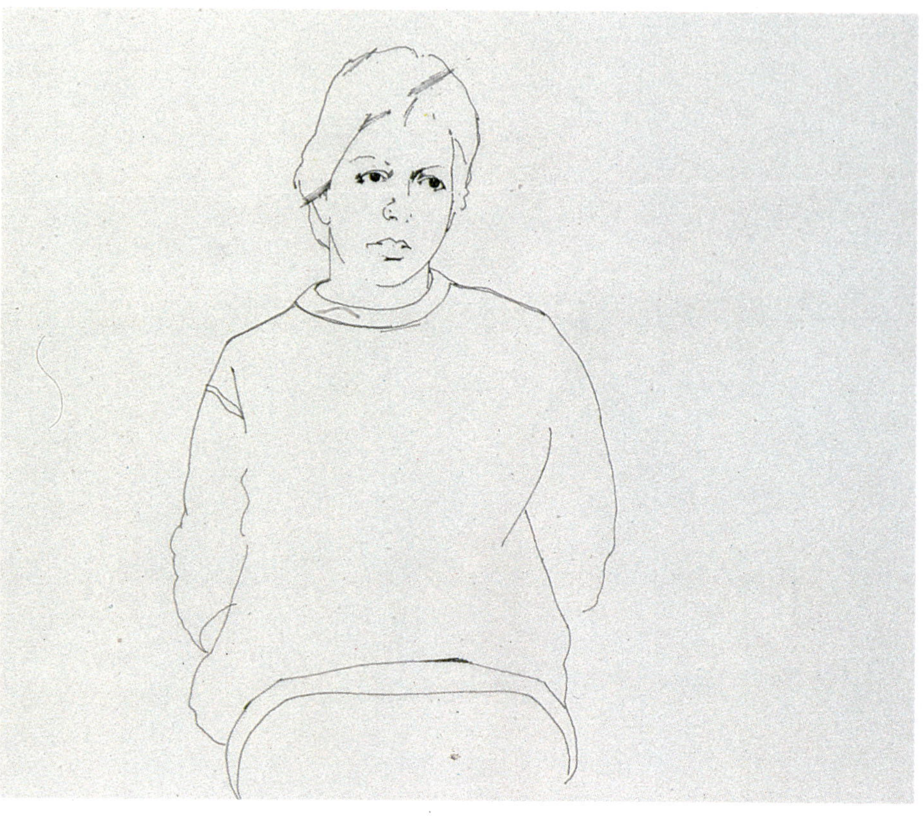

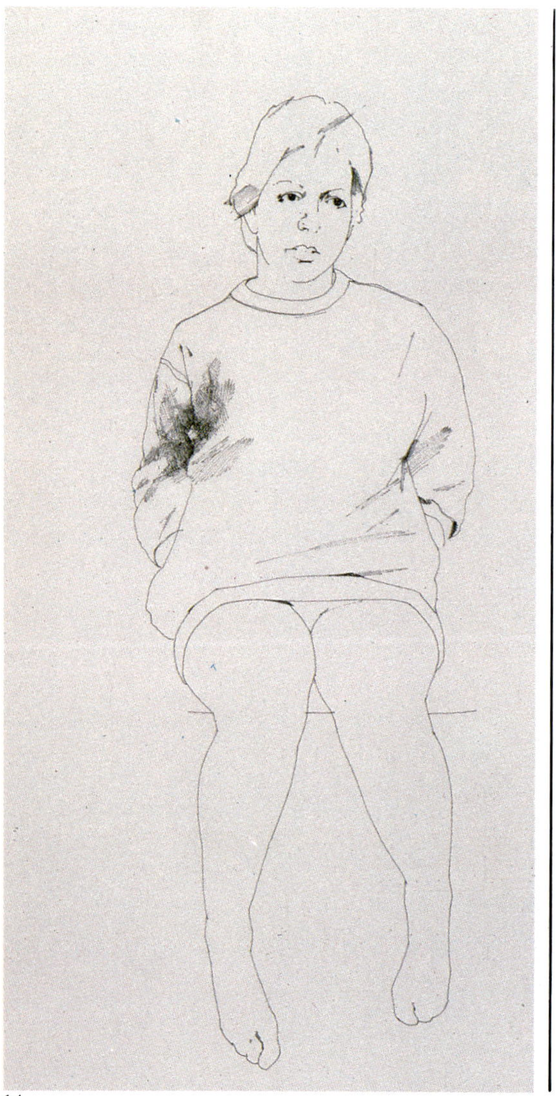

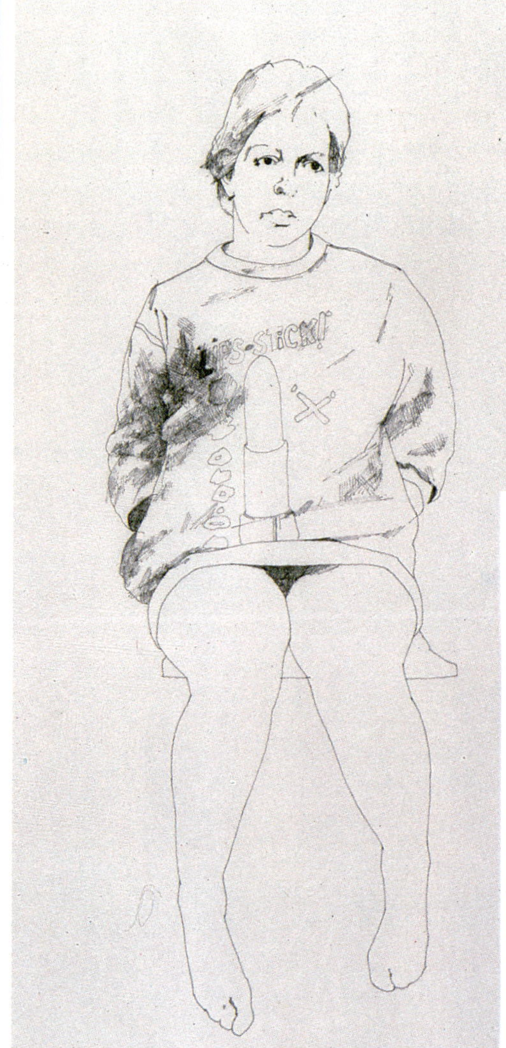

Use a rapidograph for this portrait drawing, and work on good quality cartridge paper. Holding the pen almost upright to keep the ink flowing, start to draw in the outline of the subject **(above)**. *Begin to develop the shadow area on the upper arm by lightly hatching and cross-hatching in small areas. Work the line in different directions* **(far left)**. *Draw into the figure and hair, developing other shadow areas* **(left)**. *Put in the dark areas of the seat with dense cross-hatching* **(below)**.

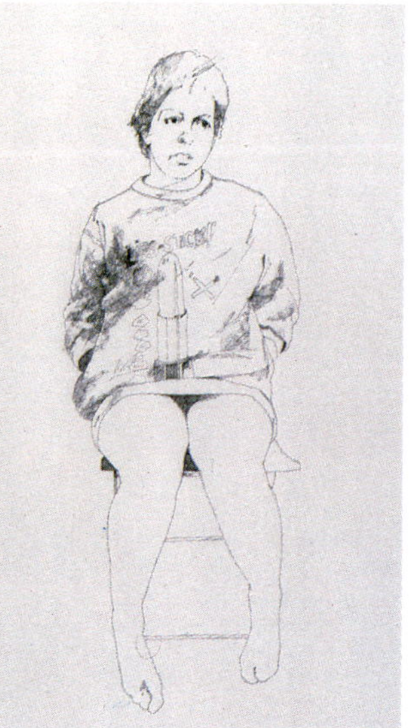

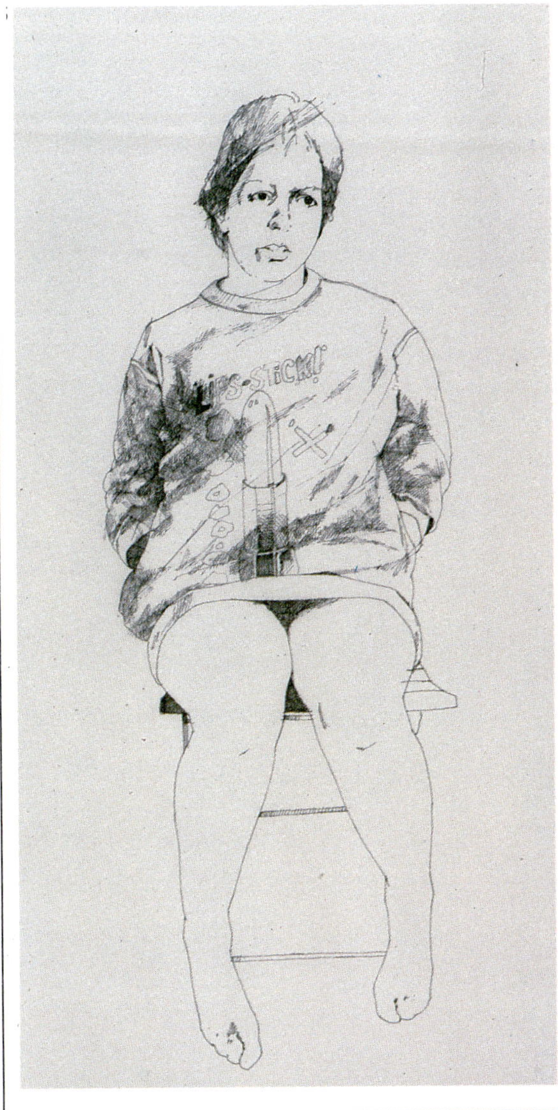

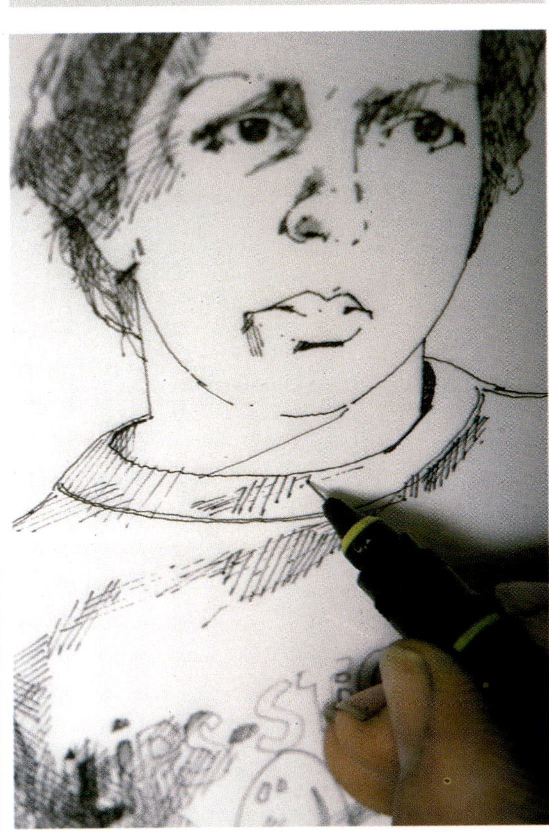

Work into the face, and with a very light stroke put in the shadows around the nose and eyes **(left)**. *Shake the pen frequently to make sure the nib does not clog. Use fine lines of cross-hatching to create subtle tones and small shadow areas* **(bottom left)**. *These delicate lines can be achieved by holding the pen in a sensitive way and applying very light, even pressure. To finish the drawing, continue to work on the shirt and head, heightening dark areas by overlaying strokes in different directions* **(below)**.

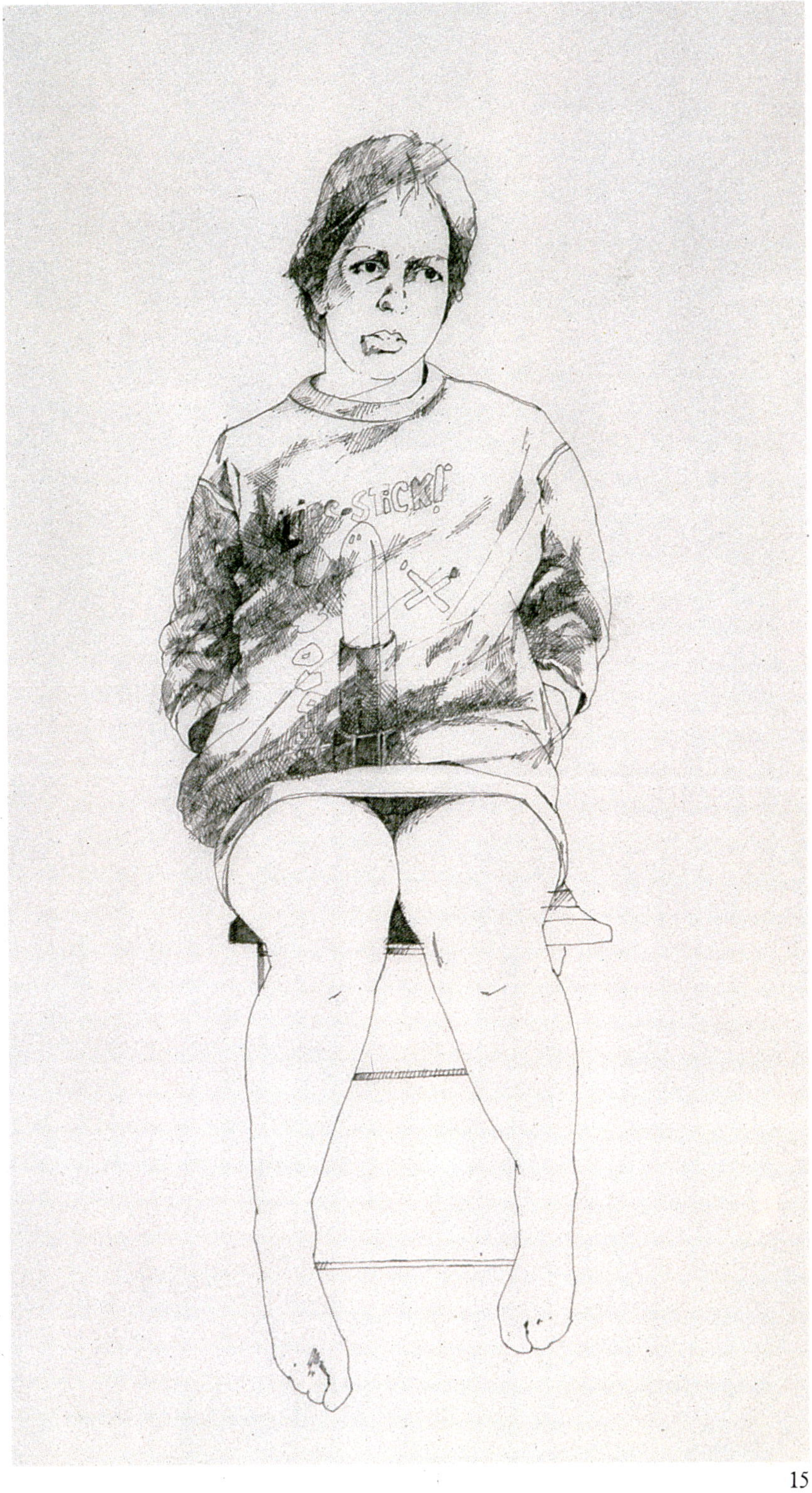

NUDE SEATED

Although pen and ink may initially prove awkward to work with, you will soon develop a feel for the medium and be able to exploit the natural flow of the ink. The pen and ink artist creates a drawing using the white of the paper and the black of the ink, and creating many tones between the two extremes. These tones are usually created by the use of individual lines of ink which, when laid over one another in various directions, create a mesh-like effect giving an impression of shadow and depth. Unlike many other drawing and painting media the pen and ink artist is limited to the use of line alone for developing tone but — as this drawing demonstrates — highly modelled, accurate work is possible.

Sketch in the figure very roughly with a 2B pencil, put in the general outlines in ink and begin to describe shadow areas **(left)**. *Continue the outline of the figure and work into these putting in shadow areas. Use a hatching stroke to define muscles* **(bottom left)**. *Continue the outline of the arm* **(below)**. *Moving outside of the figure, very loosely put in broad strokes of background shadow, working in one direction* **(right)**.

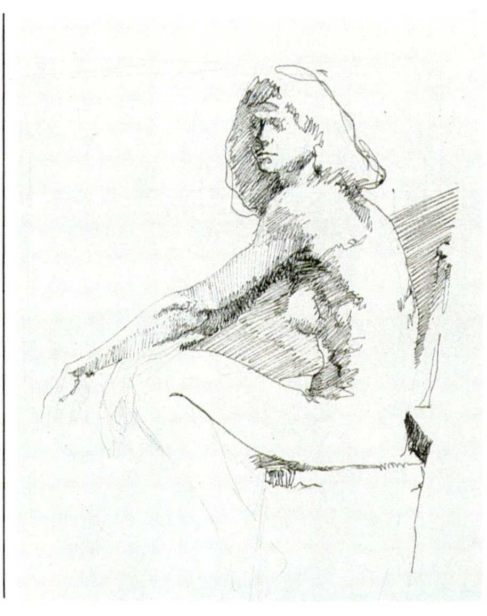

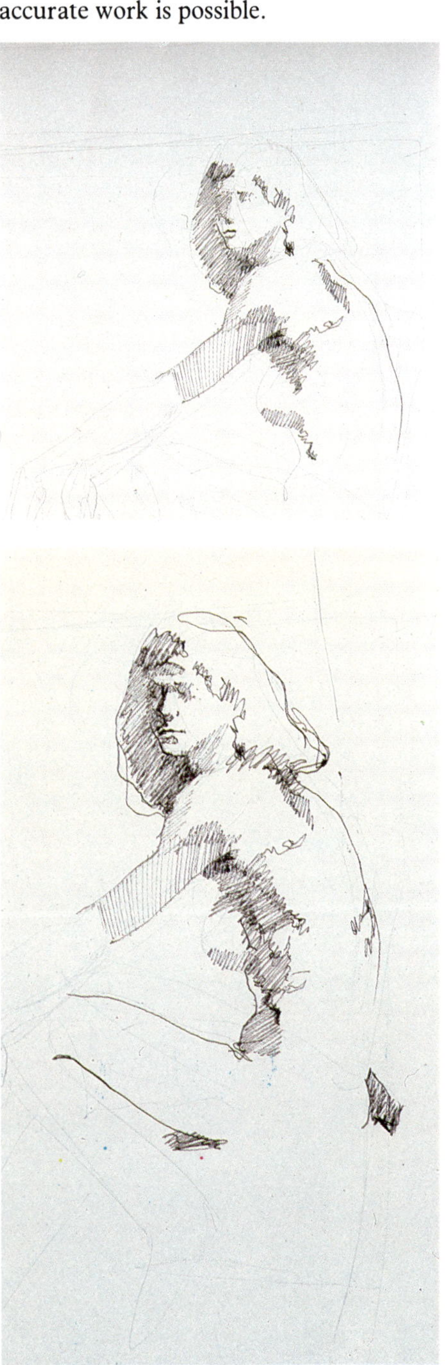

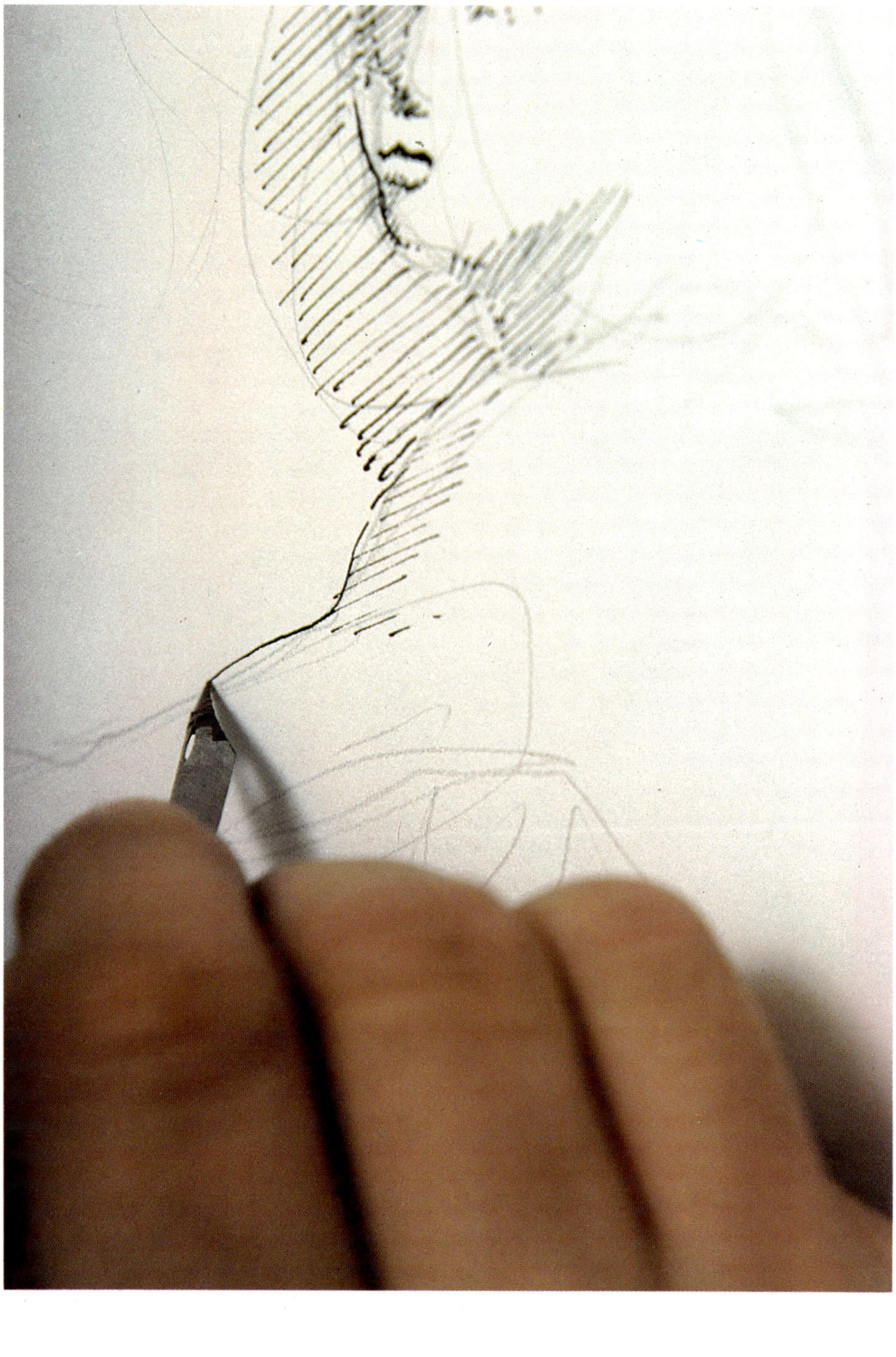

Changing the direction of the line, put in general shadow over the leg. Cross-hatch over the background shadow to create a denser tone **(below)**.

Carry the background area down behind the chair using the same directional strokes. Leave areas of white paper to define the chair shape **(right)**.

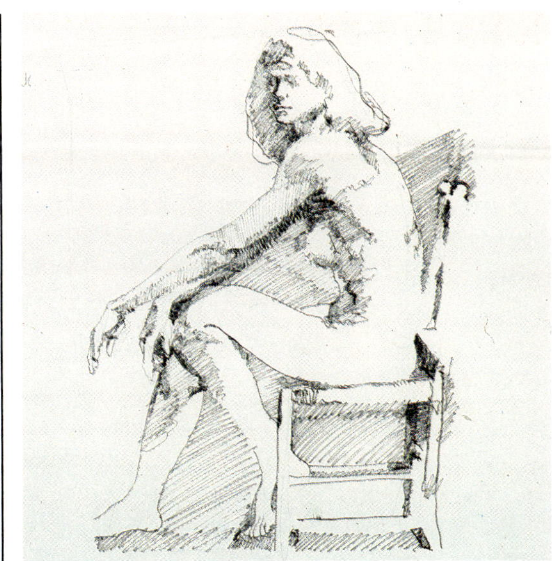

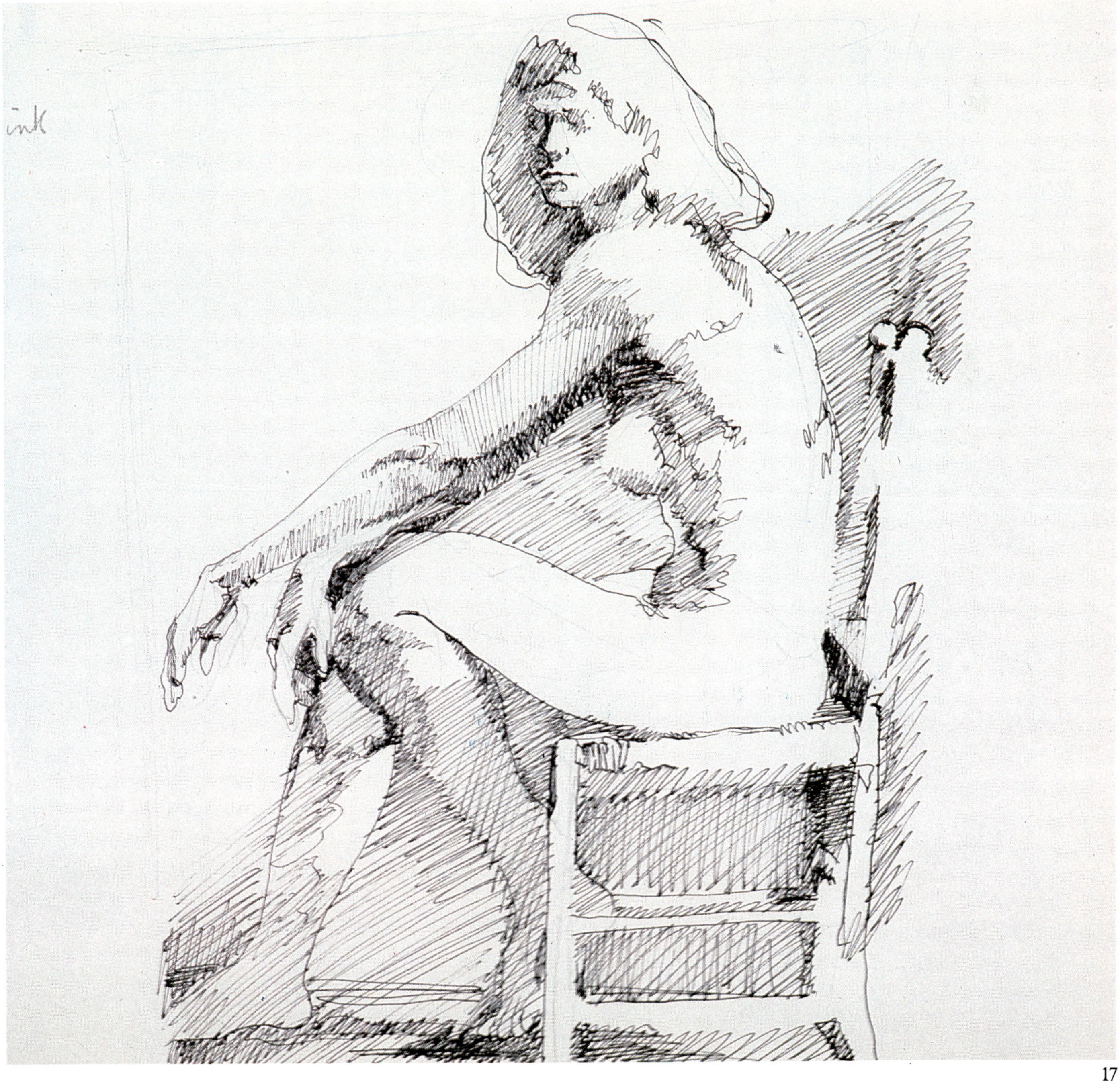

STILL-LIFE WITH HAT

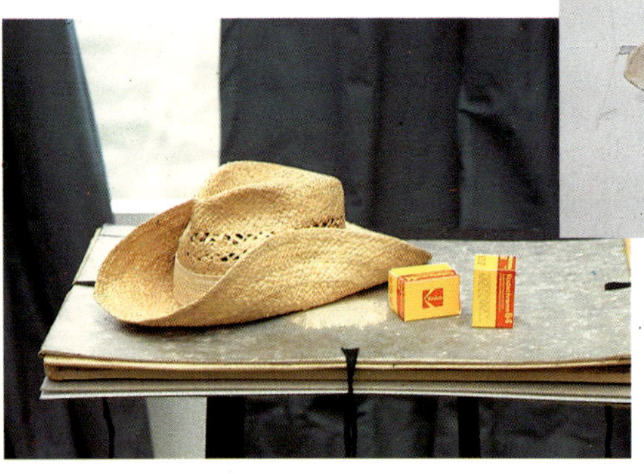

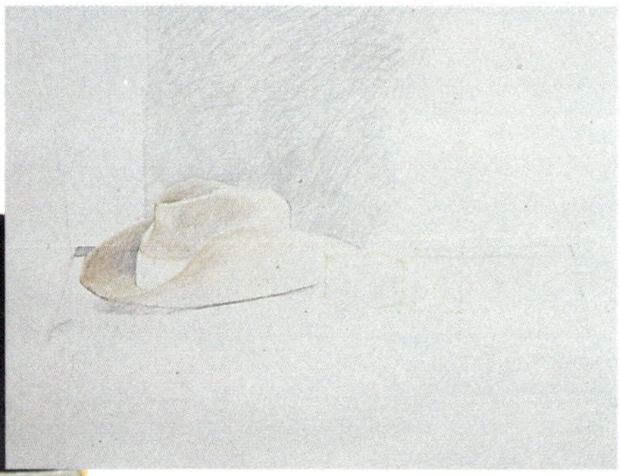

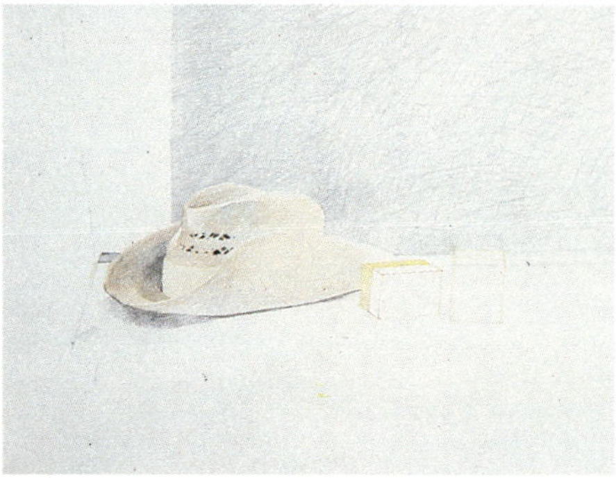

Make a selection of objects randomly selected from whatever is to hand **(top left)**. *Start by laying in a block of light blue shading behind the hat, varying the direction of the pencil strokes. Use the same blue for shadows on and around the hat* **(top centre)**. *Strengthen and broaden the background colour, developing the shadow and pattern details of the hat. Draw in the shape of the boxes with yellow and red pencils* **(top right)**.

Create subtle colour variations by overlaying light pencil strokes, using warm and cool tones together **(right)**. *Using a finely sharpened pencil, describe small detail areas in a darker colour* **(below)**.

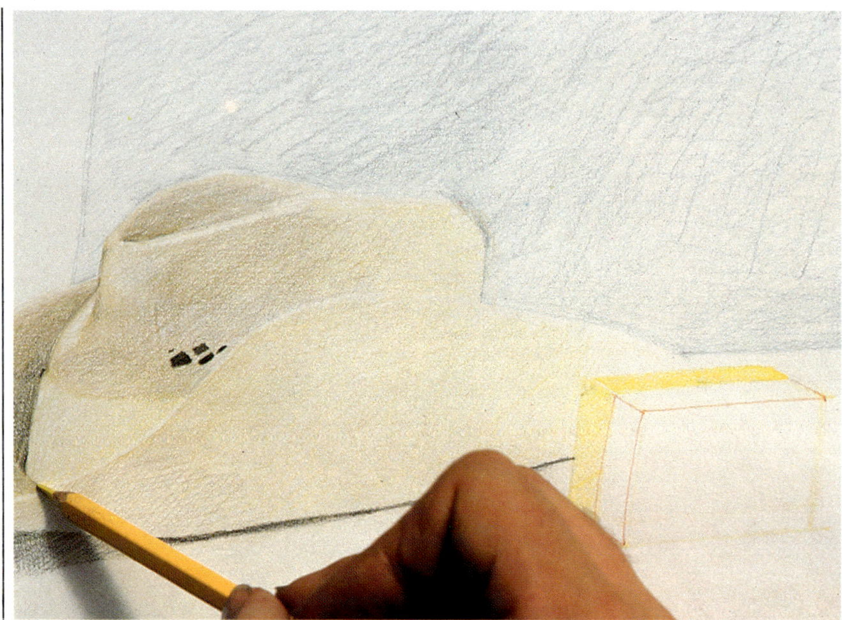

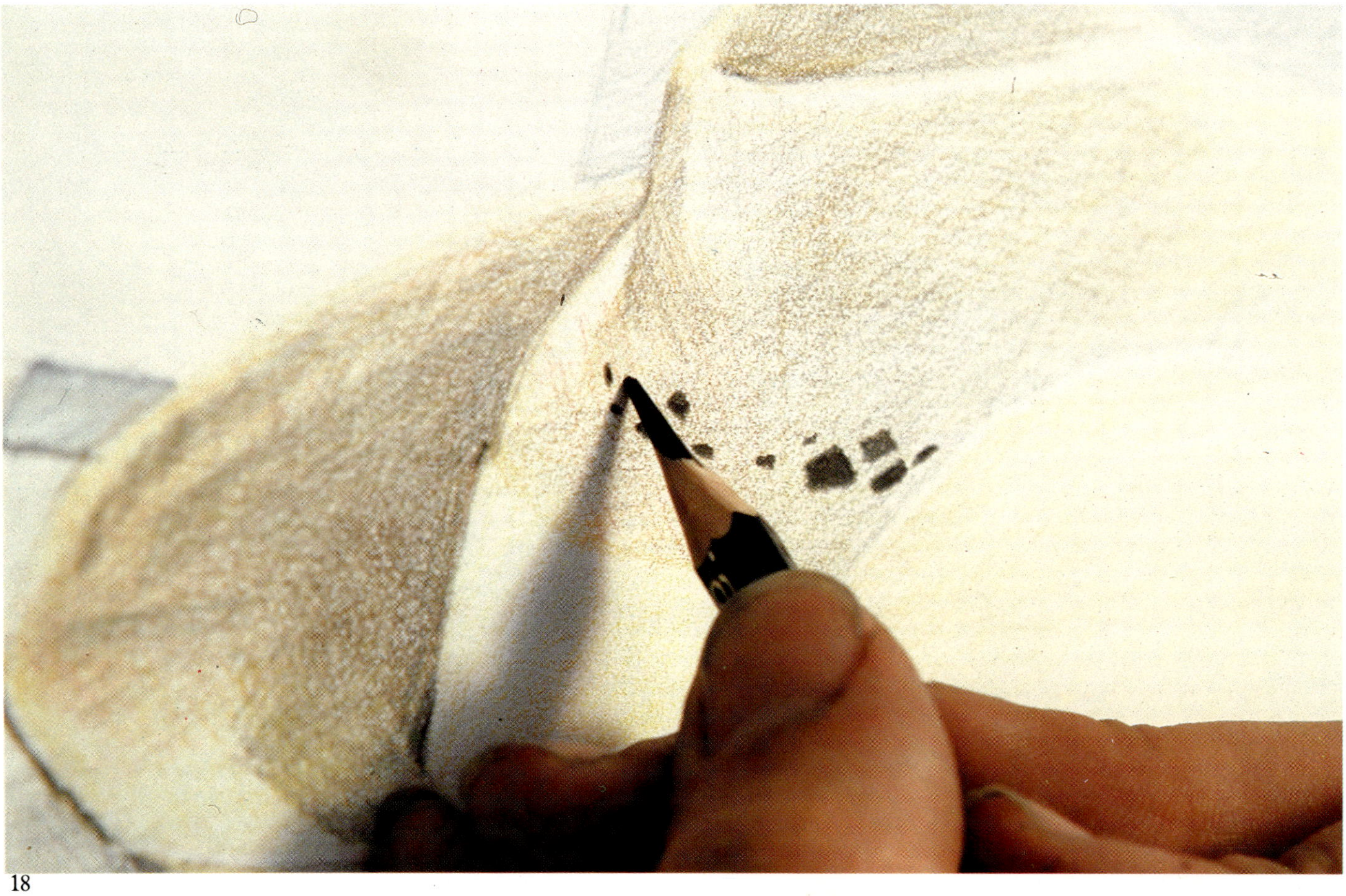

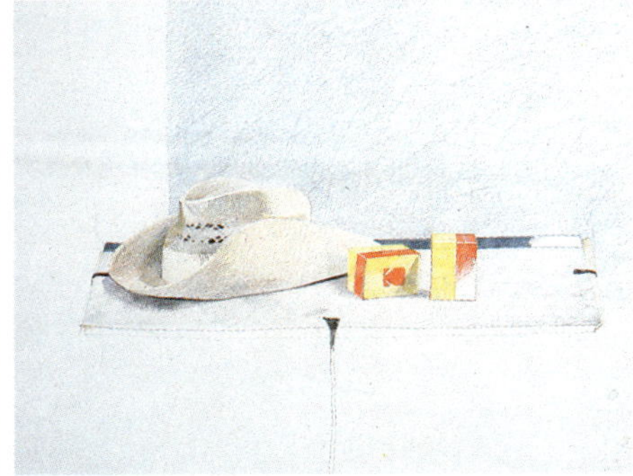

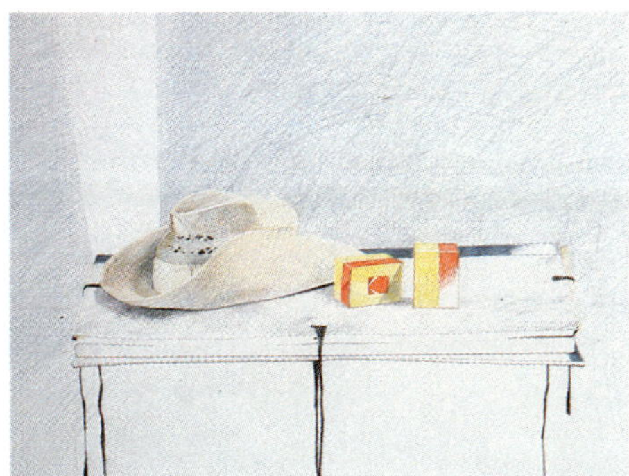

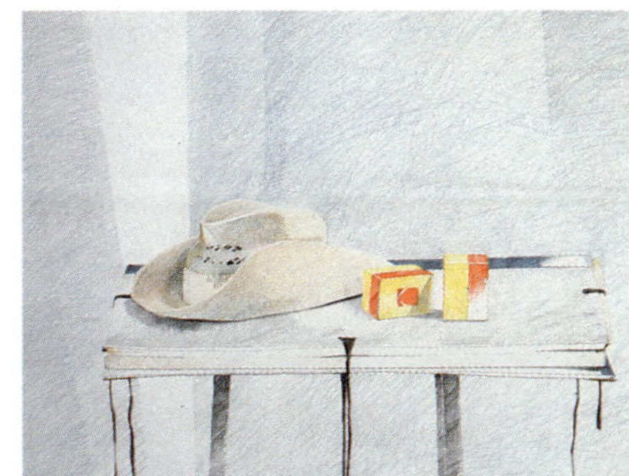

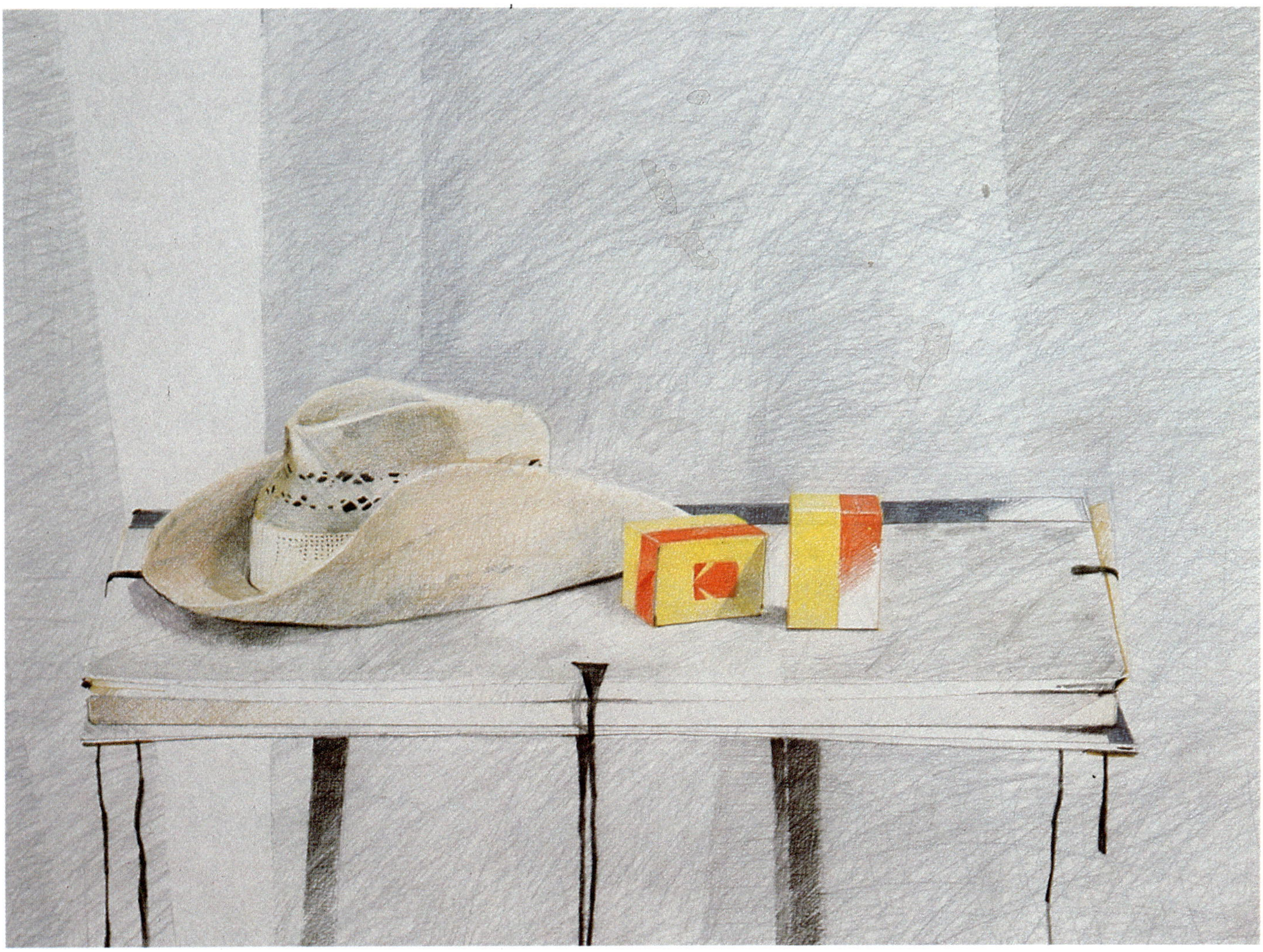

A still-life arrangement is an excellent opportunity to study form and colour in your own time, from an arrangement of objects of your own choice. Your subject may be a traditional one such as flowers and fruit, or it may be a random selection of things which are near to hand or which you particularly like. The artist chose these items for their simple colour range and the contrasting geometric and irregular shapes.

The delicate appearance of this drawing is created by successive overlaying of lines in different colours, which blend together to form a vast range of subtle hues. Each layer of colour is laid in light cross-hatching to gradually build up the finished effect. Purple and blue combine to give rich deep shadows on the yellows, echoing the colours of the background; red over yellow provides the rich shadow tone on the boxes.

Coloured pencils are waxier than traditional graphite pencils making them difficult to erase. This waxiness also tends to clog the paper if the colour is overworked. For this reason it is best to use the pencils lightly, never laying more than two or three colours over each other.

Building up the colours with contrasts of tone. Use purple in the shadows under the hat, and darken the blues to make the objects stand out **(top left)**.

Outline the portfolio and sketchbook in black, and strengthen the bright colours **(top centre)**. *Lay in the rest of the background area in blue, varying the tones with heavy reworking. Build up the details of line and tone with black and yellow ochre* **(top right)**. *The finished picture shows how coloured pencils can create a subtle yet clearly defined image.*

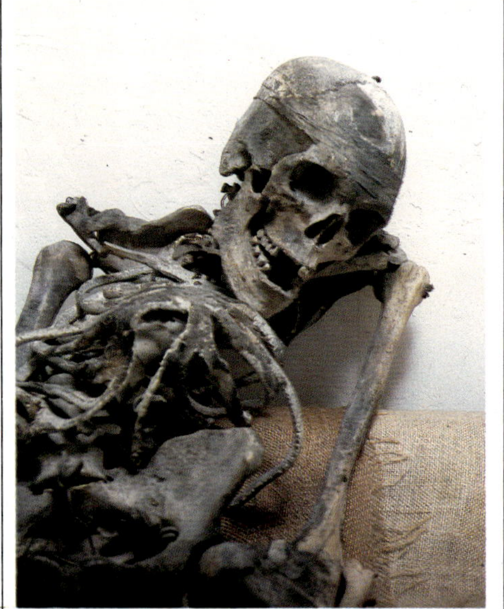

HUMAN SKULL

A human skull is an ideal subject for a pencil drawing. It has a fluid and well defined outline as well as a variety of linear and tonal detail within its complex form. The smooth, rounded dome of the skull demands subtle changes of tone which contrast with the dense black shadows in the sockets of the eyes, nose and mouth.

The forms are described by overlaid layers of cross-hatching; crisp, delicate lines outline the shapes and depict the small characteristics of the surface. Allow the image to emerge gradually by first developing the structure as a broad view of the whole shape and then breaking down each area to show details.

Take this opportunity to look closely at the shape of the skull. Knowledge of the underlying structure of the face will stand you in good stead and is invaluable when painting and drawing portraits. The cranium, the larger part of the skull, is almost egg shaped. The bones of the face which influence the surface appearance are the nasal bones, the cheekbones, the two upper jawbones and the lower jawbones. Viewed from the front, over a third of the area of the skull is taken up by the frontal bone of the cranium. Beneath this, and separated by the nasal bones, are the eye sockets, or orbits. These are deep cavities, the margins of which are rectangular with rounded edges. The lower orbital margins are made up by the cheekbones and upper jawbones. The lower jawbone is jointed to the cheekbone at the point where it meets the temporal bone at the side of the cranium.

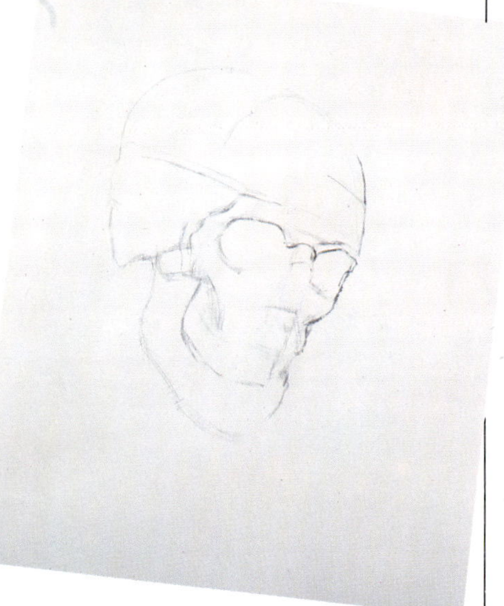

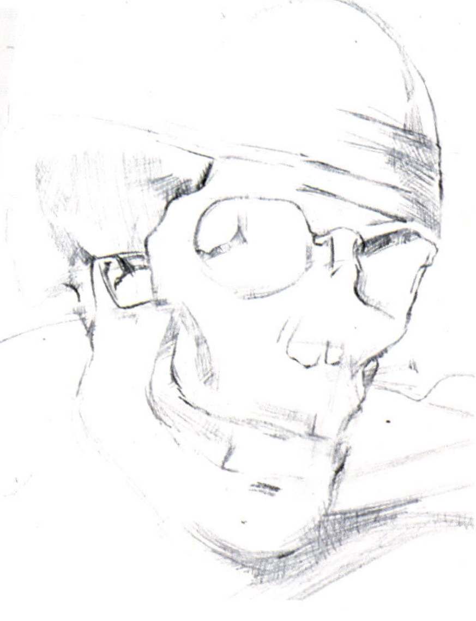

Use pencil to capture the sharp, fluid outline of the skull and the sockets of the eyes and nose, working loosely with line and light hatching **(far left)**. *Extend the outline and start to hatch in darker shadows* **(left)**. *Develop the drawing by blocking in small shapes and improving the definition of the contours* **(below left)**. *Continue to build up the drawing in more detail, drawing small shapes of the teeth and jaw socket* **(below)**. *Use an eraser where necessary to make corrections.*

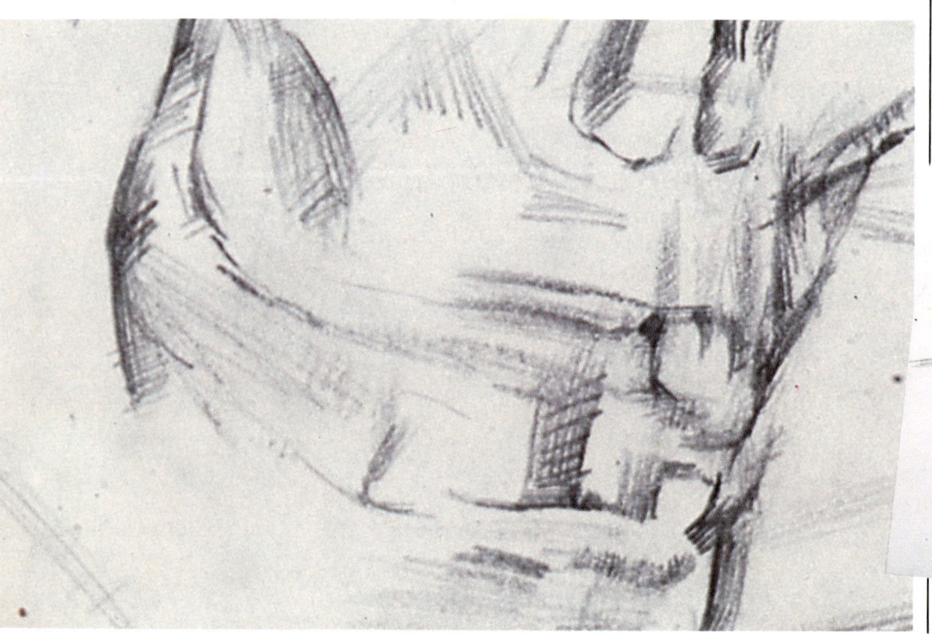

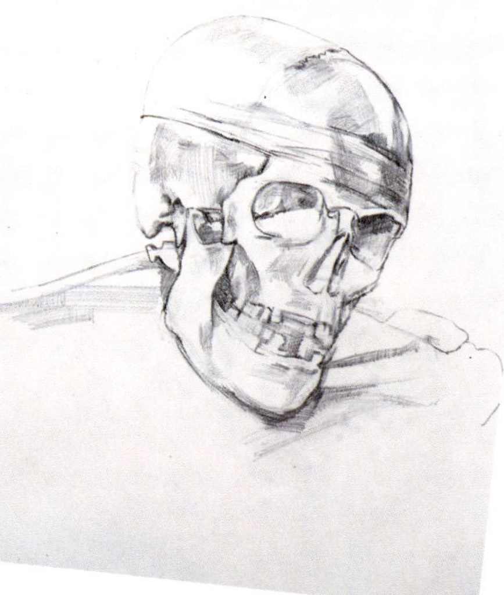

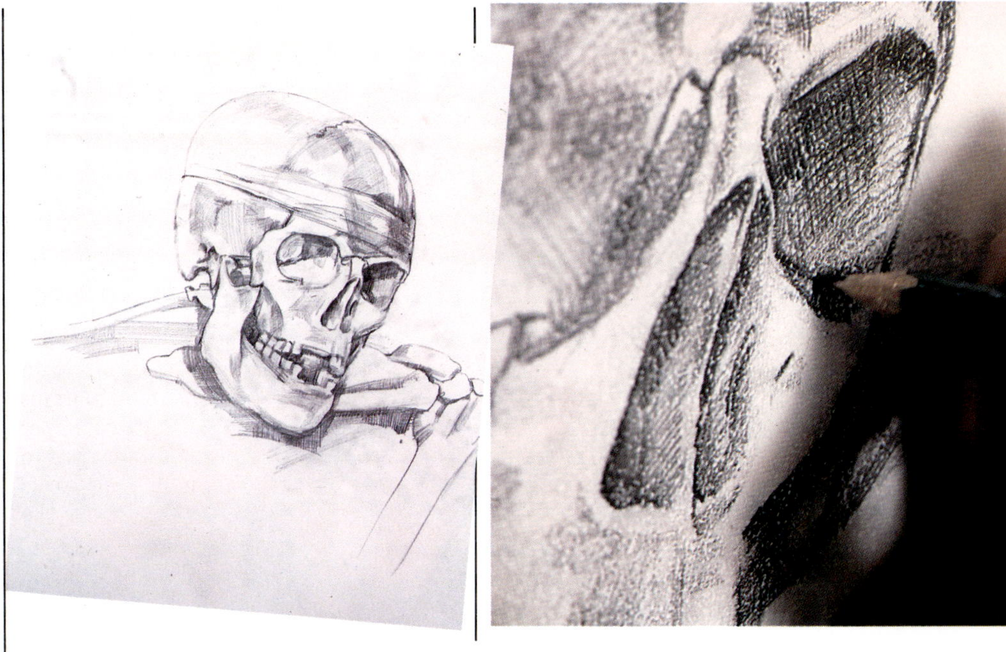

Strengthen the outline and work over dark tones with cross-hatched lines to give depth and to bring out the full volume of the form **(far left)**. *Continue to use cross-hatching to increase the shadow depth* **(left)** *— the darker the hatching, the more the shape will appear to recede.*

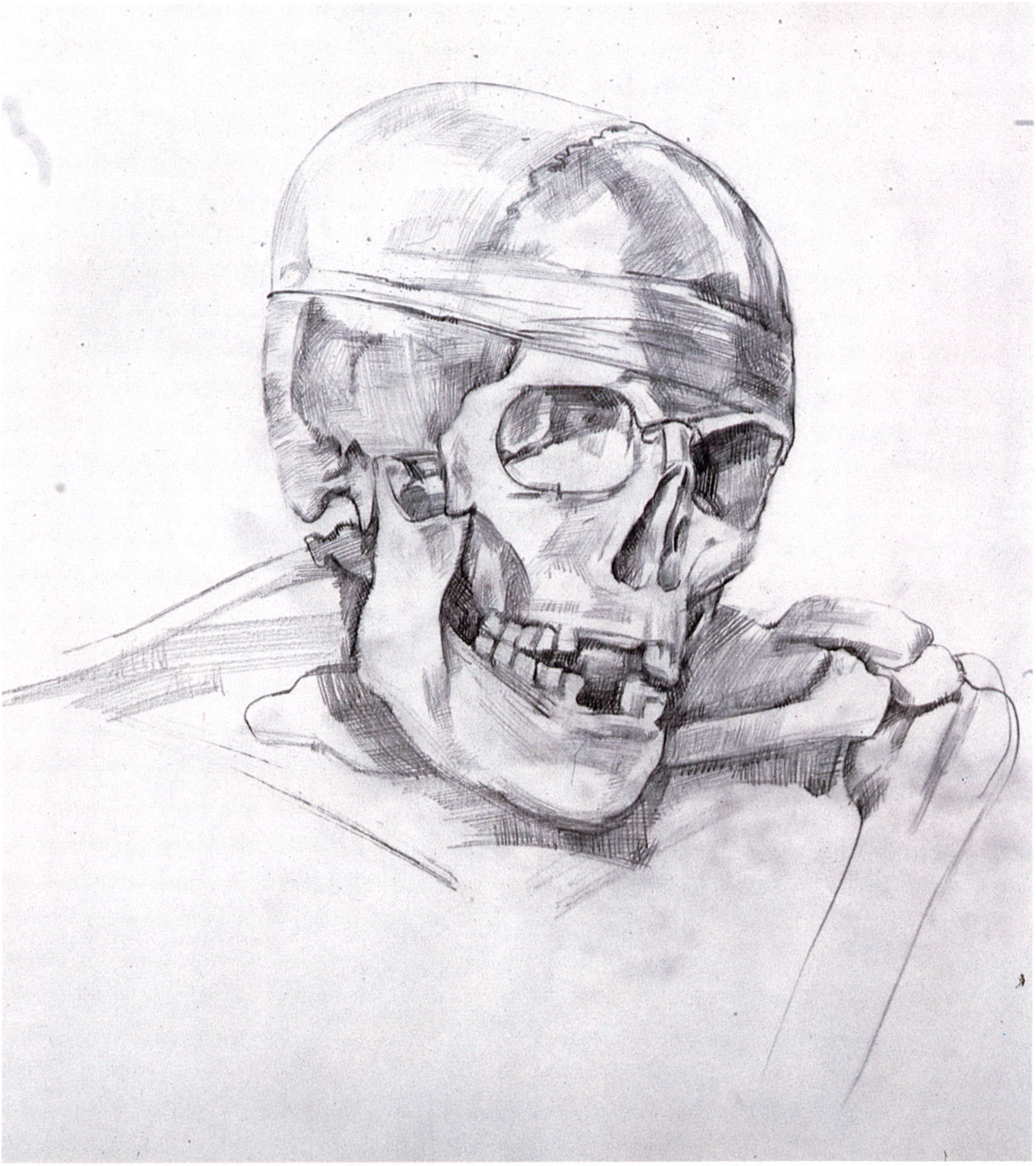

Work across the whole image making minor adjustments to the tonal balance and reinforcing the lines where appropriate to clarify the overall structure of the finished picture **(left)**.

URBAN SCENERY

The stark lines of the modern urban landscape, interspersed with the mellower and more weathered shapes of older buildings, can provide the artist with a challenging and varied series of subjects.

Styles of draughtsmanship here can vary dramatically. On the one hand, you can use techniques which are almost identical with those of an architect, with a carefully measured approach and precise mathematical lines. Alternatively, the classical methods of drawing, concentrating on subtle differences of tone and using a more organic approach, can be extremely effective.

Just because you are drawing buildings, often embellished with such tiny components as windows and bricks, you should not be deterred from seeing the main, overall shapes and masses of a structure. You are still free to approach the drawing in any way you wish. The drawings on this page show that it is possible to look at buildings in an illustrative way, taking and developing those aspects which appeal to you personally; or you can take in an overall scene — observing how the volumes of the buildings and other angular shapes relate to each other and produce abstract shapes in the sky and background.

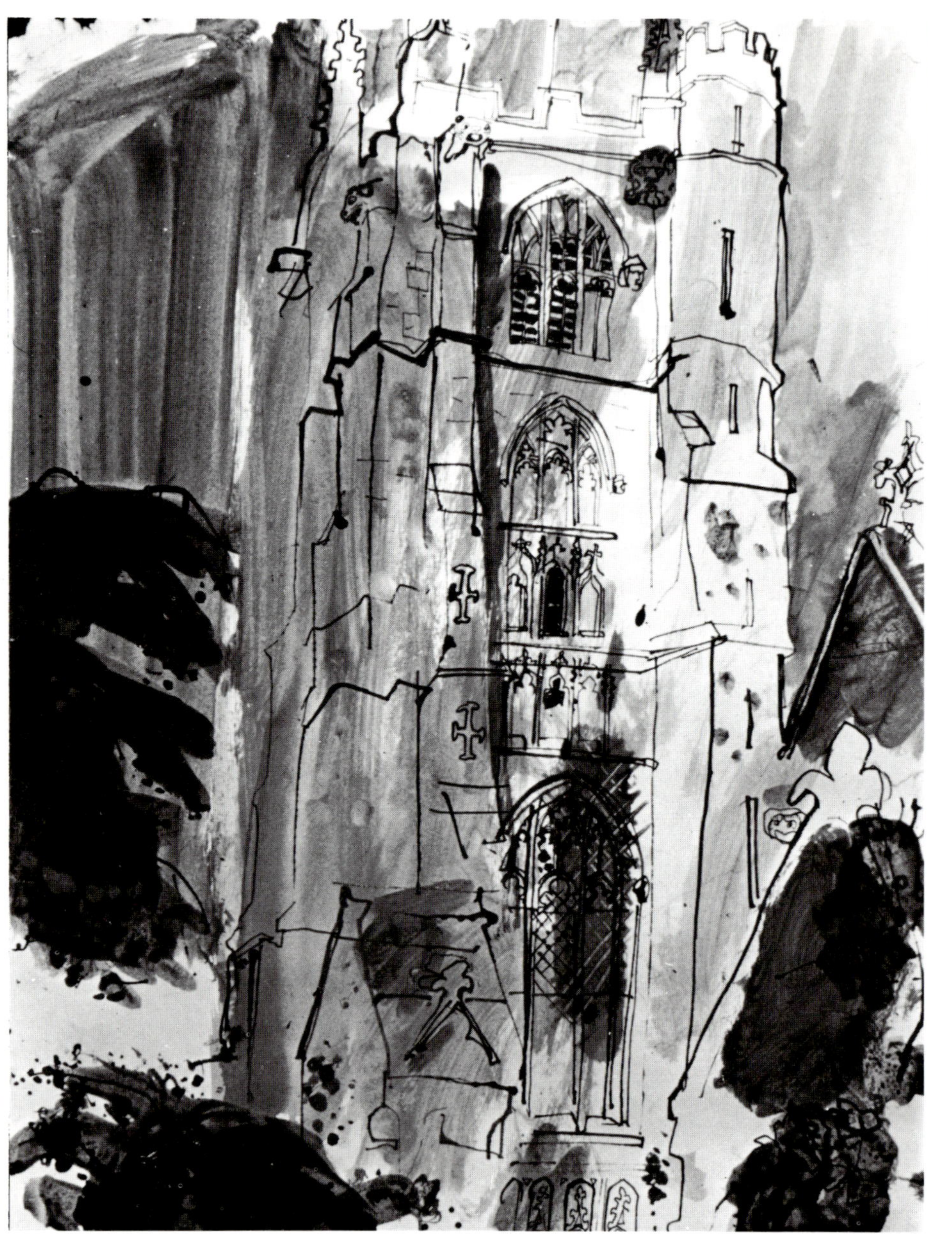

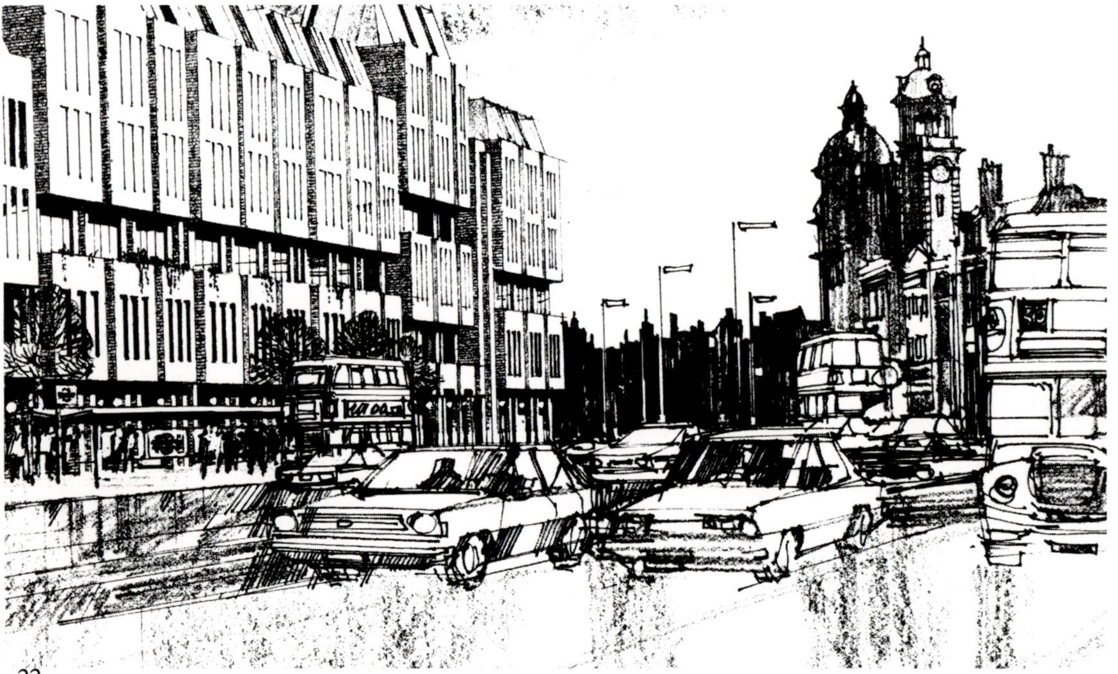

In this imaginative drawing the artist has used a combination of ink and pastels. The architectural lines have not been allowed to dominate. Instead, the artist has used his own characteristic drawing technique, with lines of varying width, flowing free rather than straight, and brought to life by areas of contrasting light and shade **(above).**

The architect's impression **(left)** *is in stark contrast. Buildings are precisely observed and mechanically executed.*

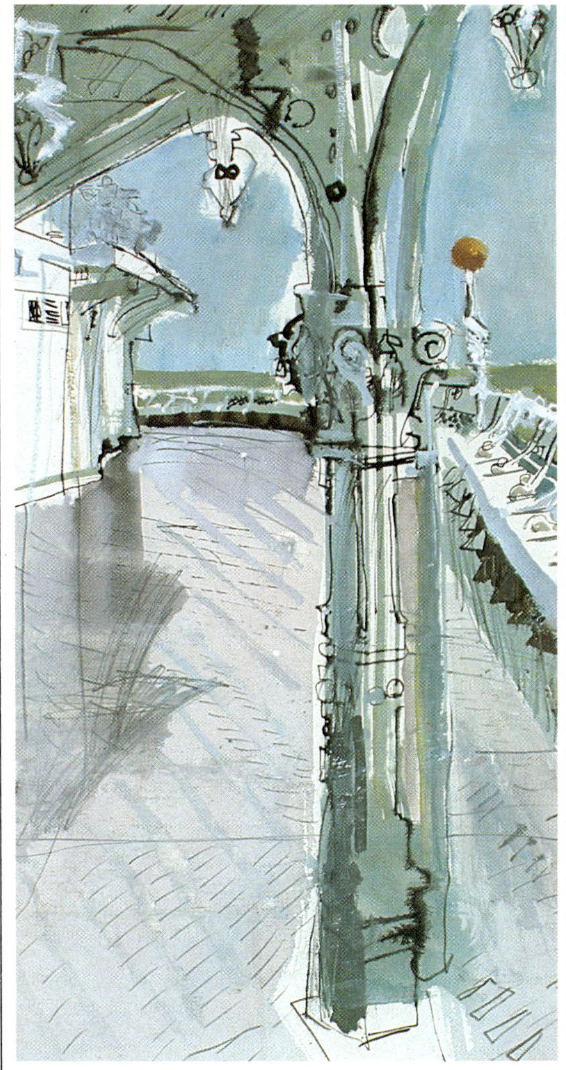

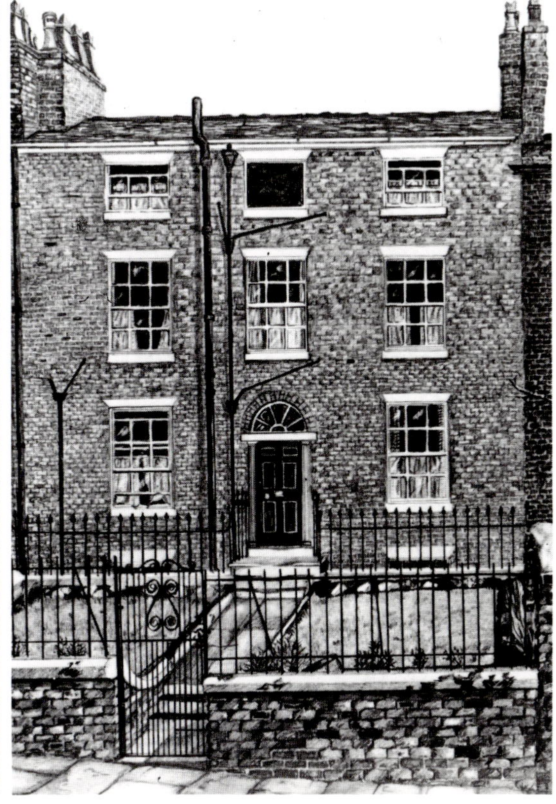

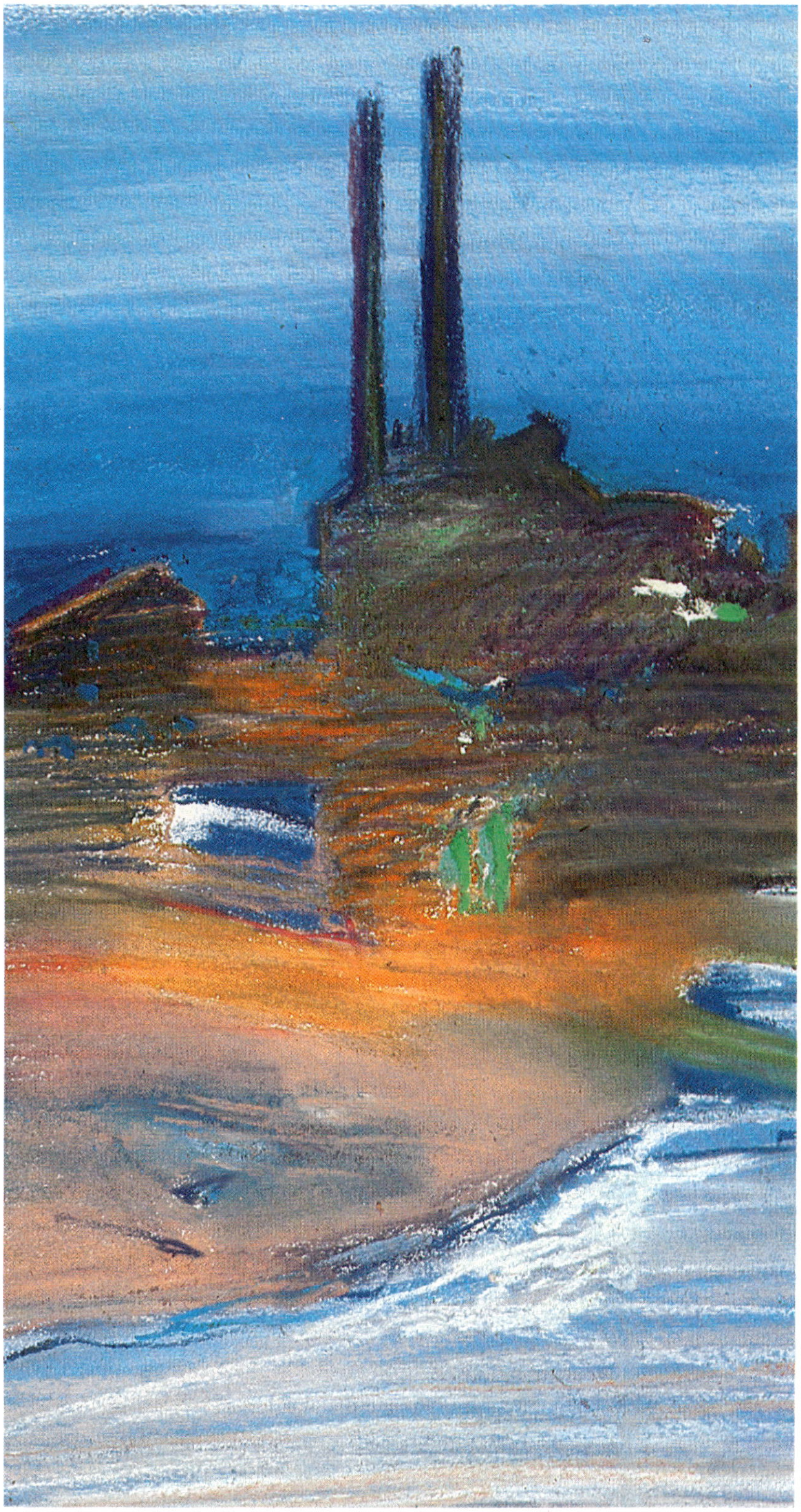

The wrought-iron pillar of the isolated seaside pier **(top left)** *inspired this ink and wash drawing. The artist recorded this architectural detail for inclusion in a painting at a later date.*

The house **(left)** *demonstrates the confusion of surface patterns such as the bricks, window panes, iron railings and roof tiles, which confront the urban landscape artist.*

In this atmospheric oil pastel sketch **(above)**, *the artist has ignored all detail and embellishment. His chief concern was the moody presence of the factory on the horizon.*

SKETCHING IN THE COUNTRYSIDE

All the drawings on this page are from the artist's portfolio and were made with a view

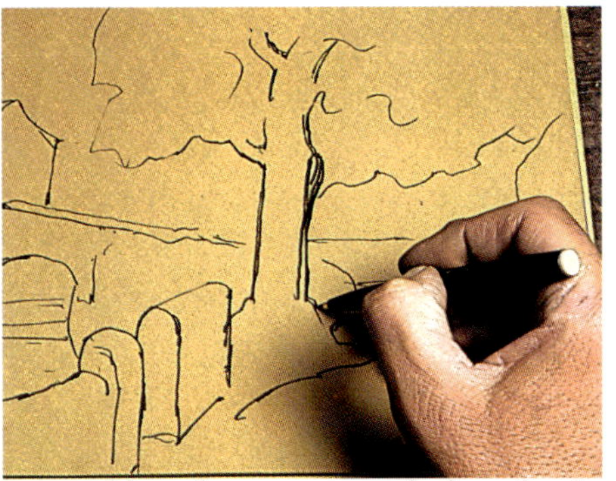

to working them up as paintings in the studio at a later date.

Before he started the drawings, the artist sat for some time looking at the subject in each case. He did this before even making a single mark on the paper. This kind of concentrated consideration will often surprise you, for even the most familiar subject will reveal new interest and your drawing will benefit immensely. For the artist, looking and 'seeing' is as important, or more important, than the marks he makes.

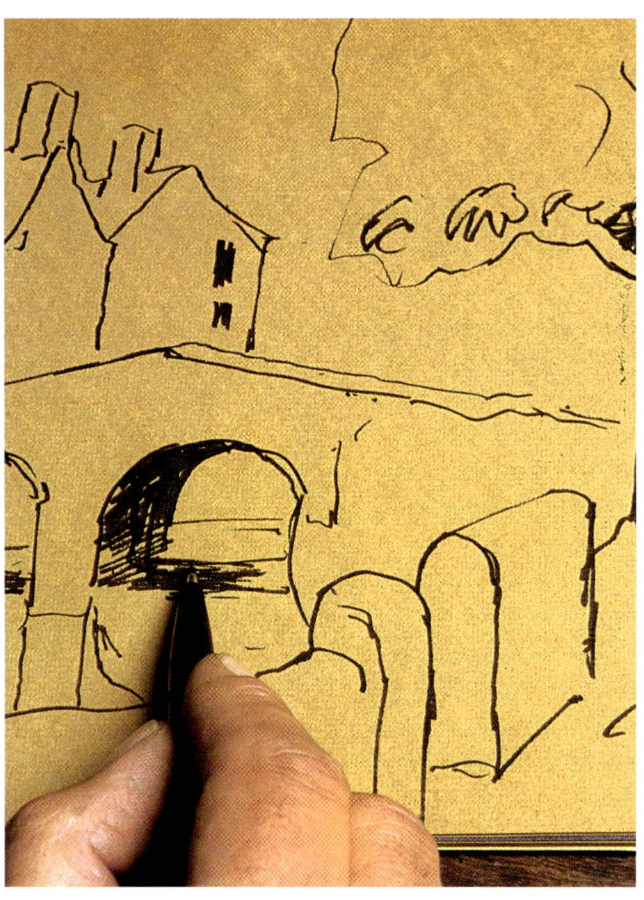

Block out the general composition of the drawing **(far left)**, *varying the line to suit the subject. Landscape sketching calls for greater versatility than most subjects — buildings, trees and water all requiring a different approach and sensitive treatment. Working across the whole sketch, introduce dark tone into the deepest shadow areas* **(left)**. *Use regular diagonal hatching to develop the medium tones, and a free, irregular stroke for the tree foliage* **(below)**.

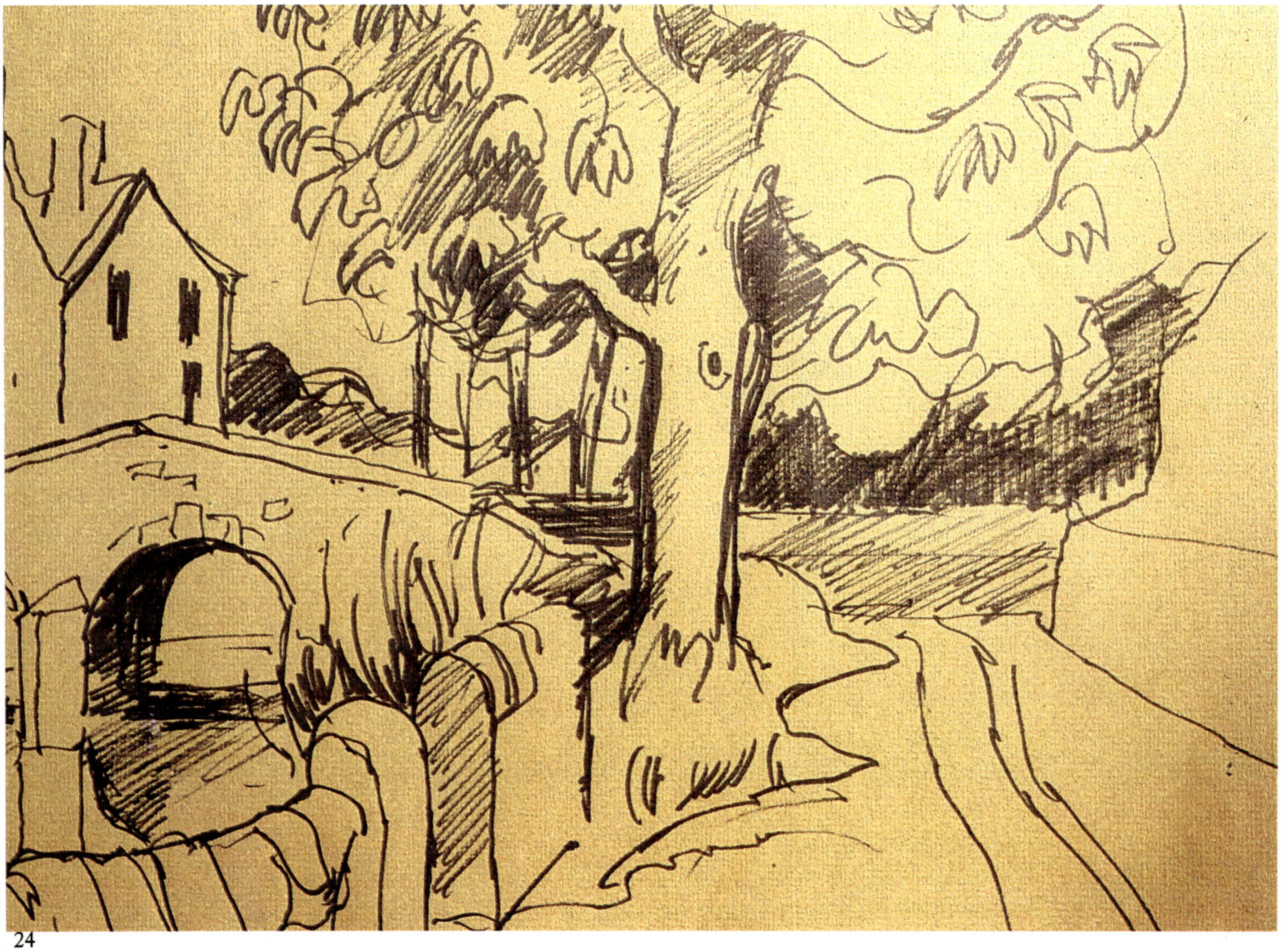

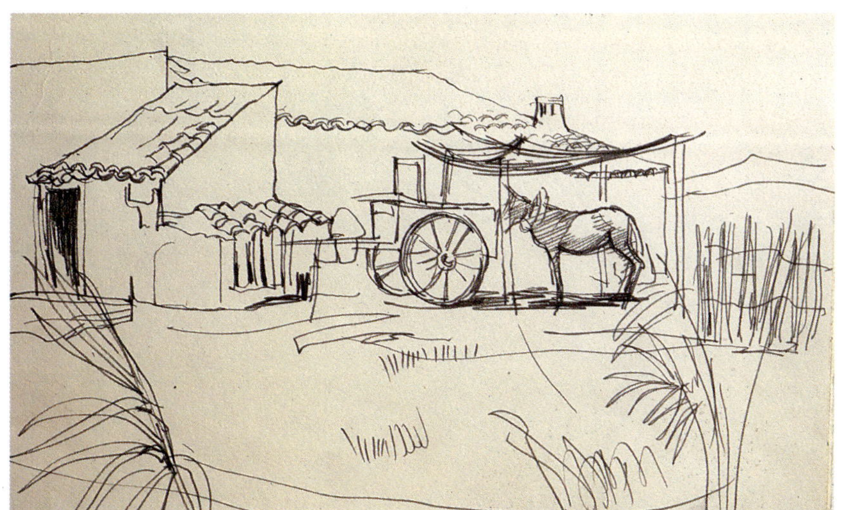

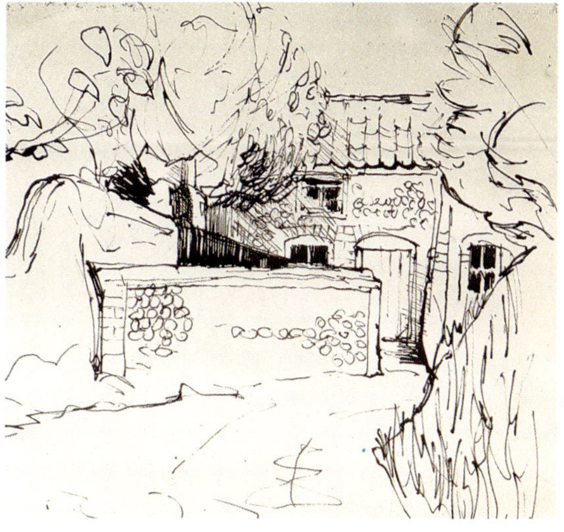

The sketch **(above)** *uses the minimum amount of information to record a passing moment on an isolated farm. The artist has accurately placed the waiting mule in its everyday setting by suggesting the layout of buildings, path and windswept trees. Simple perspective and a straightforward composition combine to convey the atmosphere of this undulating rural scene* **(right)**.

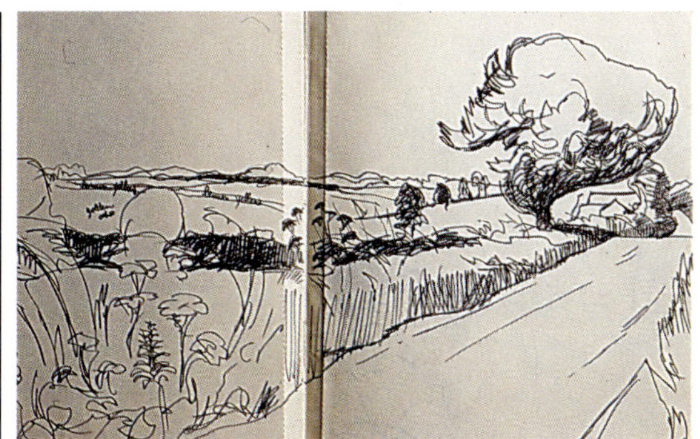

The subject chosen here **(above)** *has allowed the artist to relate the farm buildings to the shaded foliage behind. The barn, drawn in delicate line, is thrown into silhouette by the surrounding hatched tones.*

Strong shading and the repeated image of the reflections in the water lend a feeling of coolness and tranquility to this riverside scene **(below)**.

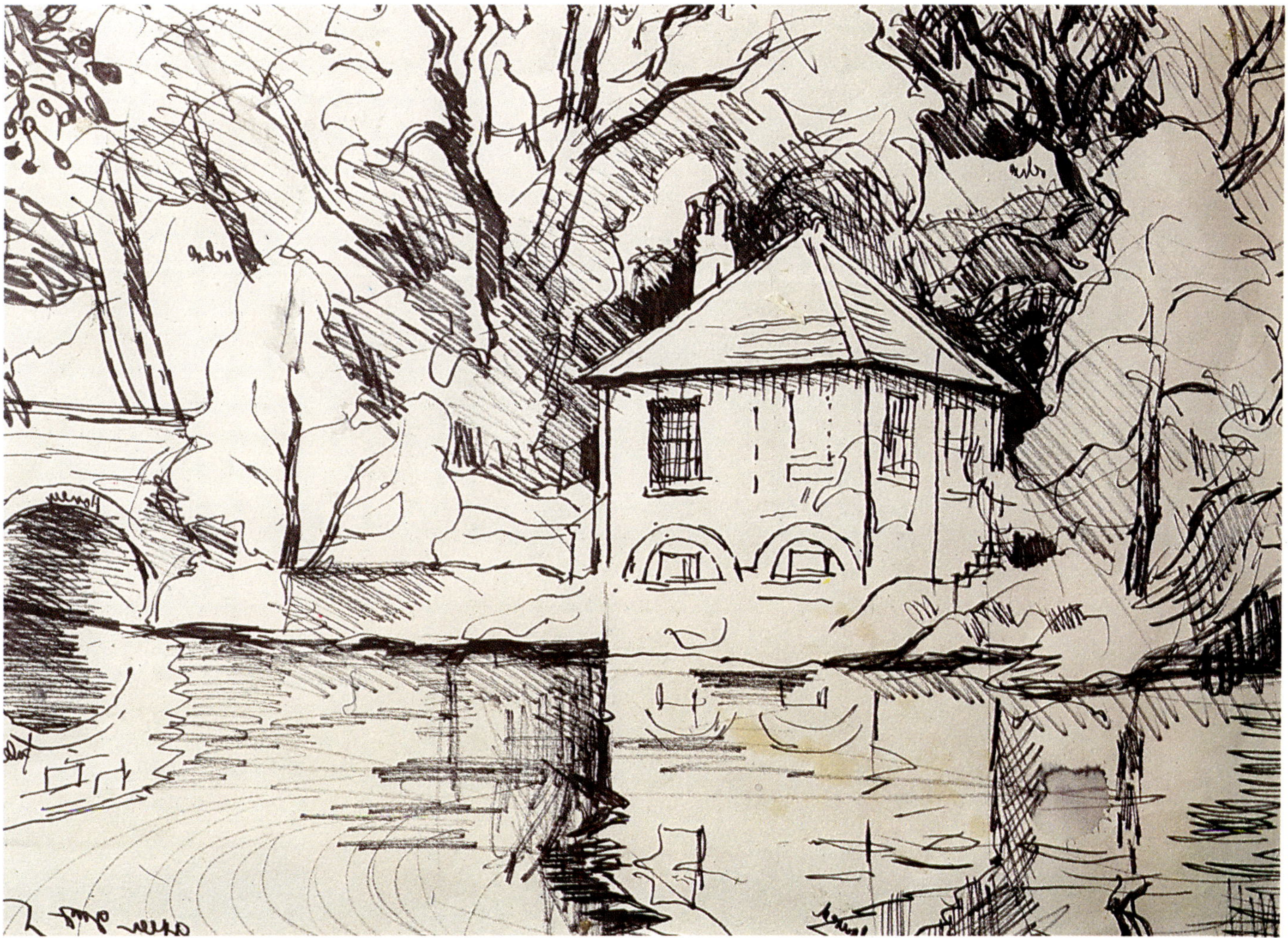

THE RED BOOTS

Liberties have been deliberately taken with this subject, to give added life to a pair of old red boots. The artist has taken the general shape, composition, and colour of the subject and through an individual use of line and colour washes has exaggerated features to make the picture more descriptive. The techniques used are washed-in colour, line, and cross-hatching, juxtaposed to create an interesting combination of textures.

One important aspect of this drawing is the use of negative space to define details.

1 *2*

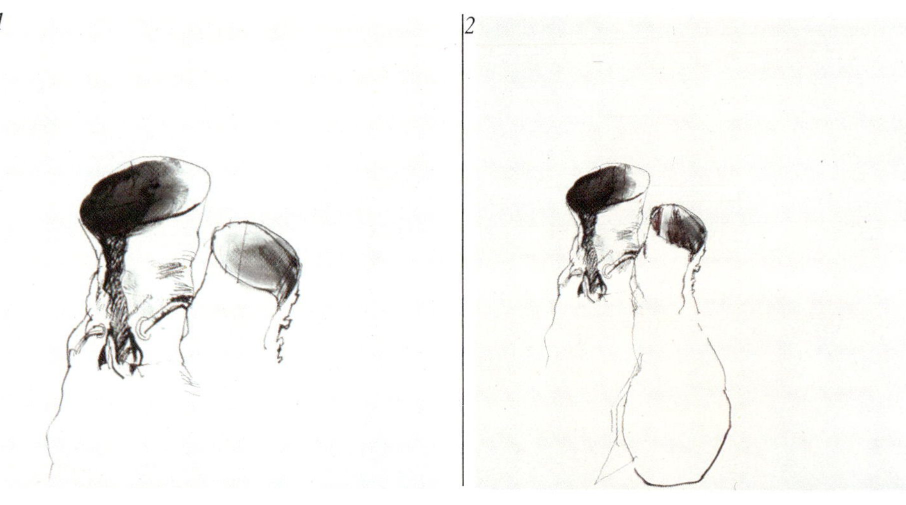

3

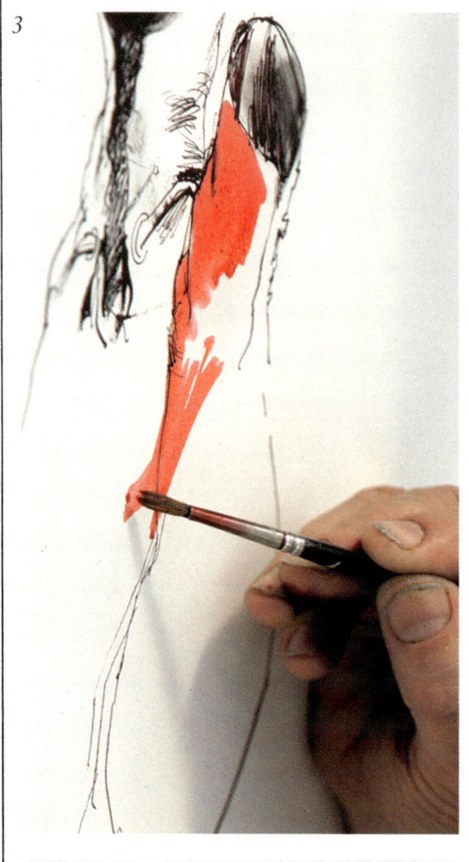

4

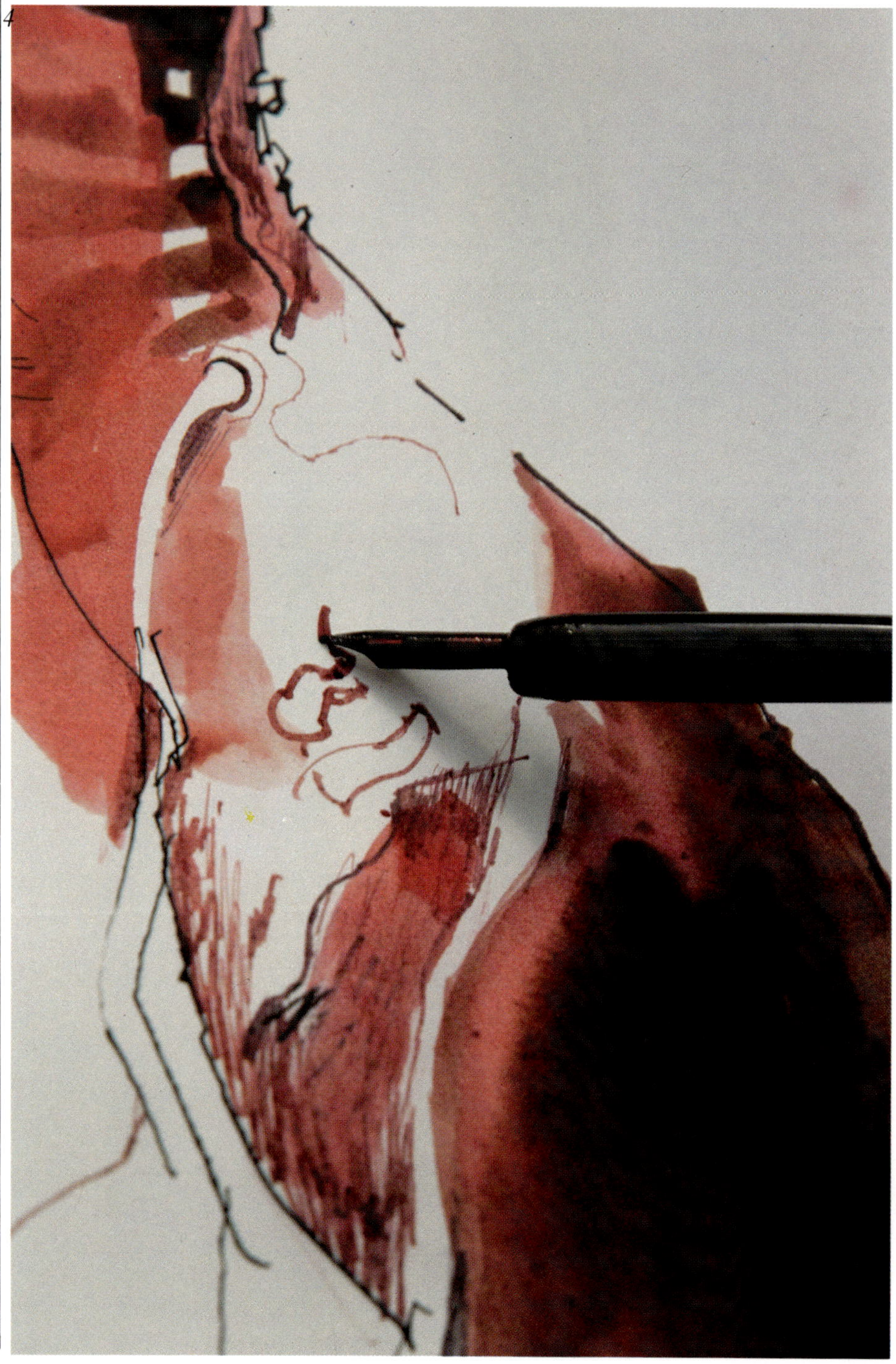

5

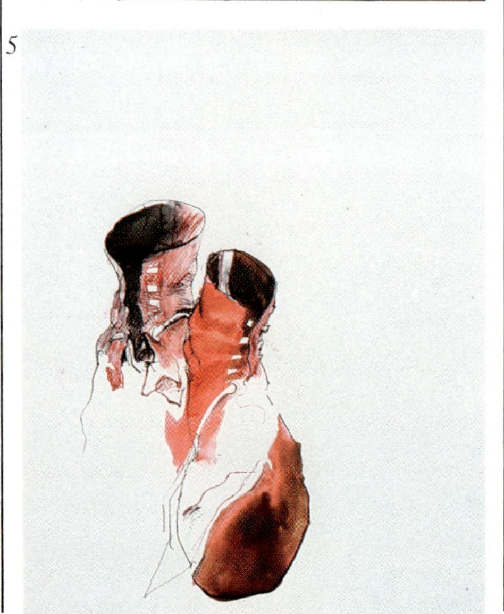

Start the outline in black ink and a dip pen. Vary the line by moving the pen both quickly and slowly. Dip a brush in water and let the pen line bleed into the wetted area, to create the shadows (1). Continue with the outline, indicating the texture of the leather (2). Put in the preliminary wash with red ink (3). Using a pen, add linear details such as the laces (4). Mix a small amount of red and burnt sienna to develop the outline of the boot (5).

6

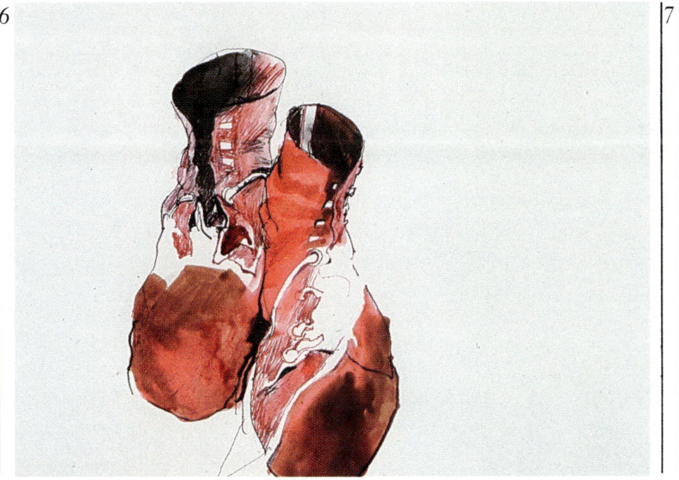

7

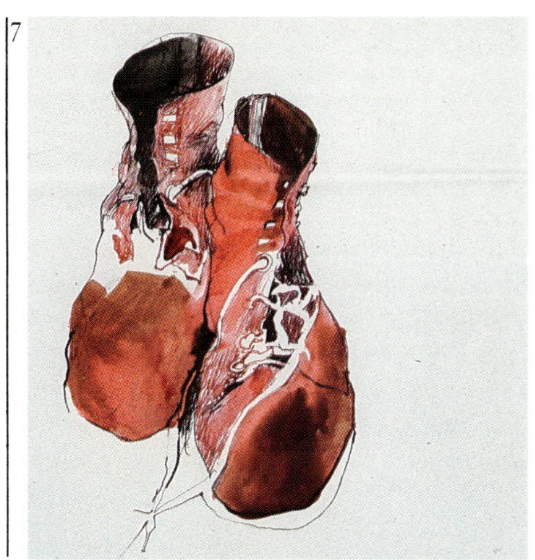

8

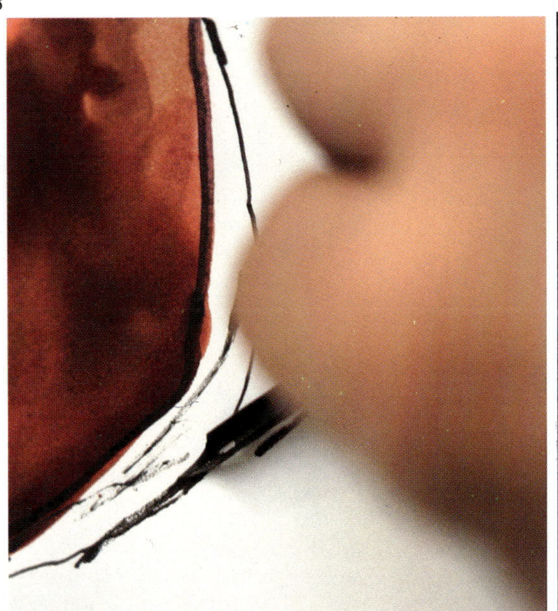

With red and black ink, cross-hatch the remaining area of the right boot, leaving parts untouched to create laces and holes (6). Using the pen and black ink, work back into the shoe with cross-hatching strokes to create the area around the laces (7). By turning the nib on its back, you will be able to create a rough jagged line (8). Use this to describe the sole of the boots (9). Complete the picture by laying a darker wash over the shadow areas of the left boot (10).

9

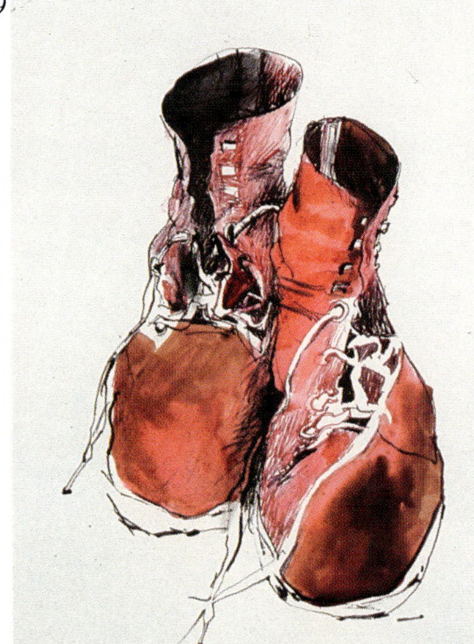

10

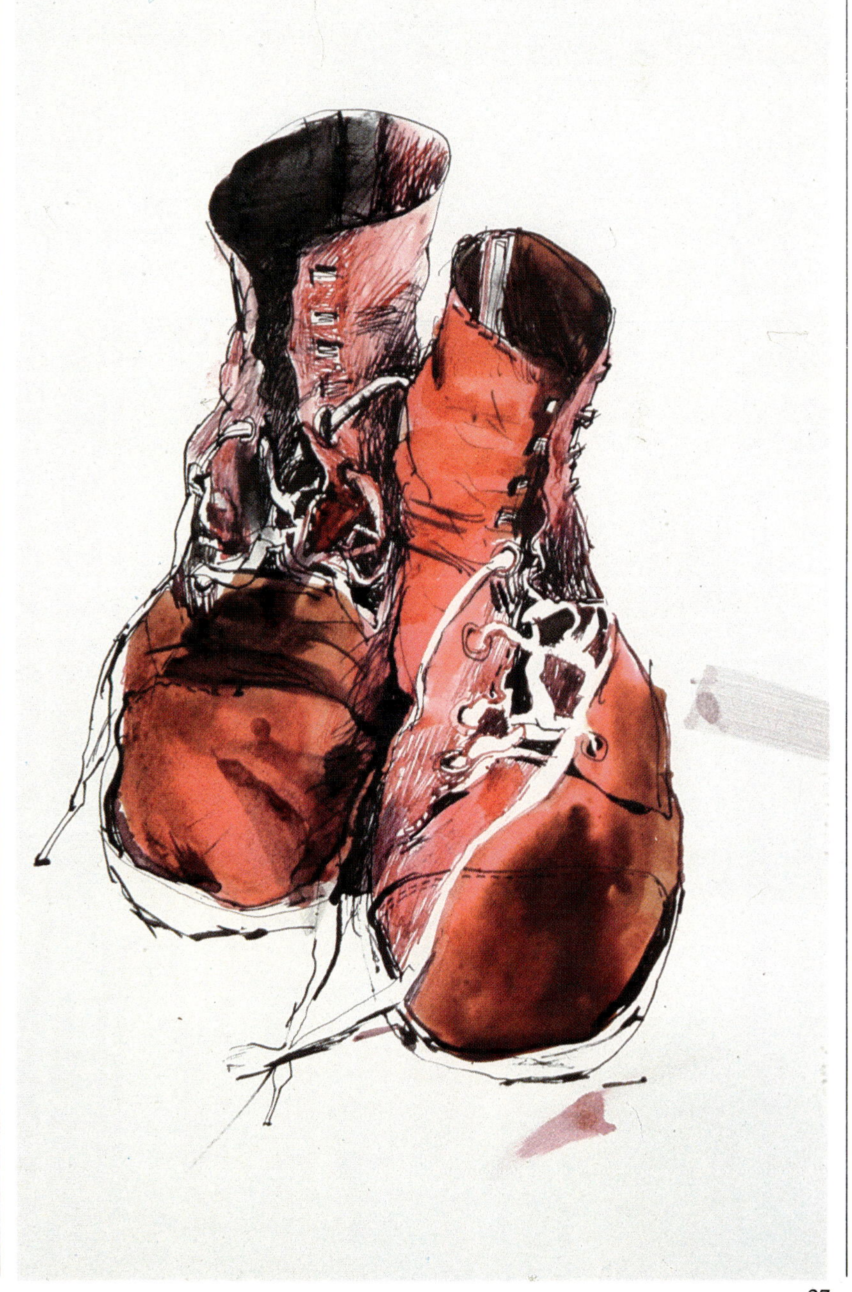

STILL-LIFE IN WHITE

An all-white still-life presents an excellent opportunity for looking carefully at tone. Our artist chose a few simple objects — a plate, mug, bottles and a box — and gave them a coat of matt white emulsion beforehand. This eliminated any distracting reflections and ensured that the subject was of a uniform white tone.

The picture is executed in coloured pencils and, although line and the side of the pencil lead were used to develop tonal areas, the method of drawing is similar to the classic oil painting technique of laying down colours, one over another, to achieve new colours. This requires confidence, because once put down coloured pencils are difficult to erase.

A striking feature of the composition is the use of the white paper within the objects to describe the local colour and highlights. The result is a convincing composition in which the individual objects are securely located in space, and the character of the composition is accurately conveyed. An exercise such as this where observation and accuracy are called for is taxing, but it is an excellent way of sharpening your perception, noting and recording the fine gradations of tone around an object.

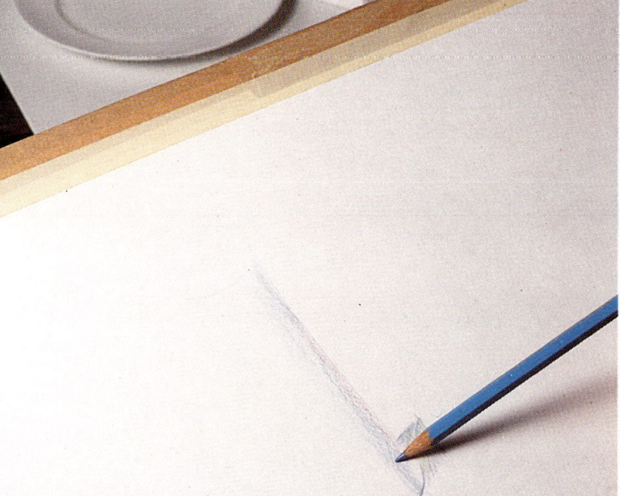

Use a wide selection of coloured pencils for this exercise, giving yourself plenty of scope to make an exciting composition from the all-white subject. Use blue to sketch in the outlines **(left)**, *keeping the objects large and central on the paper.*

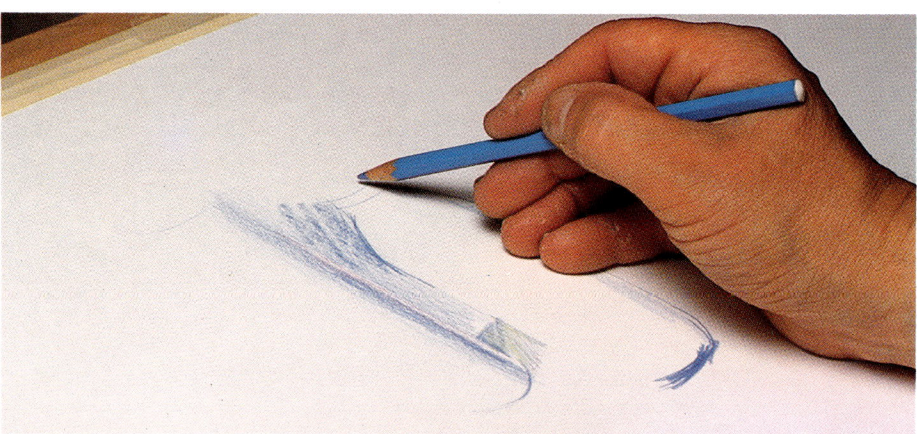

Block in the background in the same colour **(above)**. *This provides a solid tone to work into later with other colours.*

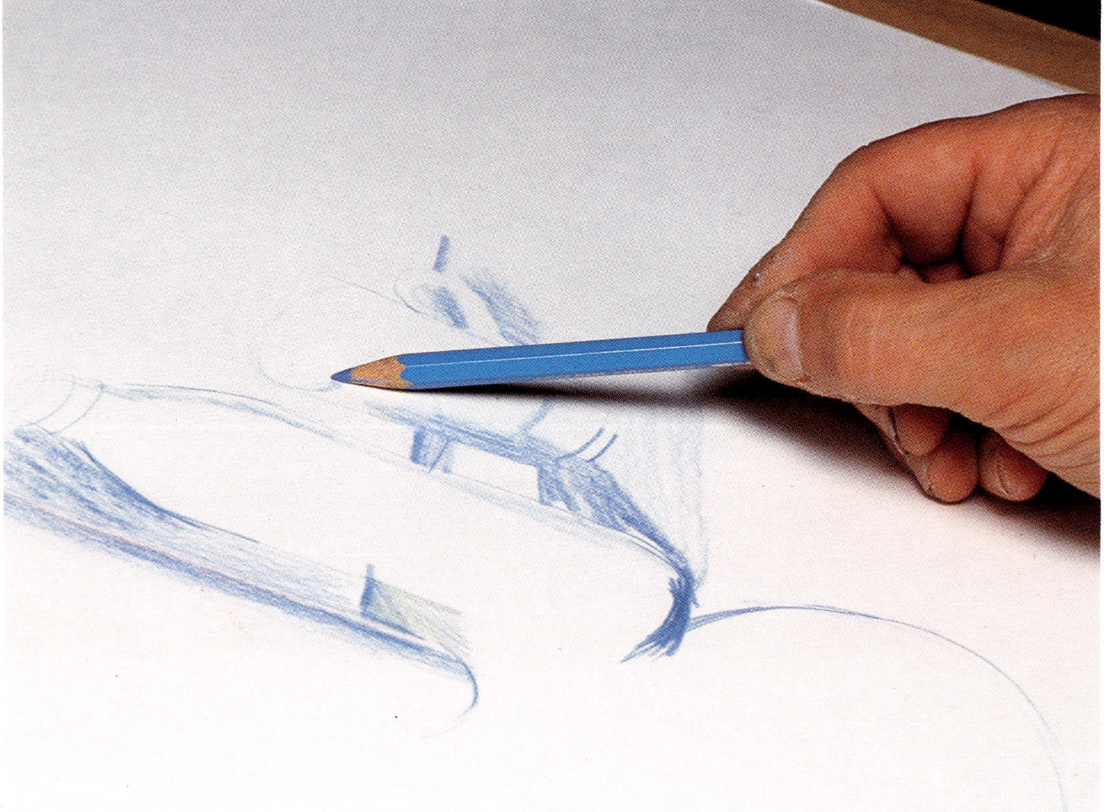

Using the white paper as a light tone, draw into the outlines, laying in shadows to show the form of the objects **(left)**.

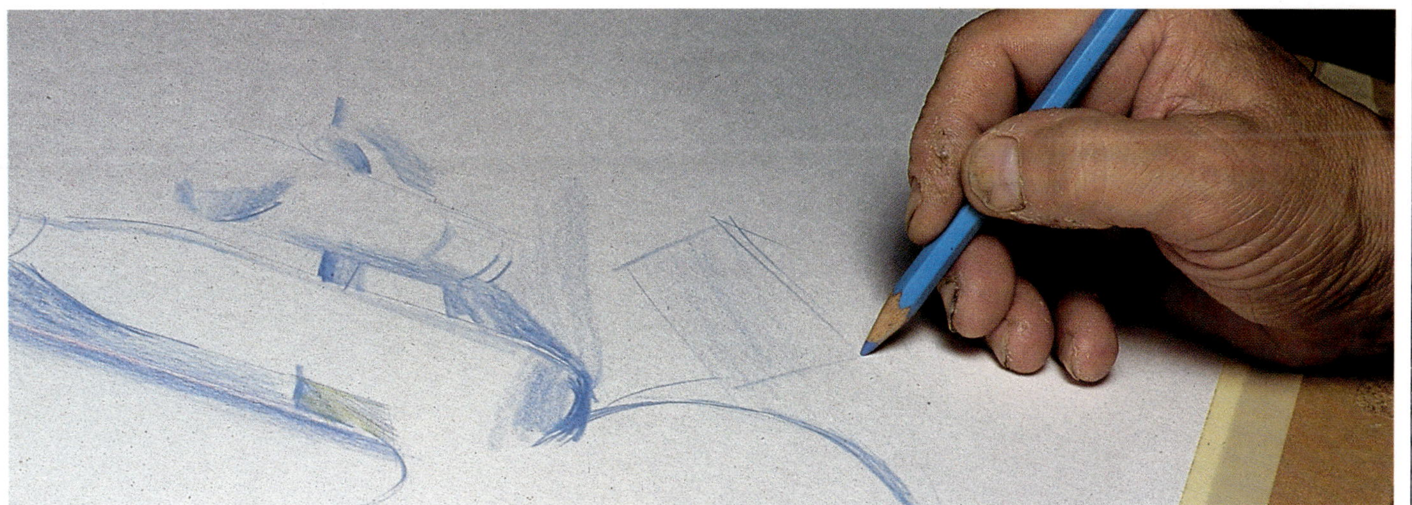

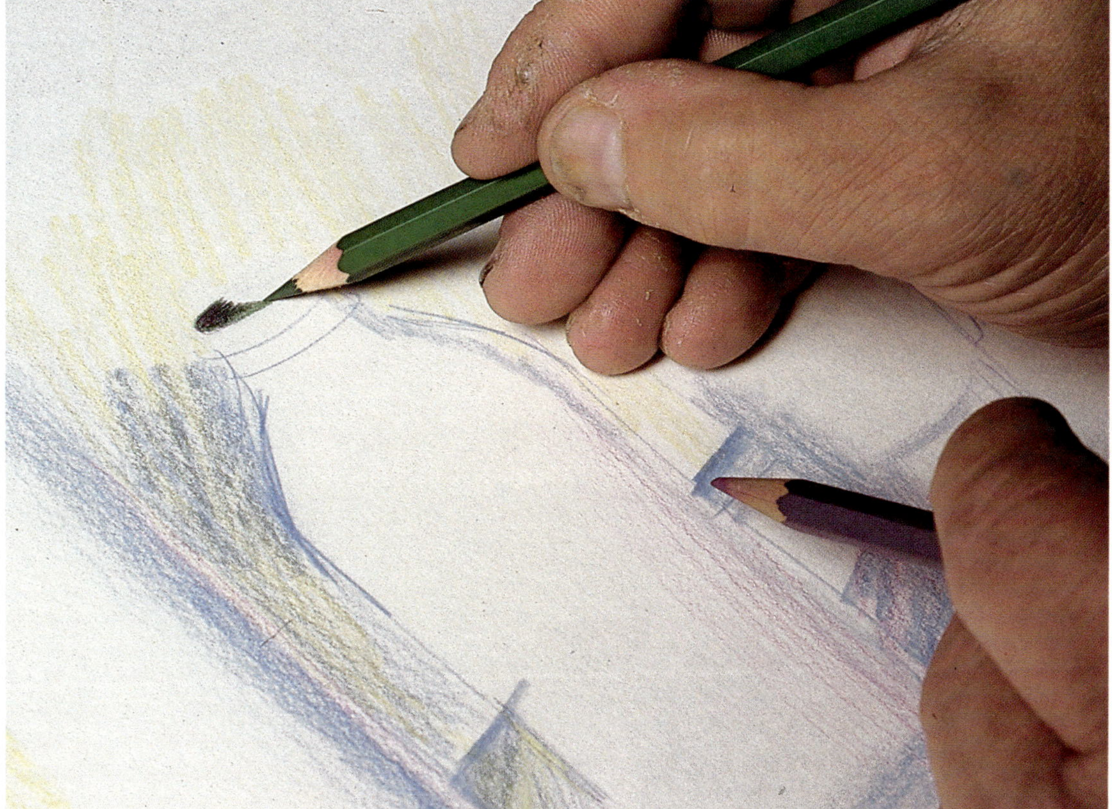

Continue to define the drawing, making the lines and shadows quite hard and definite **(above)**. *Look closely at the tones and reflections on the white objects. Try to differentiate between cool and warm areas, and to pick out any colours which may be reflected from the surrounding room. Close observation will often enable you to find subtle colour differences on the white surfaces. Introduce other colours into the drawing* **(left)**, *exaggerating the slight differences visible on the white.*

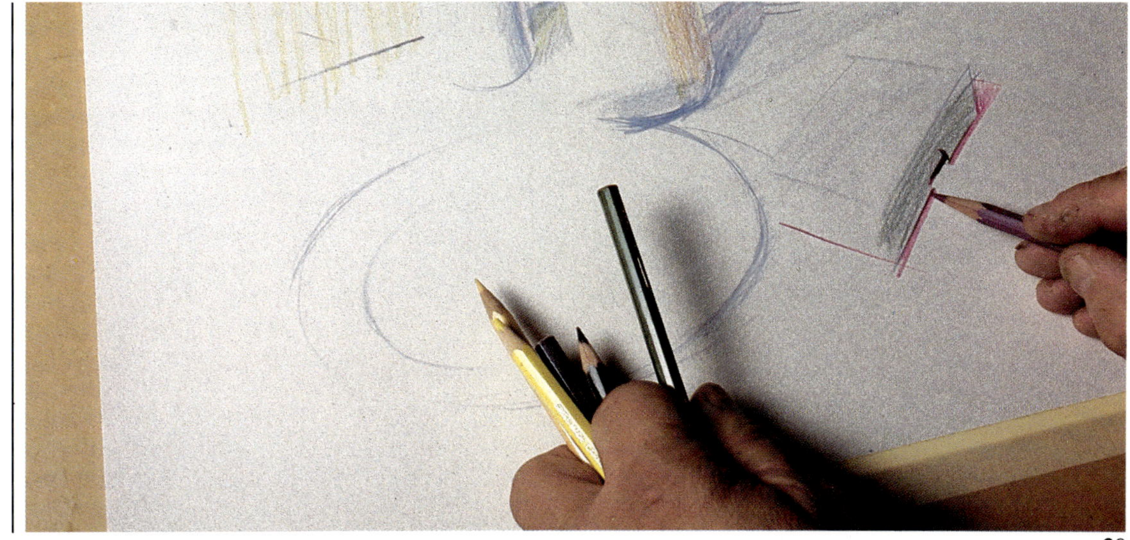

Keeping broad differences between the cool and warm areas, use the coloured pencils to build up the shadows **(right)**. *Many different colours can be used together without losing their separate identity or becoming muddy.*

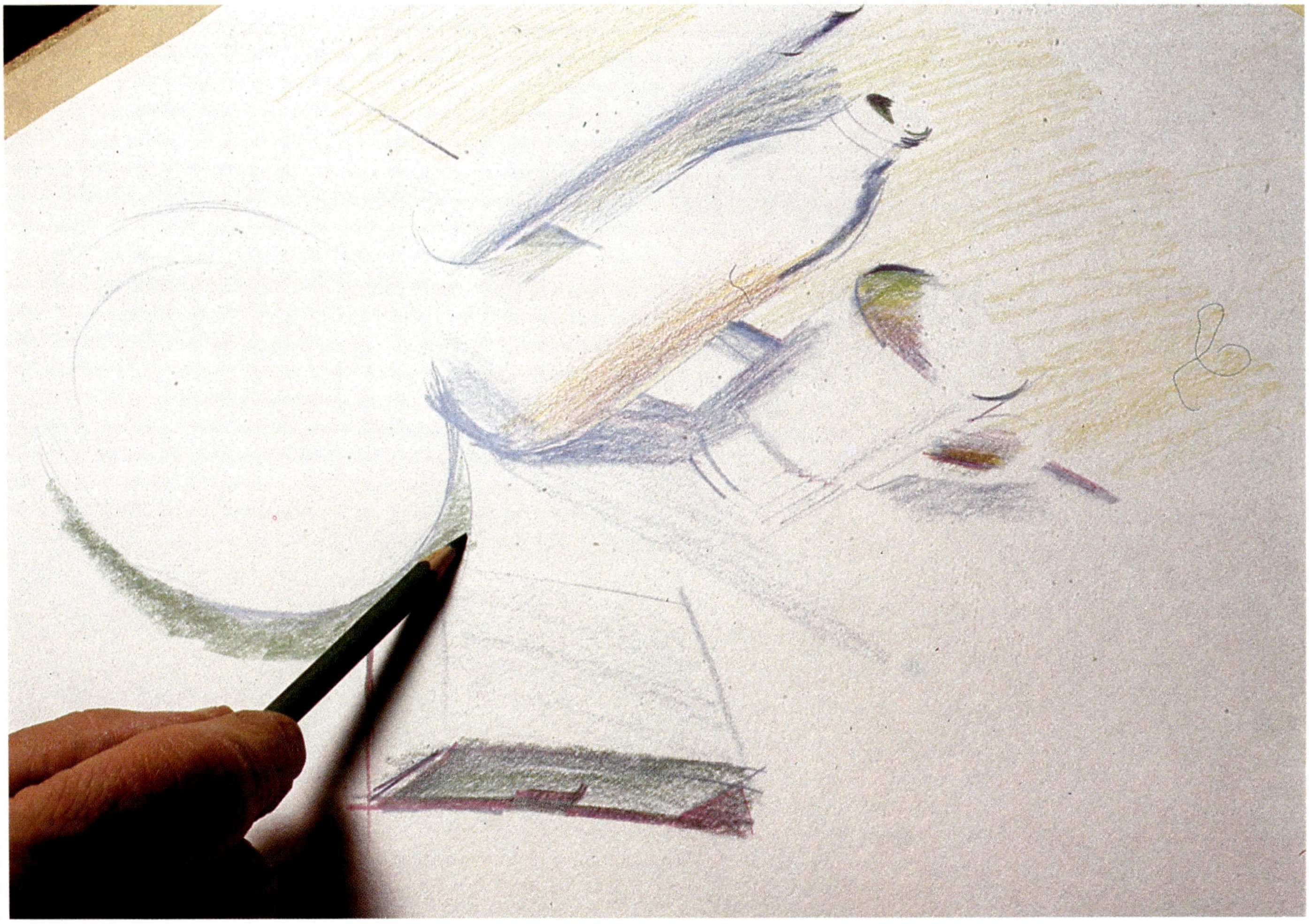

Keep the pencils sharp to ensure crisp, distinct drawing. Use the darker colours to build up the sharp, clear edges of the objects **(above)**. *Use coloured pencils to define the outline and obtain a finished effect* **(right)**. *Leave clear areas of white paper to maintain a crisp, clean quality.*

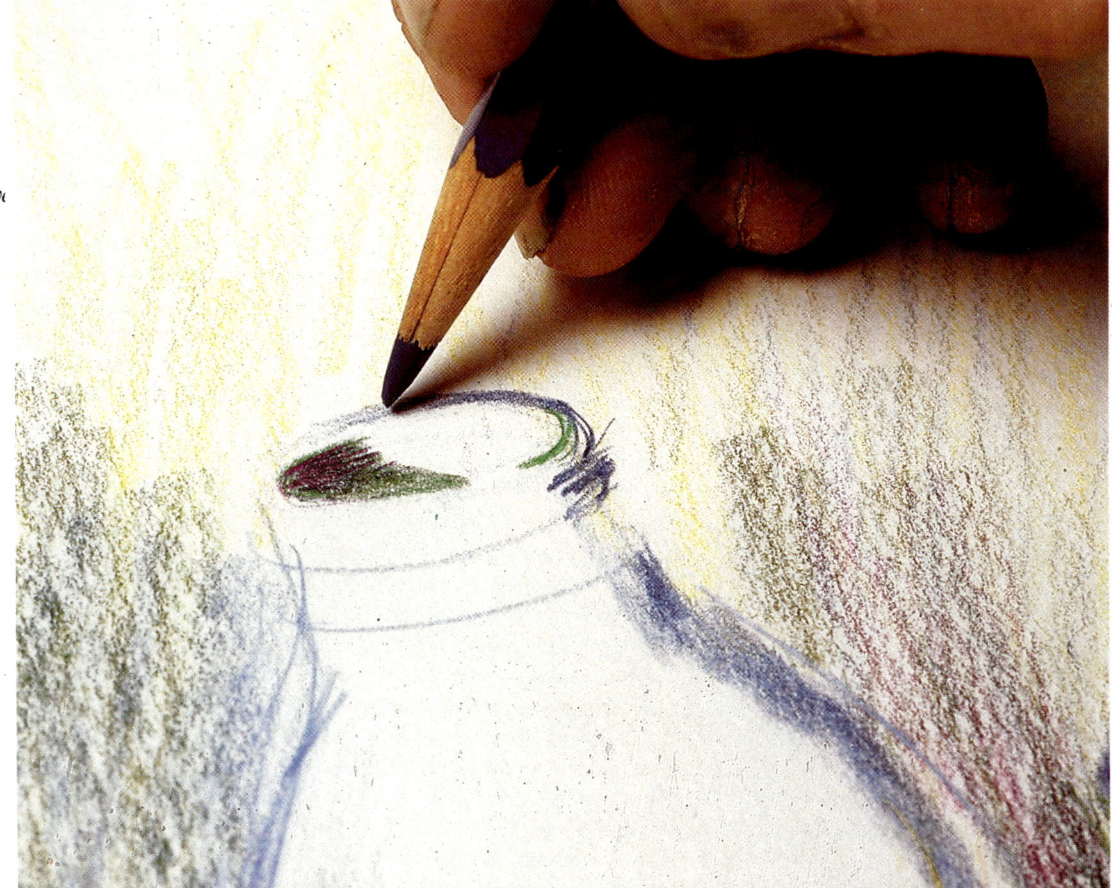

Experiment with different colour combinations. Blues and purples used together produce cool shadows **(right)**; *reds and yellows combine to make vibrant, warm tones.*

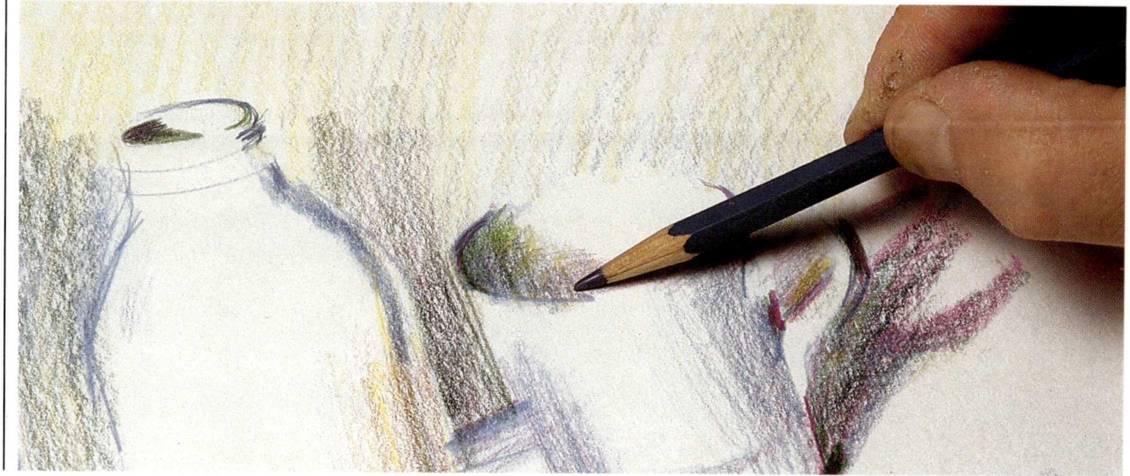

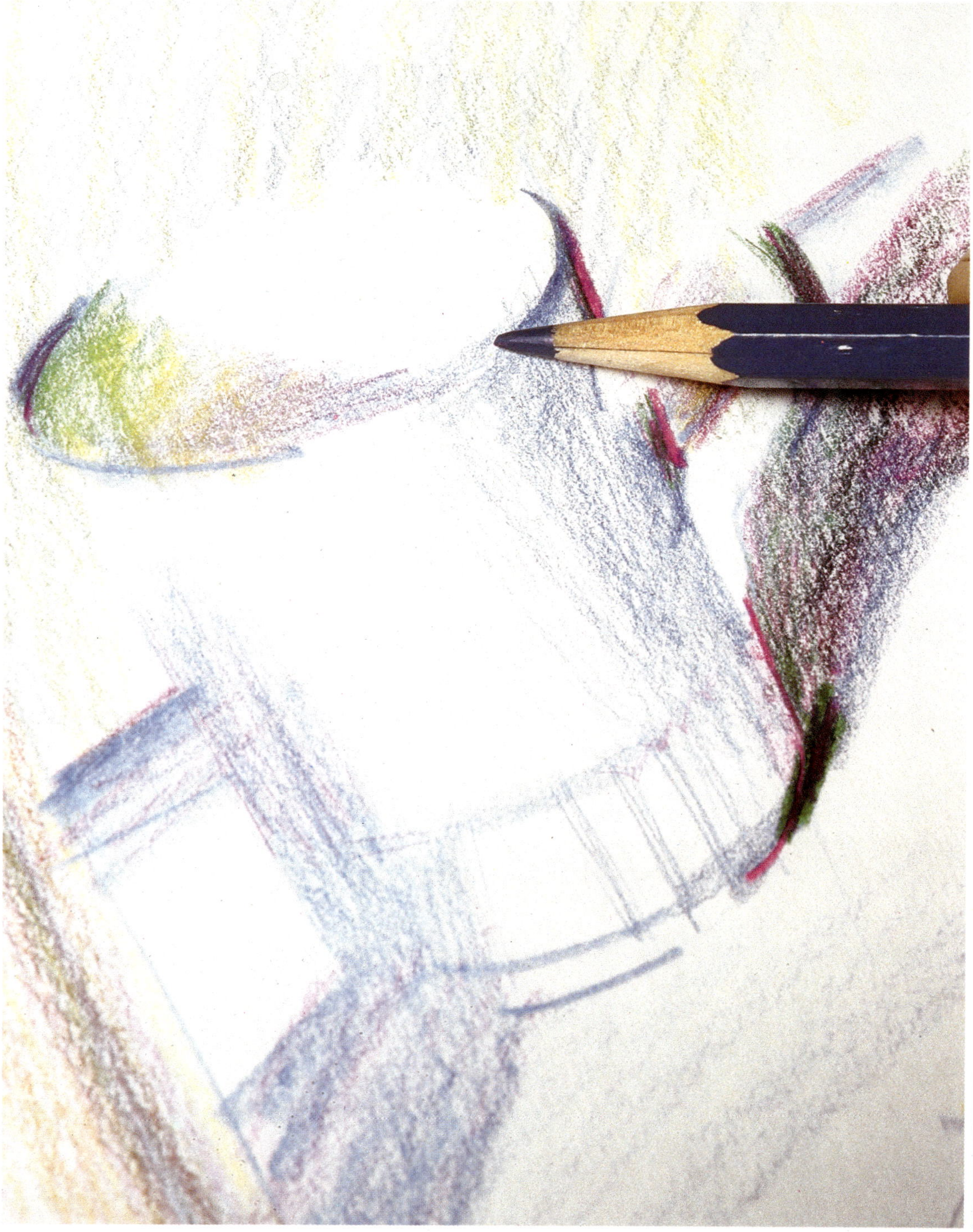

It is important not to overwork your drawing. Too many layers of colour clog the surface of the paper and cannot be easily erased. Where the outline becomes lost, carefully redraw this with a sharpened pencil **(left)**.

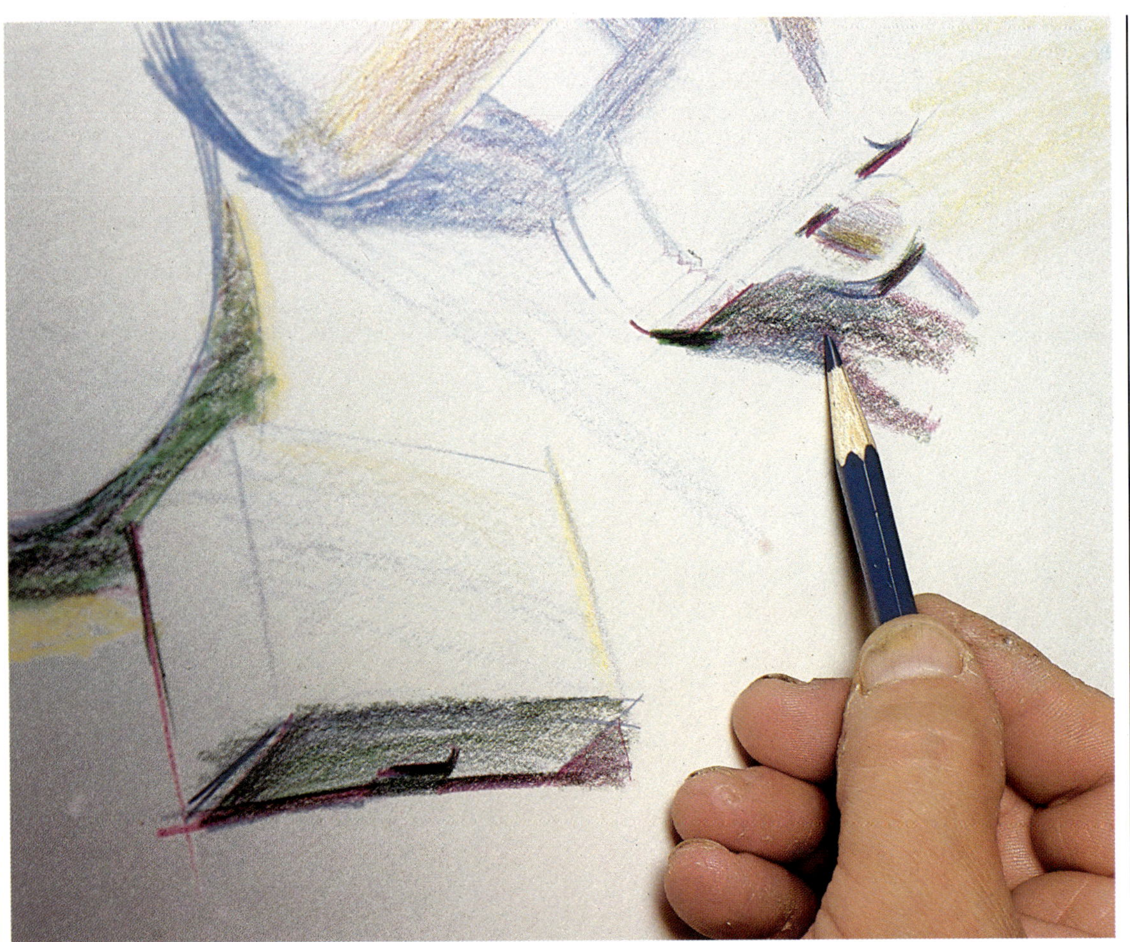

Use complementary colours together to obtain a neutral effect. These neutral tones will not become muddy or dead if you allow the separate colours to show through and do not make the pencil strokes too dense **(left)**.

The finished drawing shows how colour can be used creatively when there is very little colour in the actual subject **(below)**.

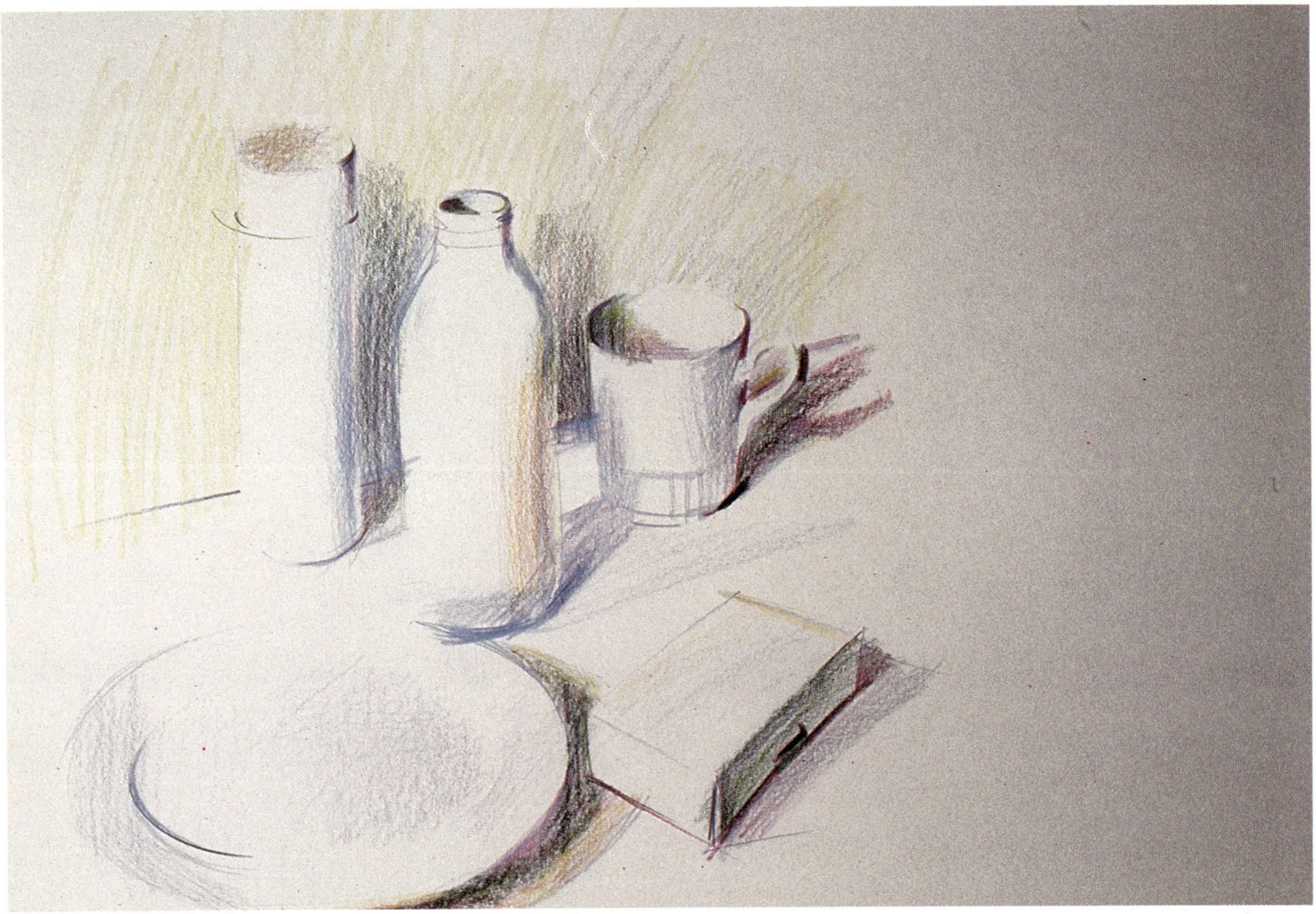

PART TWO

Drawing with PASTELS

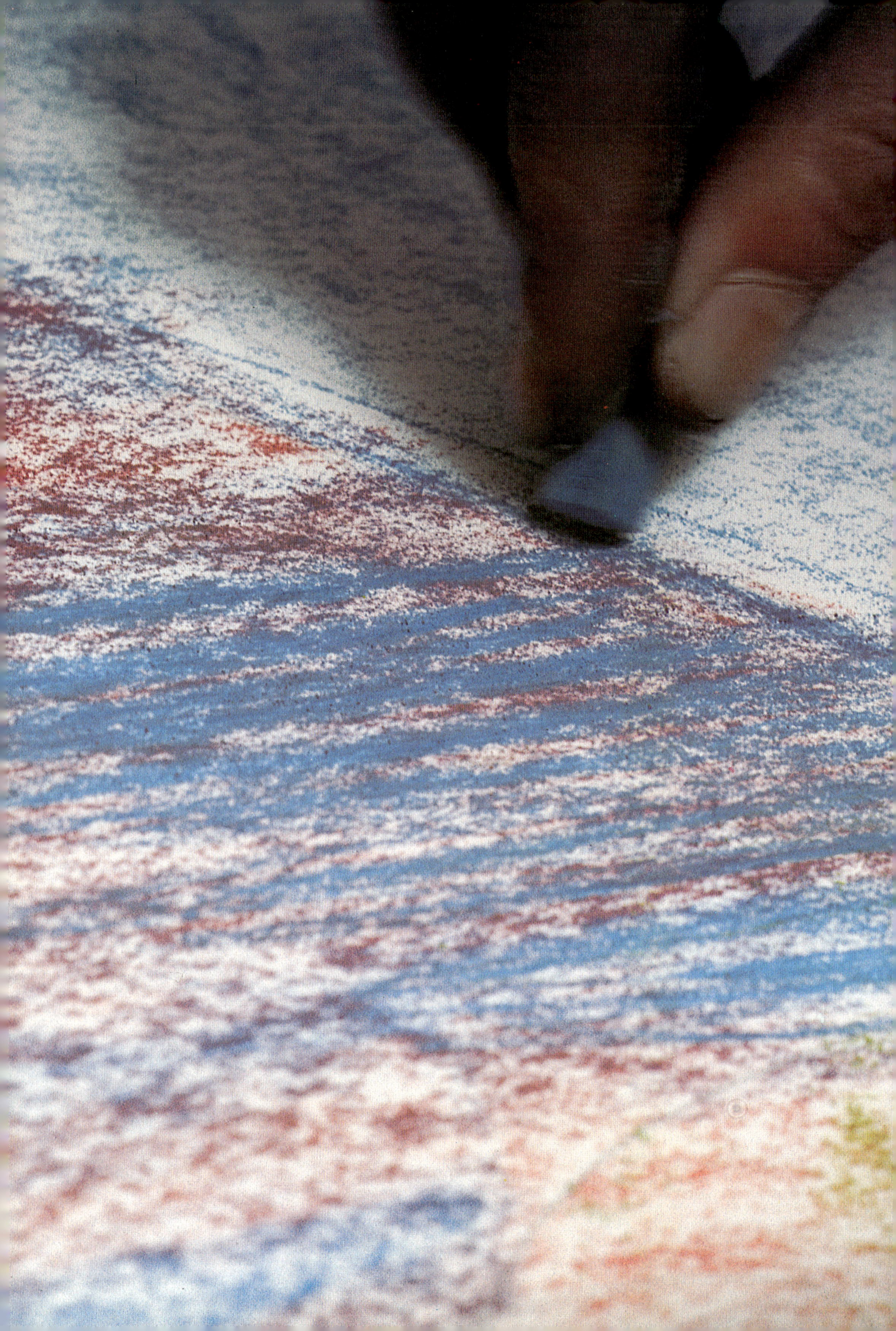

MATERIALS

Pastels are powdered pigments mixed with just enough gum or resin to bind them together. The word pastel is derived from the resulting 'paste', which is moulded into the familiar pastel sticks. The charm and freshness of pastels, their purity of colour and their immediate response when applied to paper are part of the nature of the medium and distinguish it from oil painting. Pastels can be purchased in three qualities, soft, medium and hard. Soft pastels offer the most brilliant range of colours.

Unlike watercolour and oils, pastels cannot be mixed on the palette to form other colours and tones. These have to be manufactured separately, and, in all, some 600 tints are on the market. Some manufacturers supply pastels in pencil form. Selecting a suitable range is very much a matter of individual taste. A basic selection might consist of about 48 colours, while a small range of about twelve colour sticks would be suitable for outdoor sketching. Begin with a boxed set and expand the selection as needed.

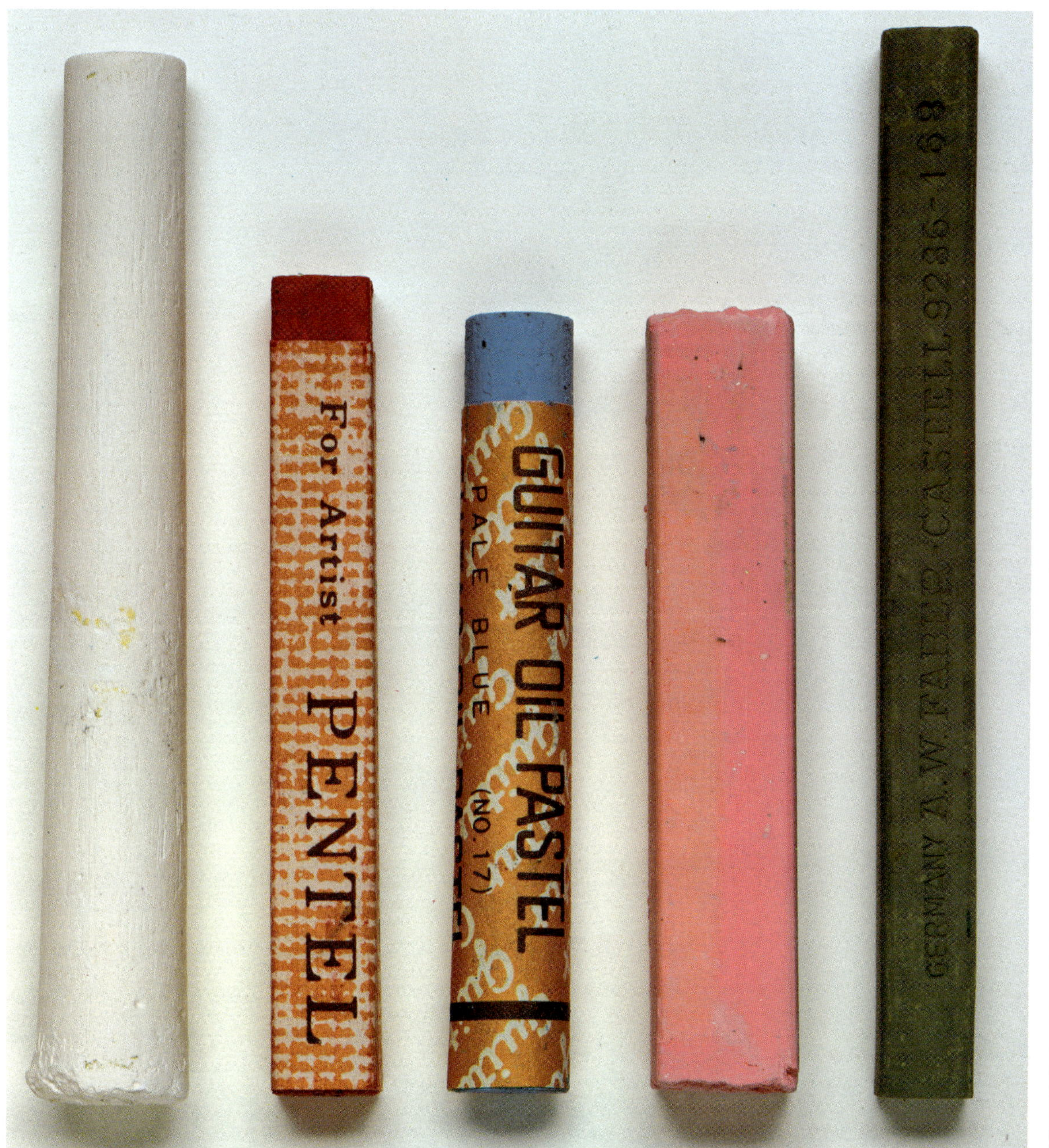

TECHNIQUES

Before beginning a picture, lay out your pastels on a piece of soft cloth or corrugated cardboard, arranging them carefully according to colour and tone. In this way you will avoid having to break off in the middle of the work to search for the right colour pastel.

Begin by practising various strokes, colours and effects on paper similar to that to be used for the picture itself. You will find that the pastel stick can be manipulated to produce thick and thin lines and textures. For instance, the sharp edge of a broken pastel, drawn lightly across the paper, will produce a fine line; by laying the end of the pastel flat on the paper a flat even area of colour can be laid down. Heavy pressure forces a lot of pastel into the grain of the paper, light pressure reveals more paper through the colour. Pastel laid on flock paper gives a velvety patch of colour, on fine canvas it produces a fairly flat colour. On glass paper and ingres paper much of the texture shows through the pastel.

Delicate contrasts can be achieved by covering a torchon or stiff brush with powdered pastel and applying it lightly across the picture. Fine hatching, cross-hatching or alternatively strokes of different colours and tones produce effective shading.

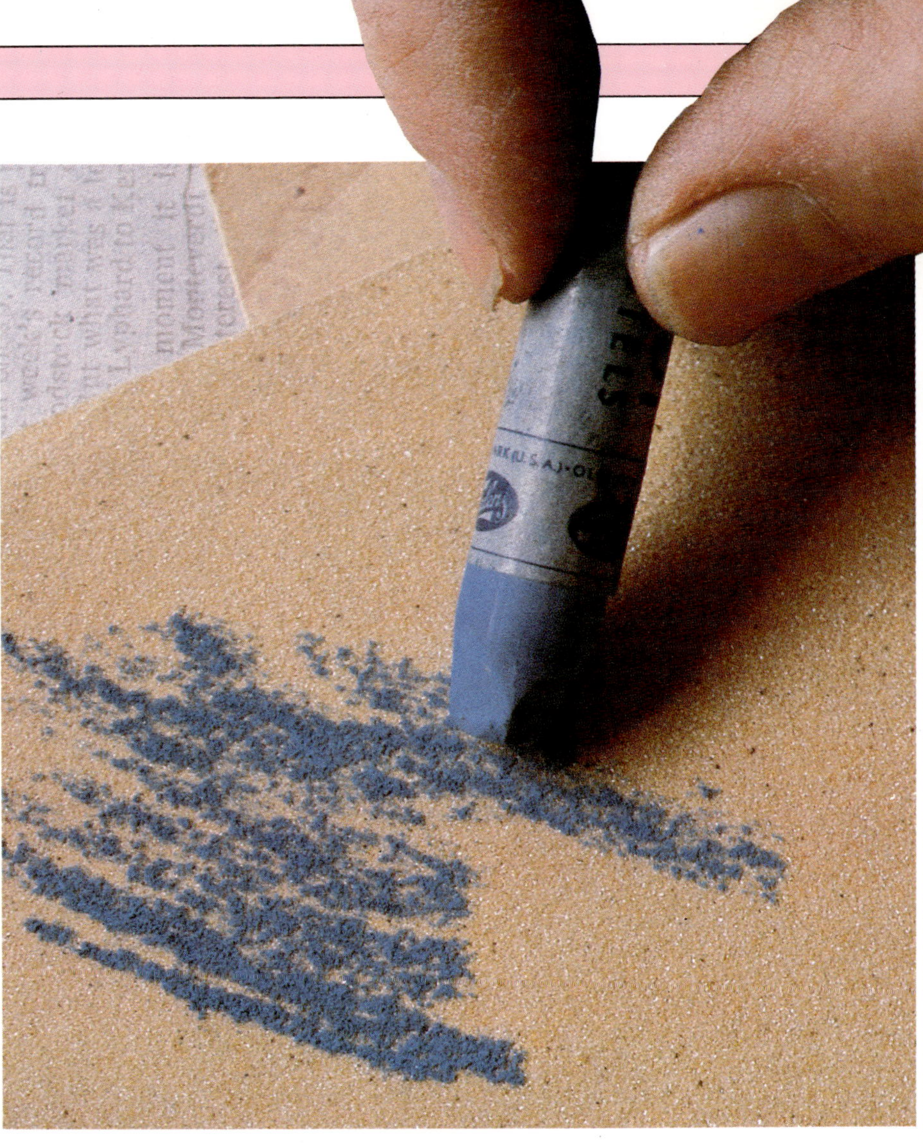

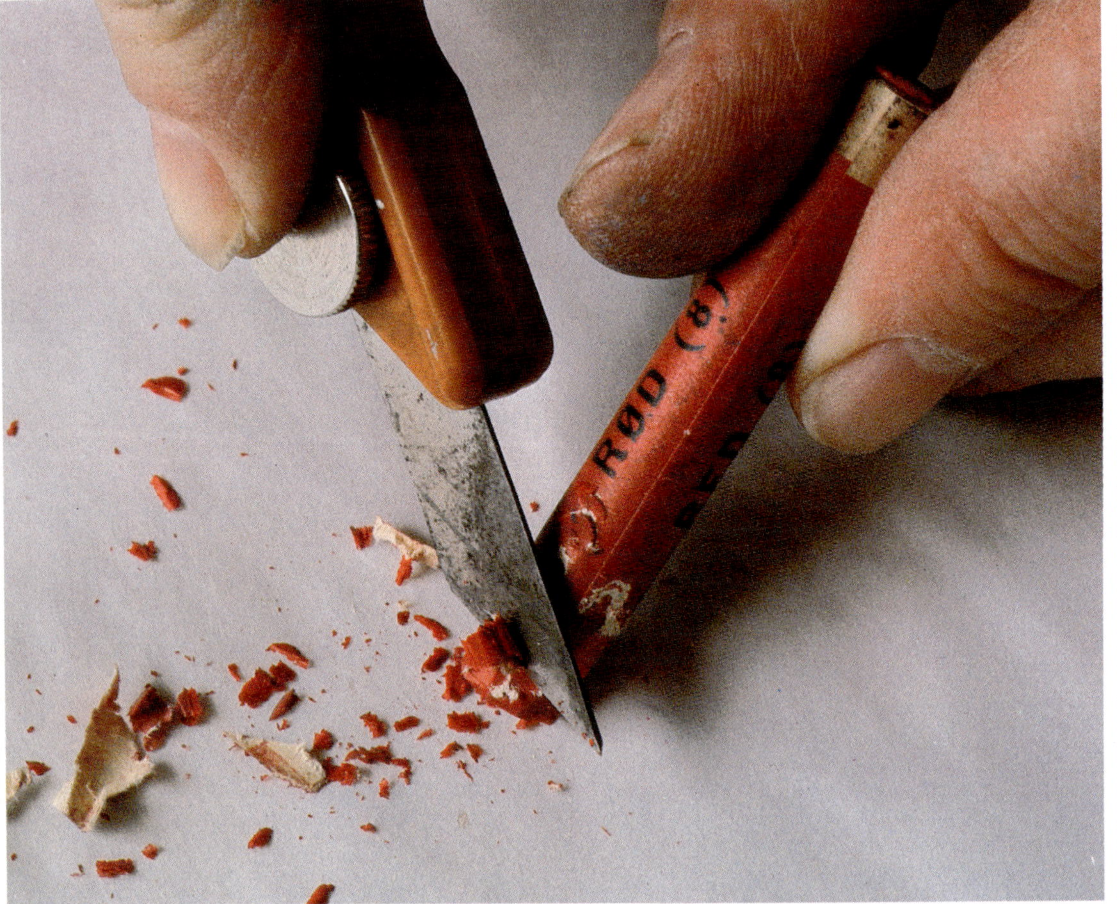

Sharpening pastels. For very fine work, rub the end of the pastel lightly on fine sandpaper to chamfer a point **(above)**. *Oil pastels are more firmly bound and harder than true pastels, so these can be sharpened with a knife* **(left)**. *Sharp pastels are useful for line work but as they are very soft you will have to resharpen them quite often if you are to avoid smudgy, ill-defined lines.*

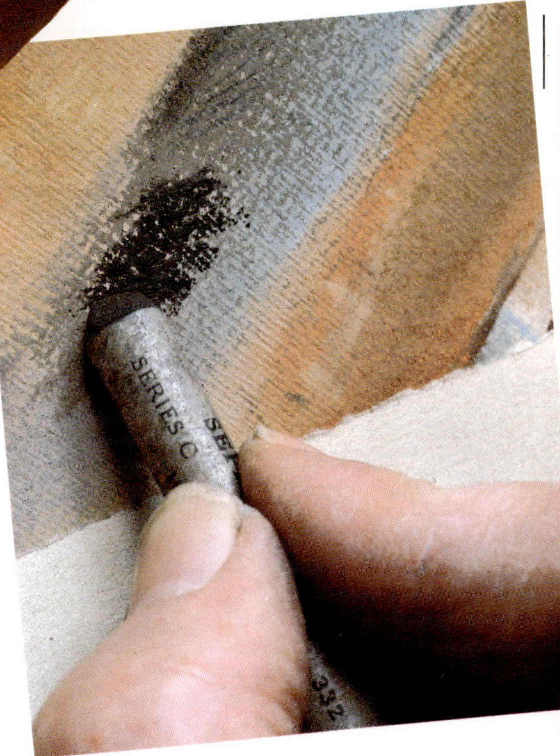

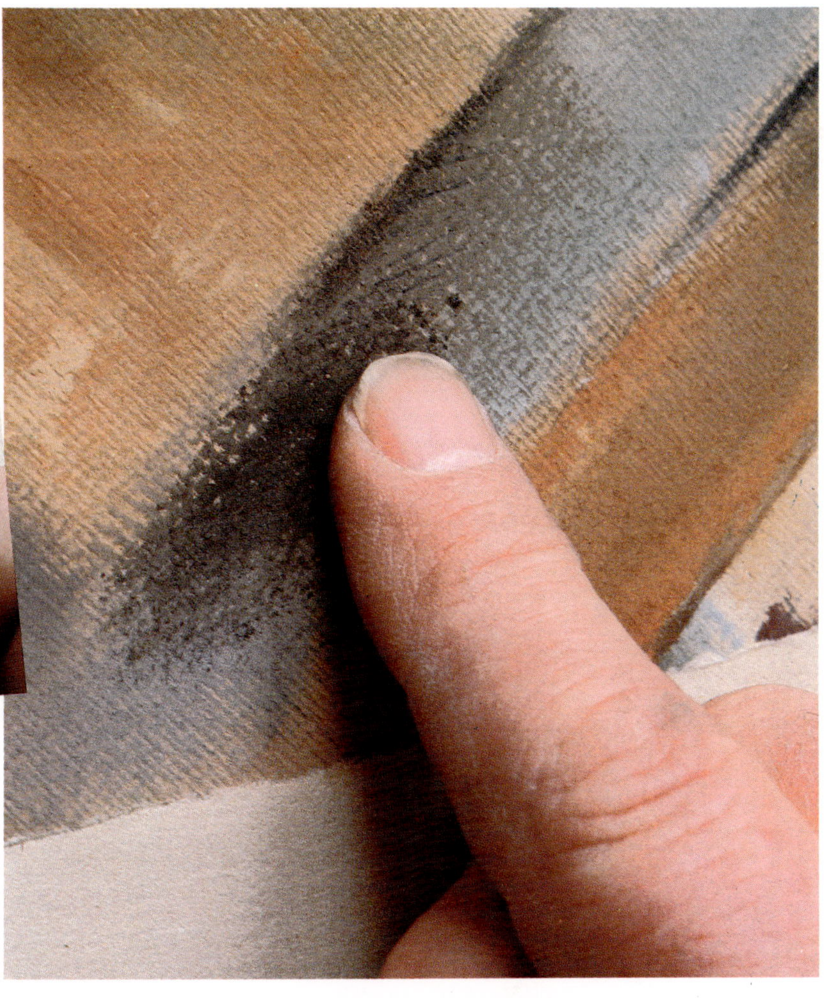

Laying an area of tone. Draw in a small area of thick colour using the blunted end of the pastel **(top)**. Using your fingertips spread the colour slightly **(right)** and work it into the area required. If necessary more colour can be added for extra density. This method can also be used to blend two or more colours. Work with the board tilted slightly so the pastel dust falls off the drawing.

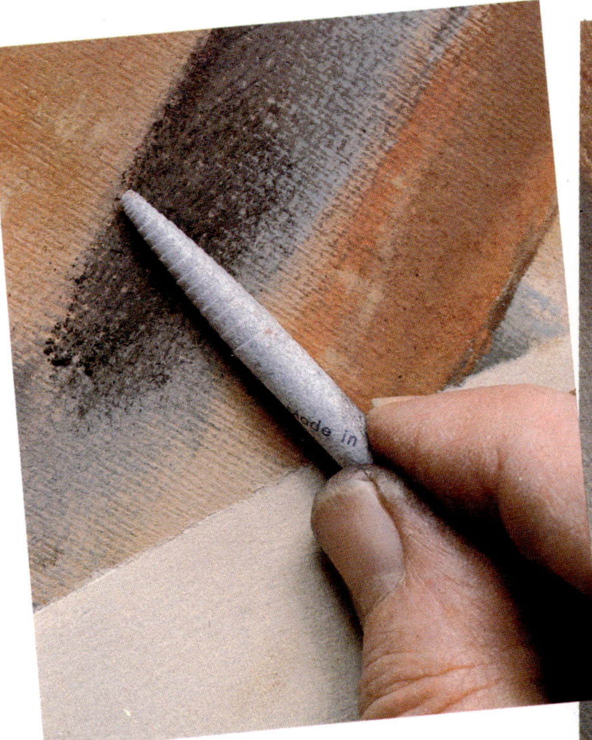

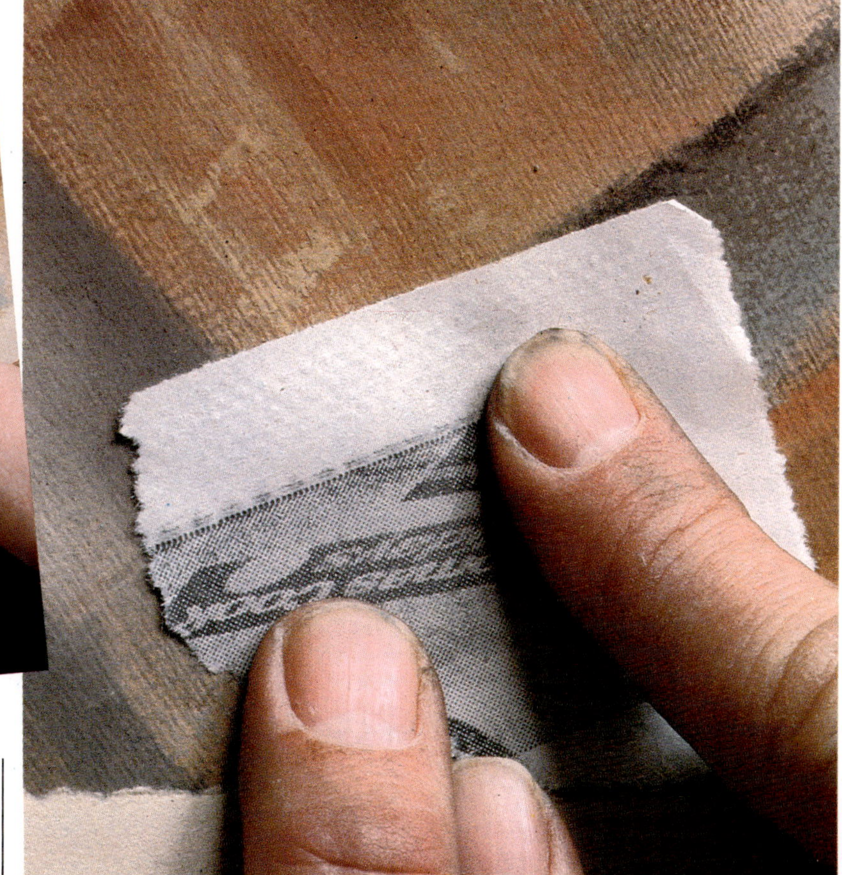

Using a torchon. A torchon is a pencil shaped tool, made from tightly rolled paper, which can be used to spread the pastel. This is useful for fine details **(above)**.

Setting the pigment. Place a piece of newspaper over the area of colour and rub it. This pushes the pastel into the grain of the paper making it less likely to smudge **(right)**.

Using a coloured support. The grainy texture of pastel is well suited to coloured paper which shows through the pigment modifying and unifying the colour. You can mix colours by laying them down as short, open strokes **(below)**. They mix optically the perceived colour being a product of the brown and blue pastels and the pink support.

Combining different marks. **Right** the artist has laid down lightly hatched strokes of colour, and beside that solid colour into which he has worked a lighter tone. It is worth spending time experimenting to see how many different marks you can elicit from a stick of pastel.

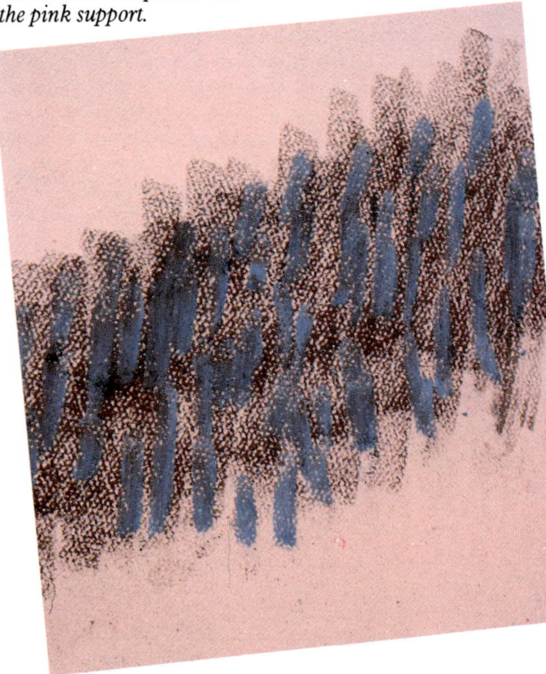

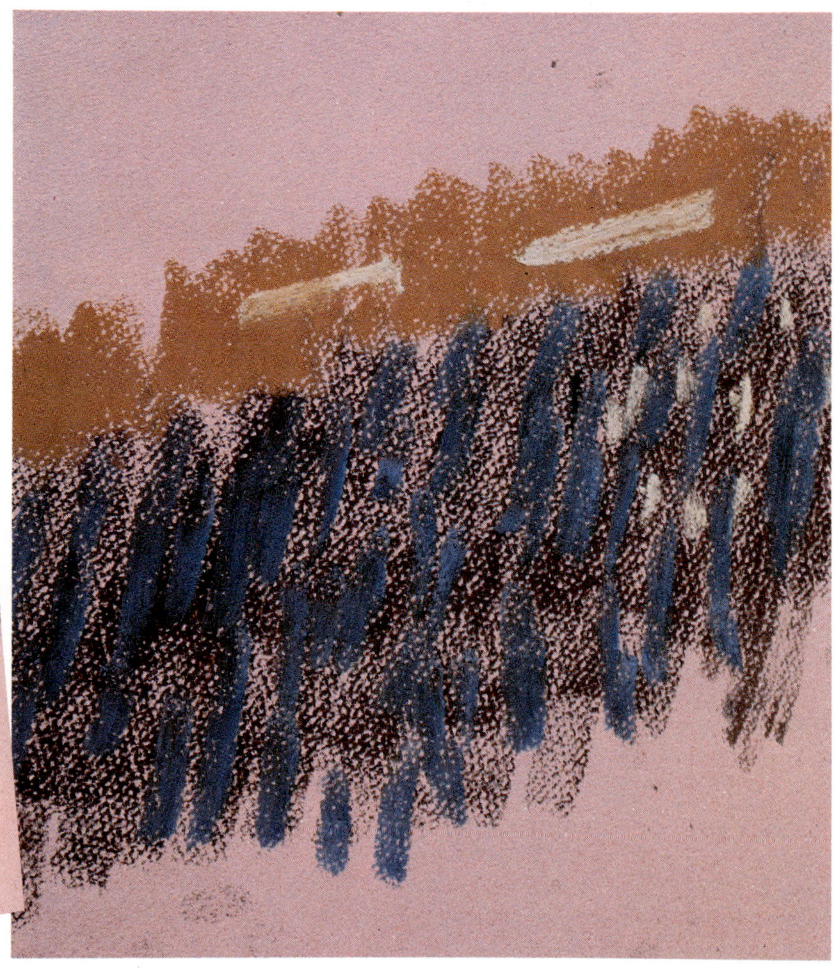

Using charcoal. Strong dark tones can be laid in with charcoal. Put down broad, black lines and spread them out with the fingertips **(below)**. Highlights can also be worked into the charcoal, but eventually the colours will clog together — so do not overwork the surface **(right)**. The clarity and tonal differences in the drawing will soon be lost if it is not fixed immediately after completion. Pastel drawings are very susceptible to smudging, especially when white and dark colours are used in the same picture.

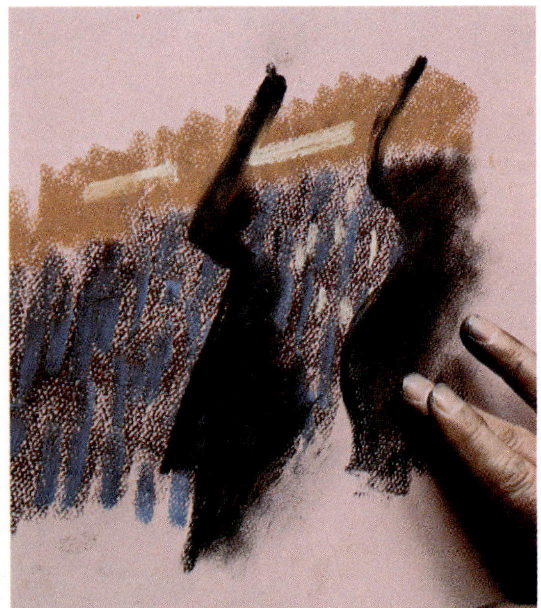

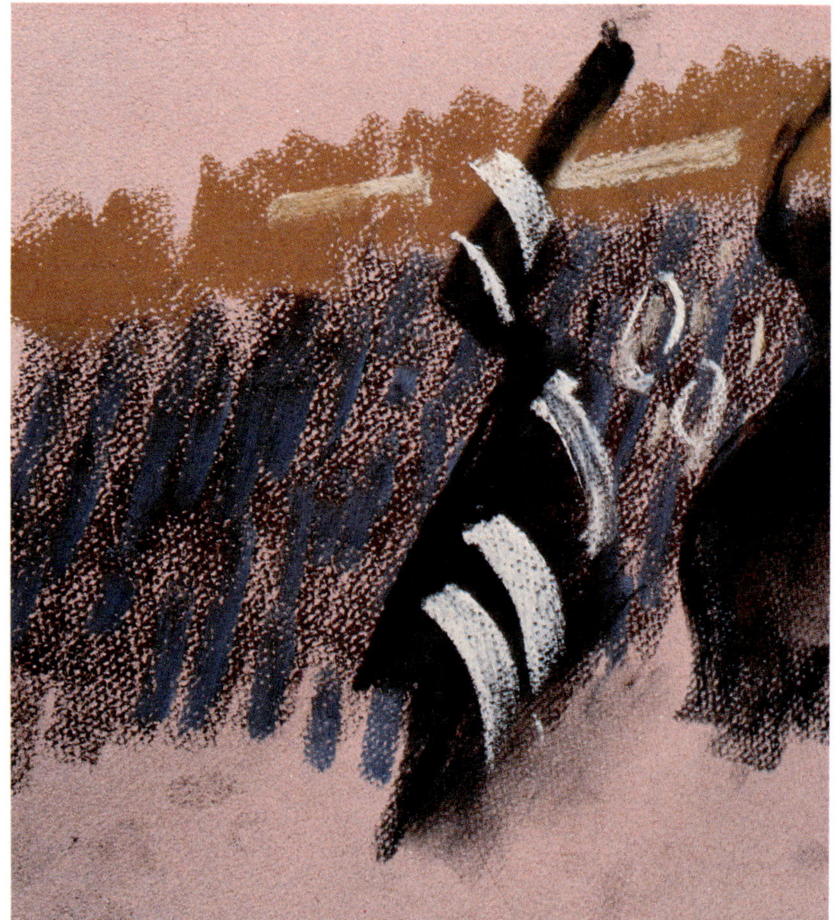

Lifting pastel with a brush. A soft sable brush can be used to lift excess pastel and to lighten the tone. Blow away surplus dust **(right)**. *Adding detail with charcoal. For fine work, sharpen the end of the charcoal by rubbing it lightly on sandpaper. Charcoal can be used to add strong, crisp detail. Pastel can be worked over the charcoal* **(below)** *and the hard line can be 'knocked back' by blending. To protect the drawing while you work you should rest your hand on a piece of paper* **(bottom)**. *Highlighting with a soft rubber. Knead the rubber to a point and lift a small area of the pastel to obtain lighter tones* **(bottom right)**.

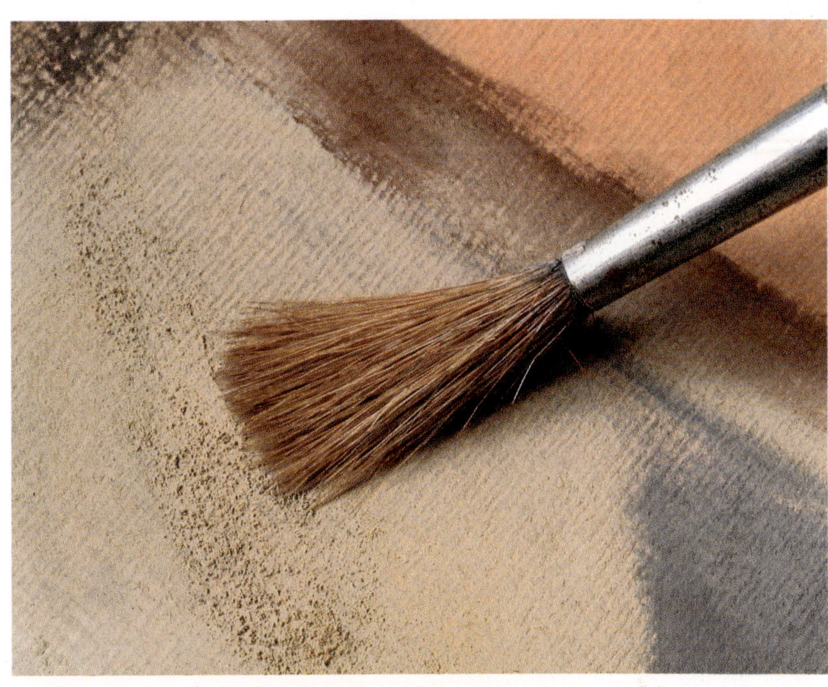

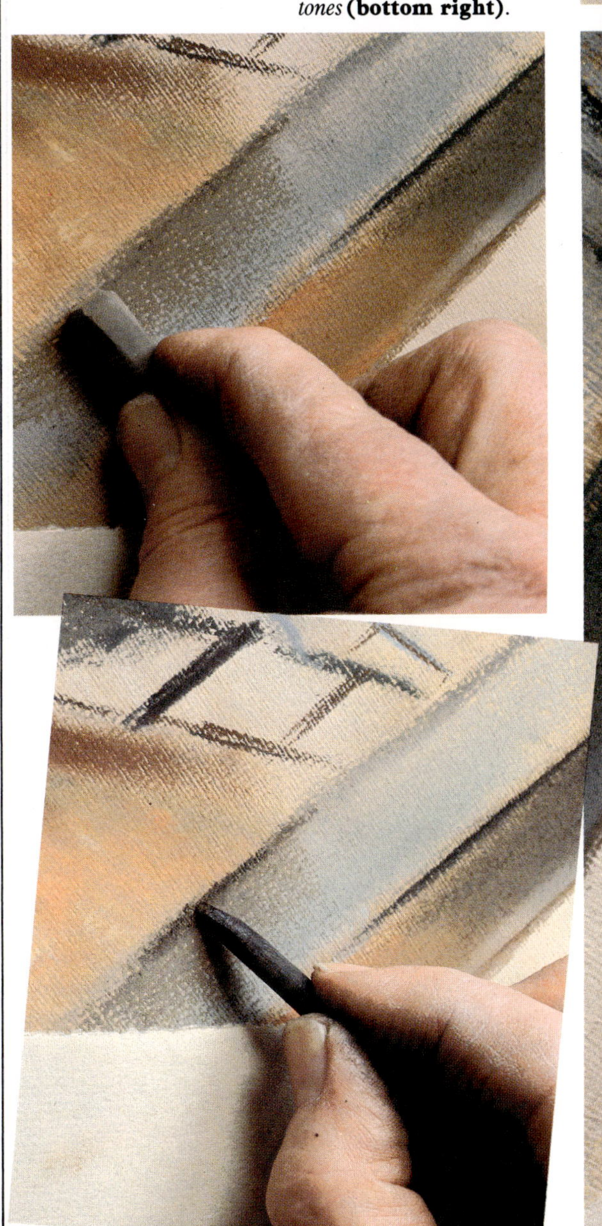

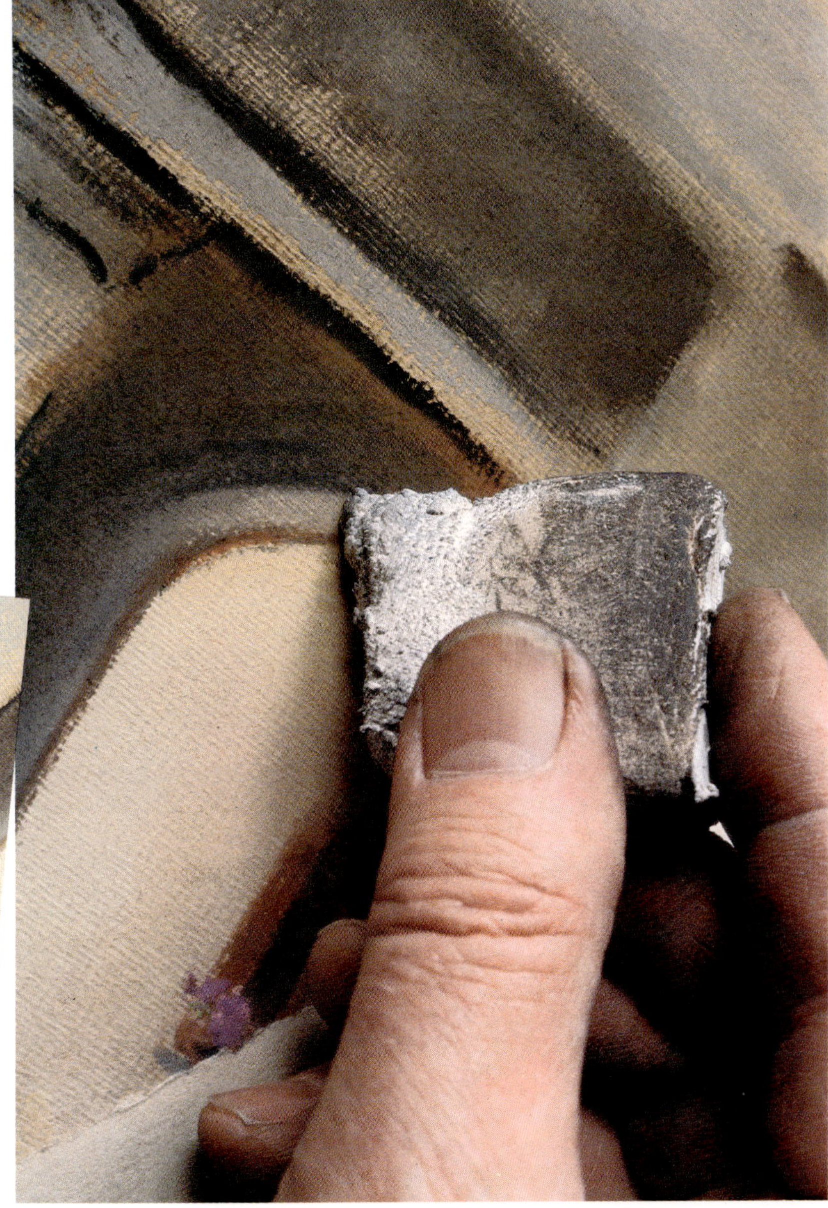

USING COLOUR TO EXPRESS MOOD

Our feelings play an important part in the way we perceive colour and these emotional responses can be used to create particular mood in a drawing or painting.

An artist uses colour for expressive reasons as well as reasons of literal representation — it is yet another means of communicating what he or she feels. What the artist is trying to say and the mood which is being conveyed should be apparent to the viewer through the choice of colours and the way they are used.

On the next pages we show an example of the way in which the atmosphere of a painting can be changed by adjusting the colours. The artist has taken a single subject and treated it in two different ways. He had used pastel because he wanted to develop his ideas as quickly as possible. How do you respond to the two finished pastels?

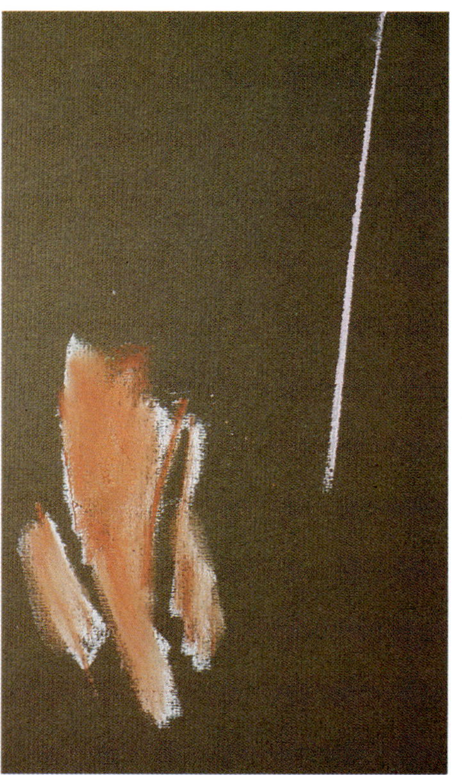

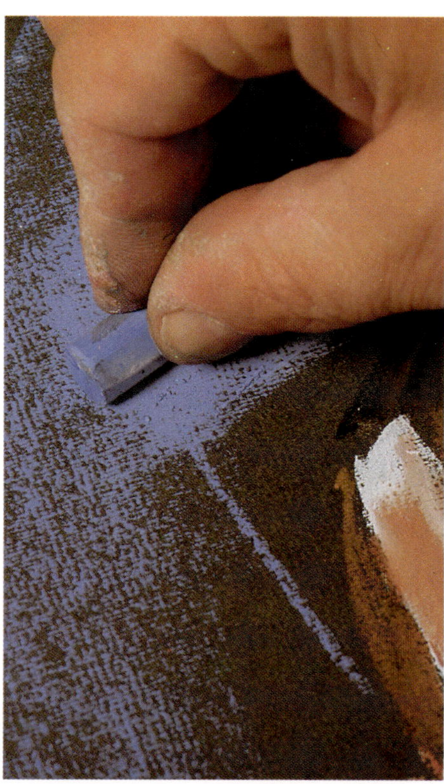

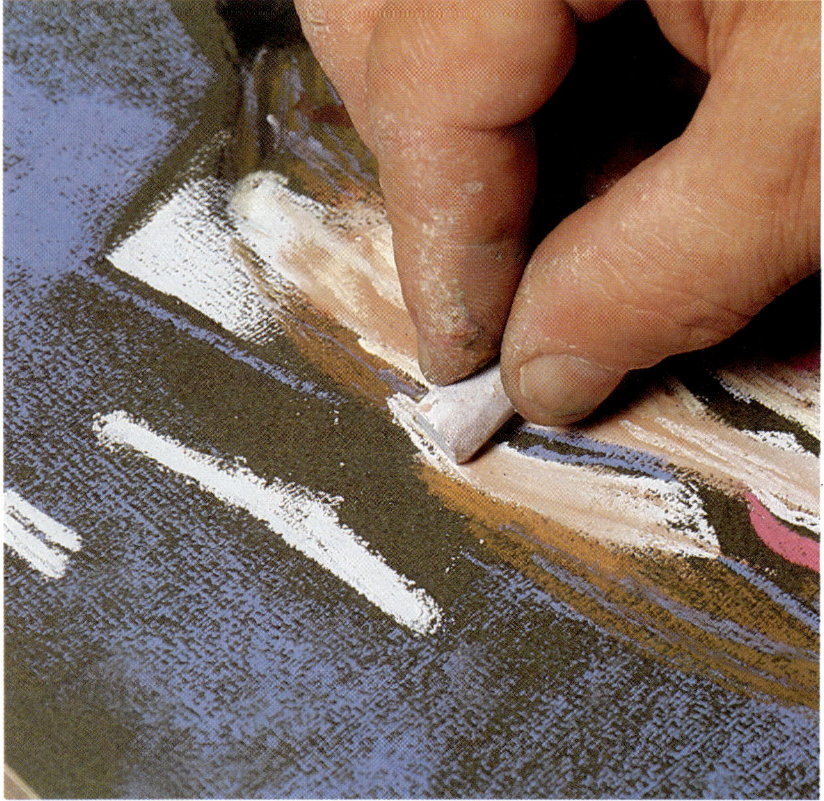

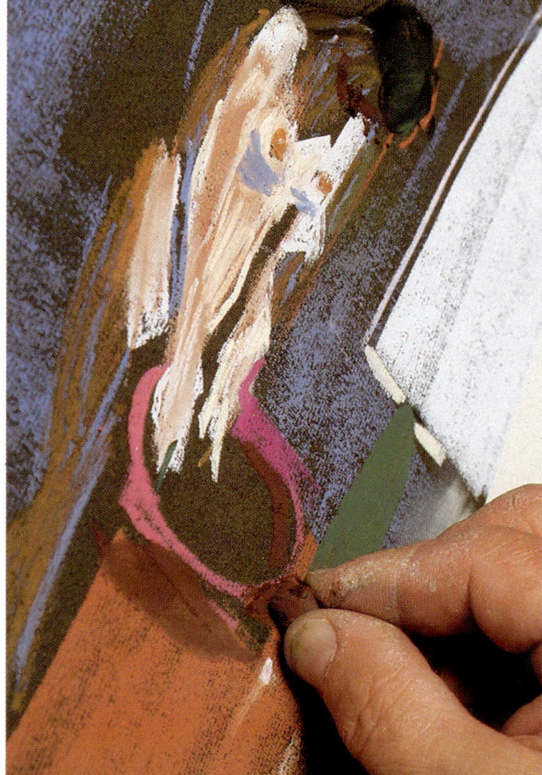

The mood of a picture is usually dictated by the colour and tone. By slightly changing either of these the feeling of a painting can be completely altered. In this exercise the artist makes two pictures of the same subject, using different colours and a different tinted paper for each one.

For the first picture he chose a dark paper. A cool colour, such as olive green, is ideal **(top left)**. *Using a set of general purpose soft pastels, and keeping the colours readily to hand, he starts to block in areas of the composition.*

When doing such an exercise do not be too self-conscious about choosing suitable colours, but try to maintain a fairly rich tone in the picture. The artist blocks in the background in a strong blue or mauve, **(top right)**. *The artist applies the colour using the side of the stick so that the colour builds up quickly. This will later be echoed throughout the composition. He develops the figure, pressing hard on the pastels where a particularly dense tone is required* **(above left)**. *He keeps the areas of colour quite simple and separate, without blending and mixing the colours.*

The artist introduces some deep, bright colours into the pastel drawing **(above right)**. *Deep reds, pinks and oranges all contribute to the overall richness of the colour theme. Some of the tinted paper is allowed to show through between the pastels.*

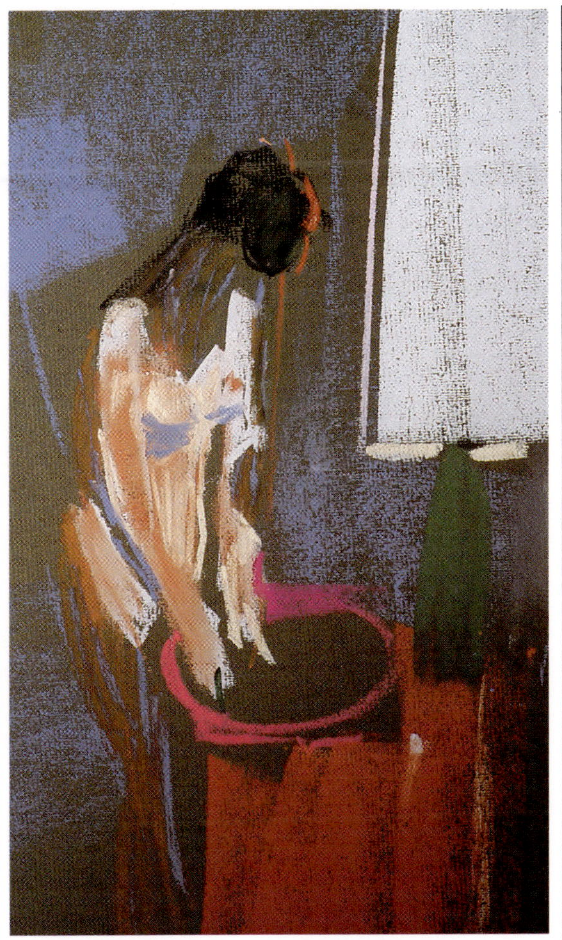

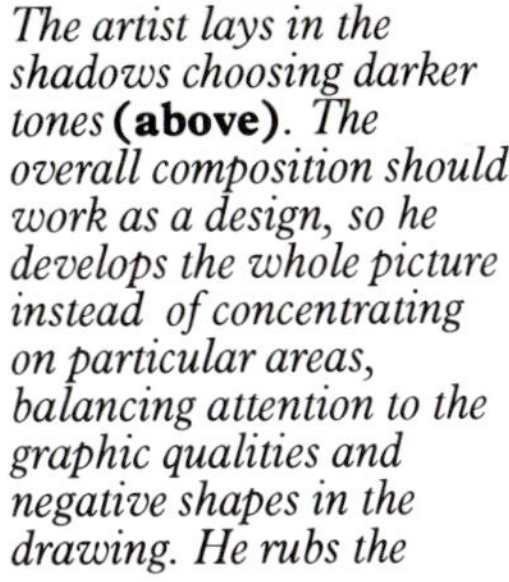

The artist lays in the shadows choosing darker tones **(above)**. *The overall composition should work as a design, so he develops the whole picture instead of concentrating on particular areas, balancing attention to the graphic qualities and negative shapes in the drawing. He rubs the background colour to get a more solid effect* **(top right)** *taking the background colour into the figure* **(below)** *and keeping the drawing simple and the shapes general. He adds details such as the flowers* **(right)** *and works into the shapes with darker tones to give form and depth.*

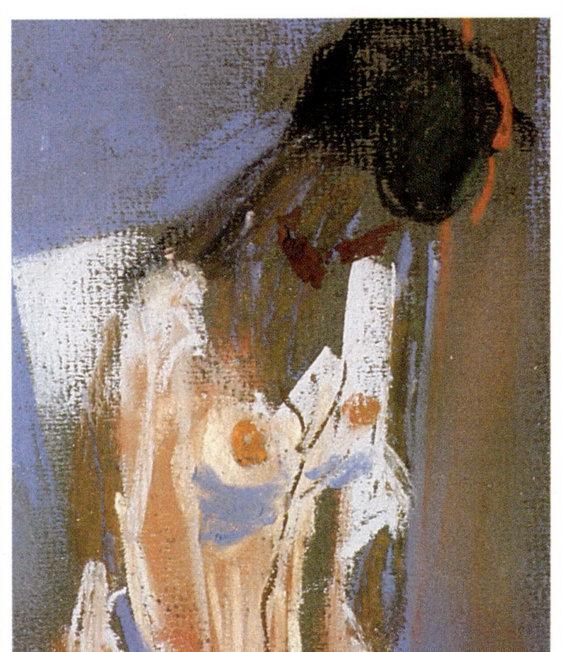

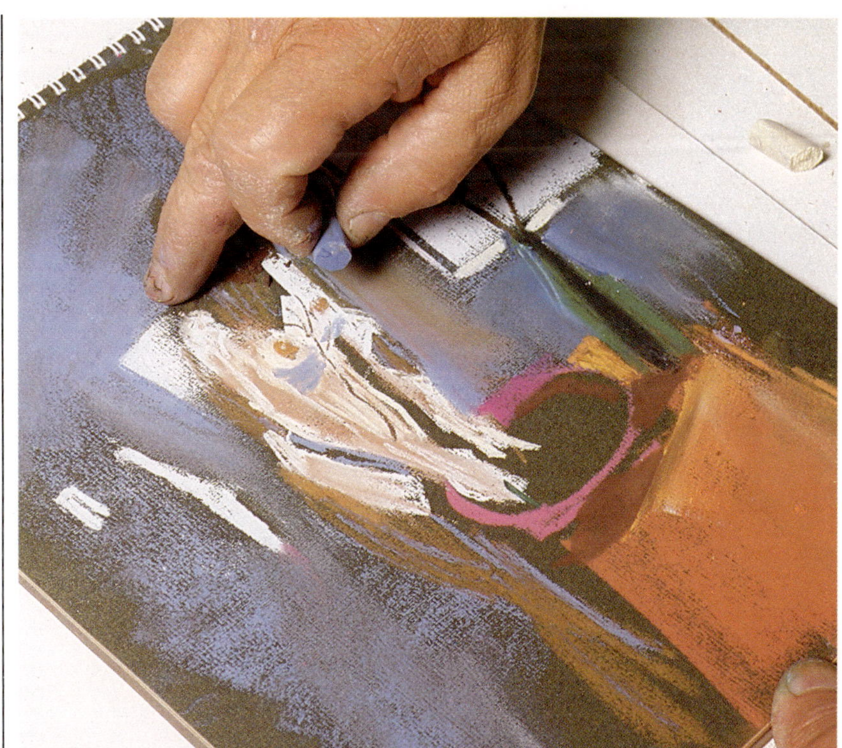

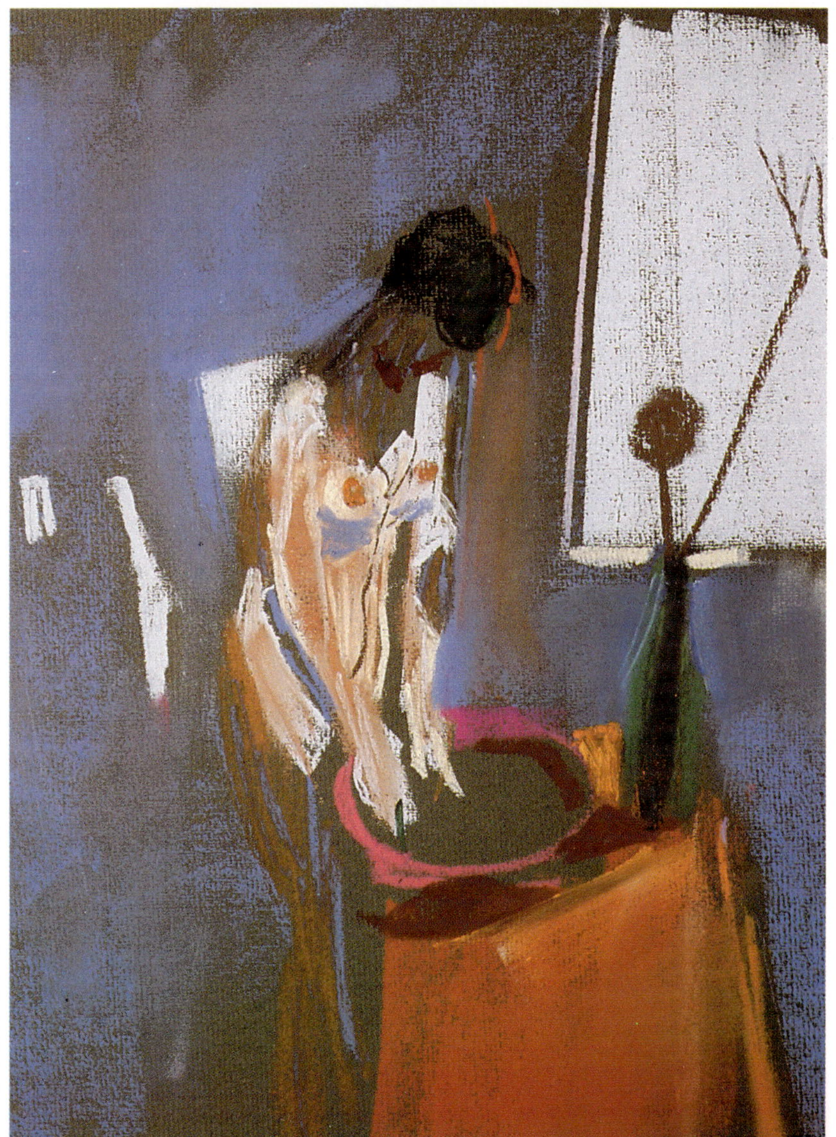

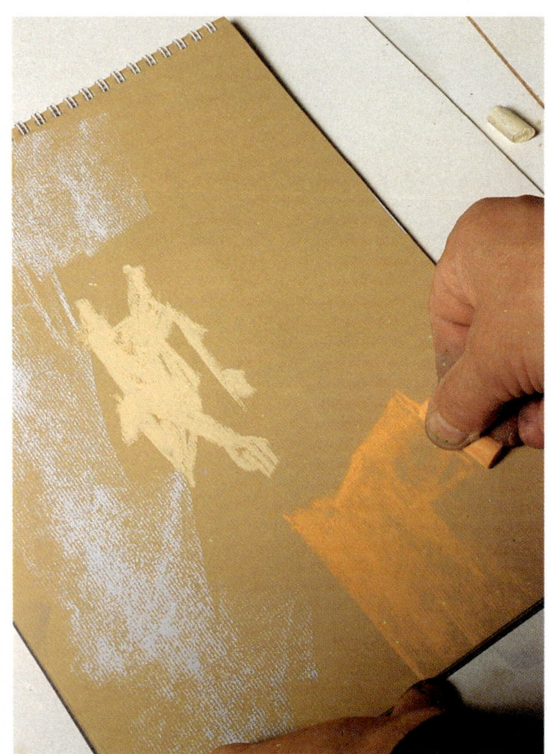

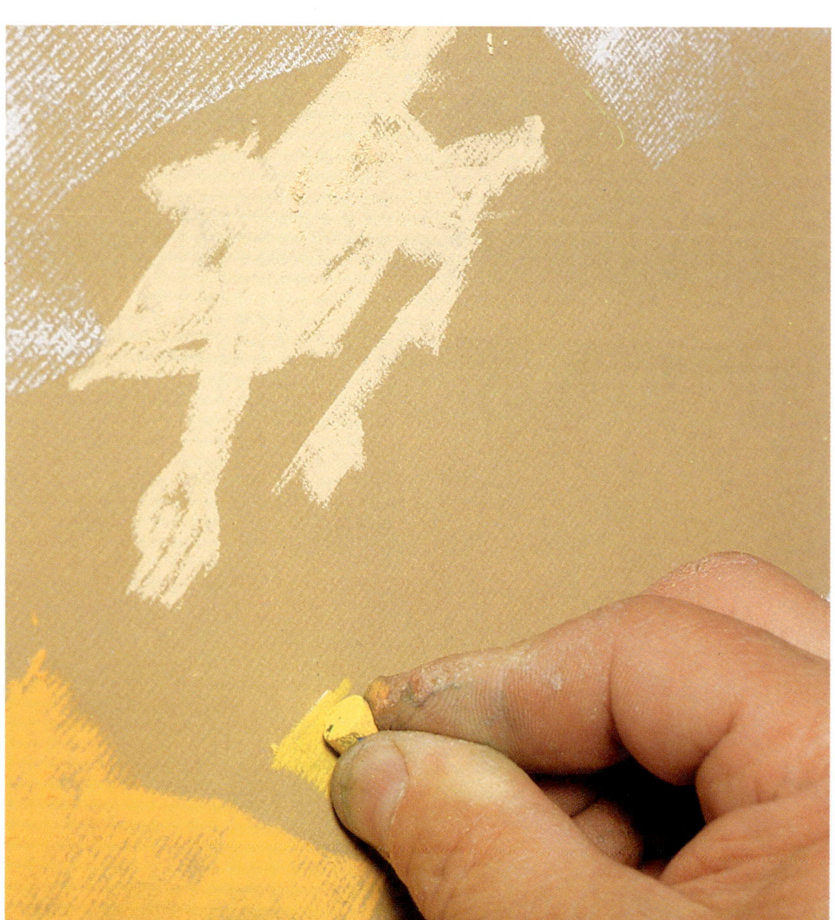

For the second picture the artist takes exactly the same composition — using the first drawing as a reference. Working in the same way as before he begins to block in the light tones **(above)**. *He uses a light, warm tinted paper, and chooses light, warm colours for the initial drawing* **(right and bottom)**.

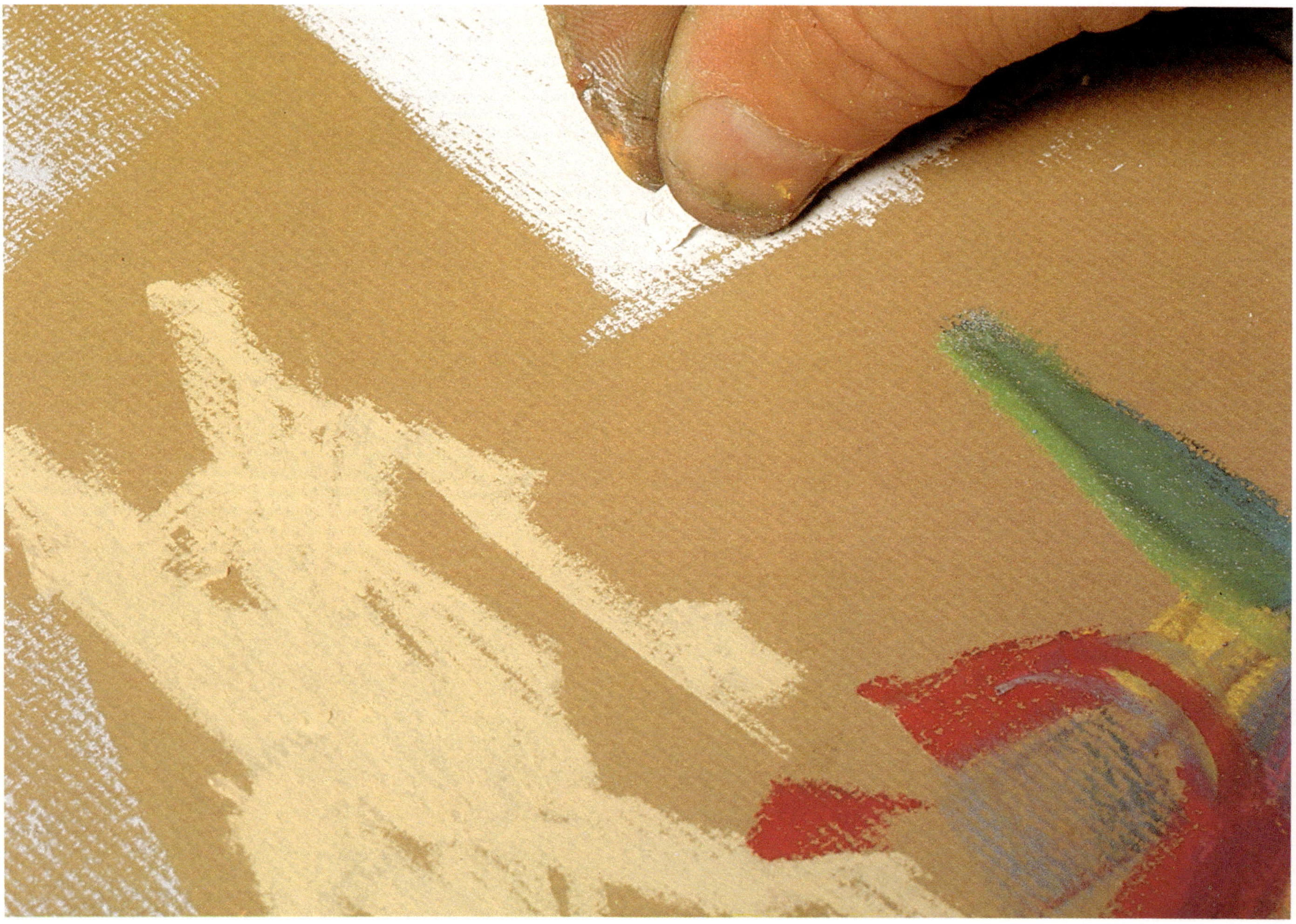

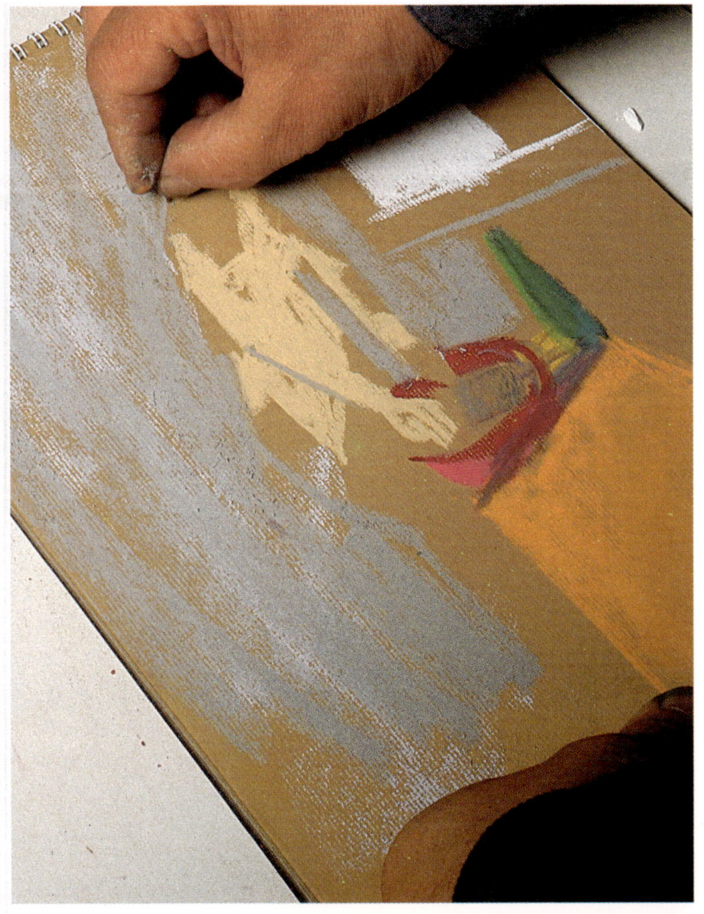

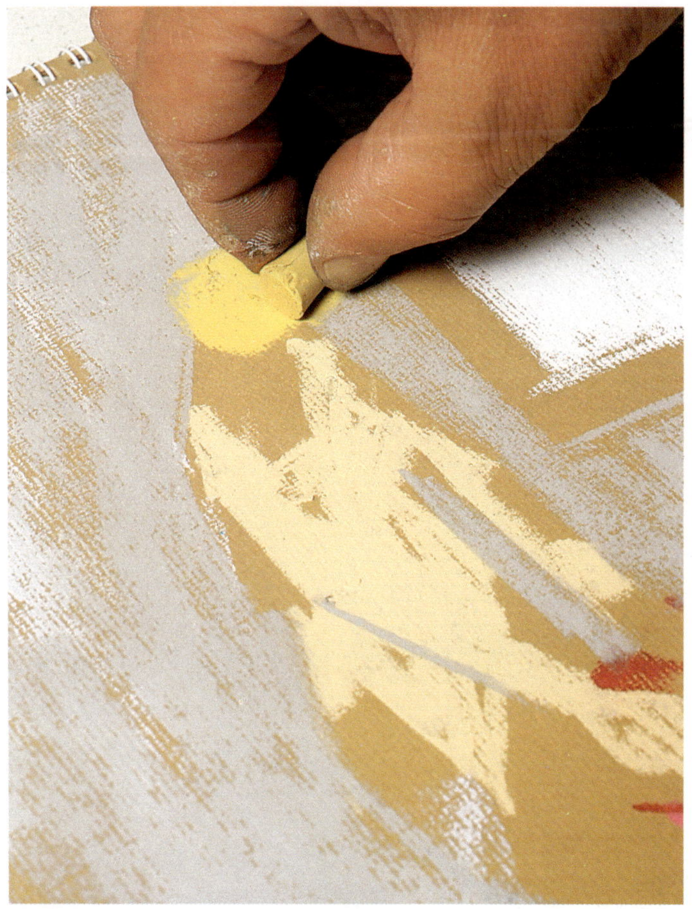

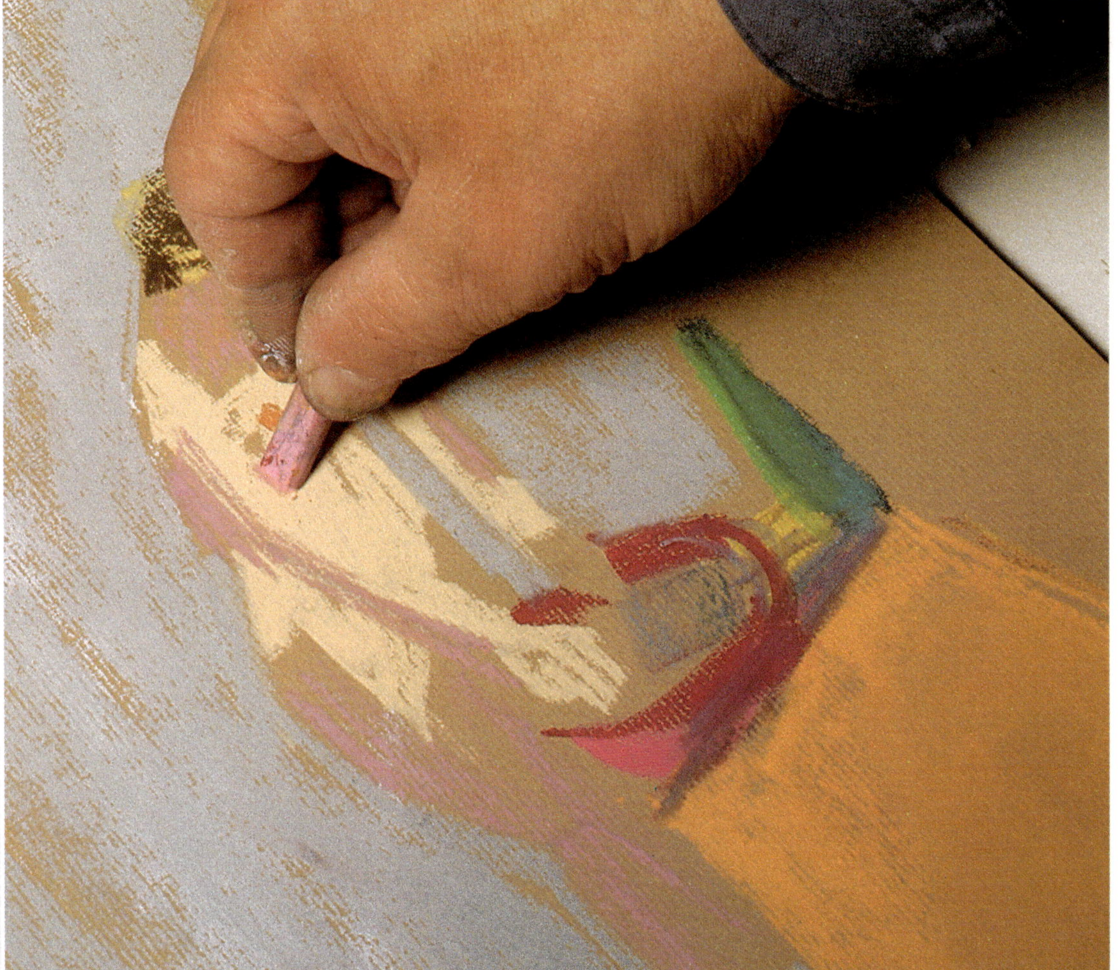

The artist keeps the colours in this picture slightly more subdued than in the first, without making them radically different. For instance he uses a neutral, light grey for the background **(top left)**. *By using lighter local colours he changes the atmosphere* **(top right)**, *working into the figure in warm, pale flesh tones* **(bottom)**.

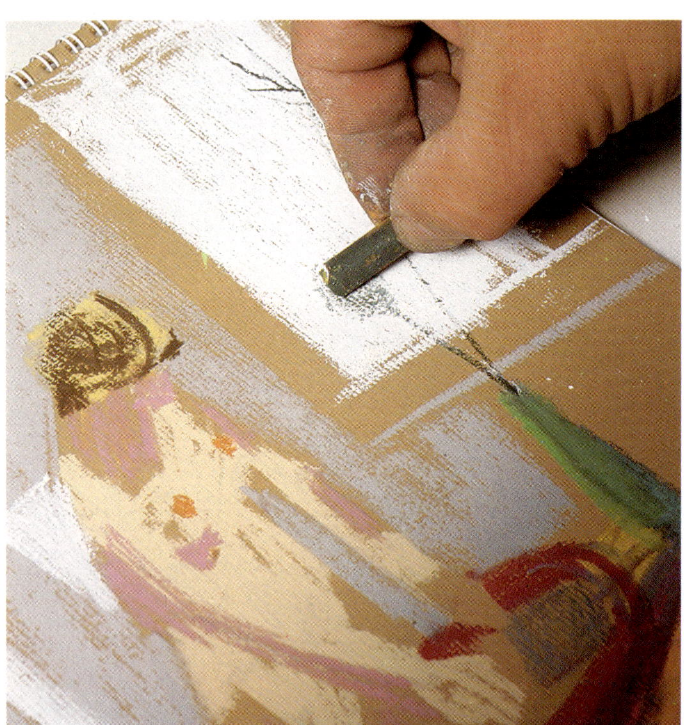

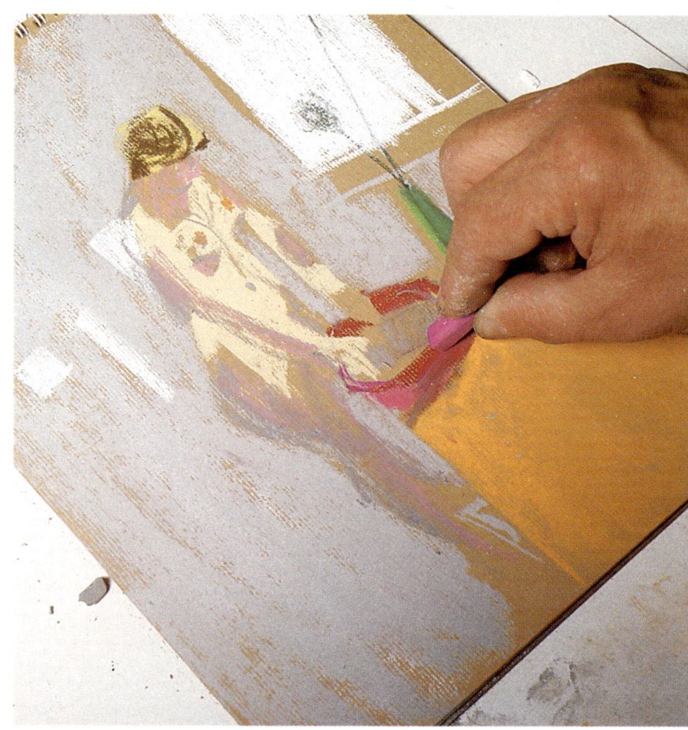

The artist adds details, making the flowers softer and less stark than they were in the earlier picture **(top left)**. *Working into the drawing he adds shadows and dark tones in subdued, muted colours* **(top right)** *to complete the picture* **(bottom right)**.

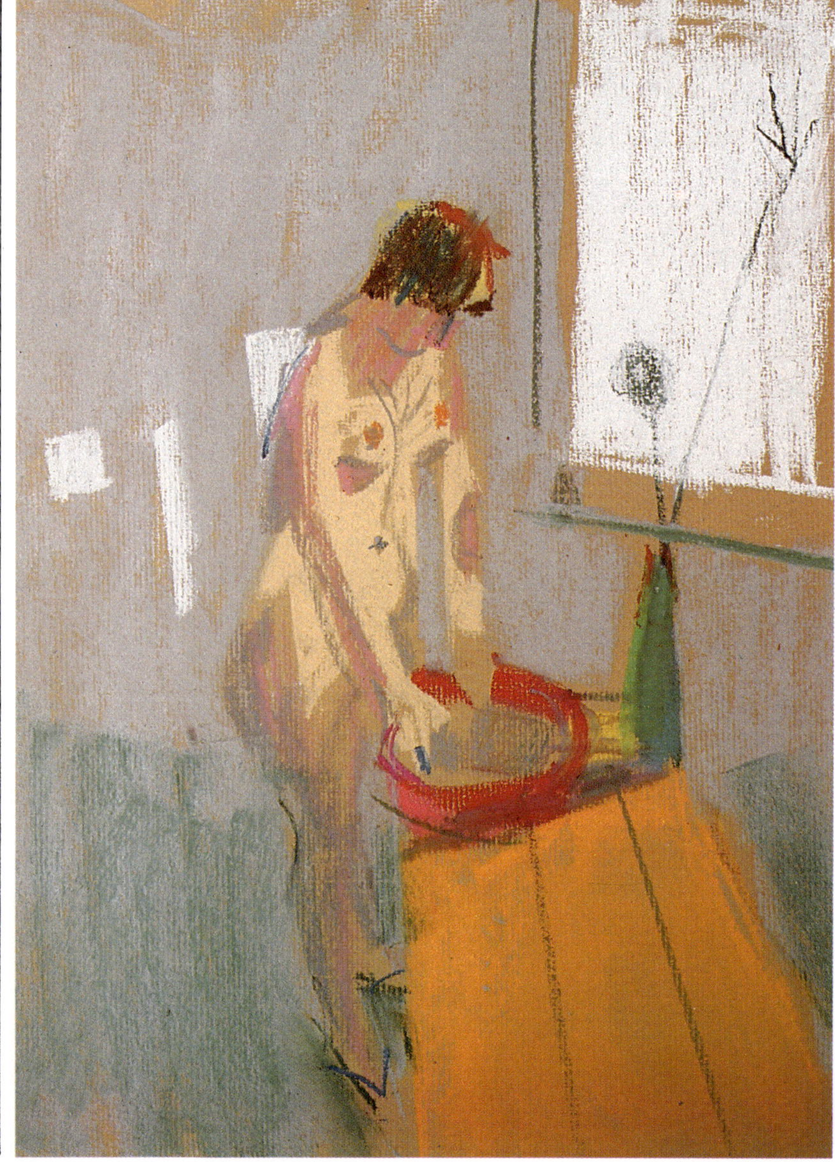

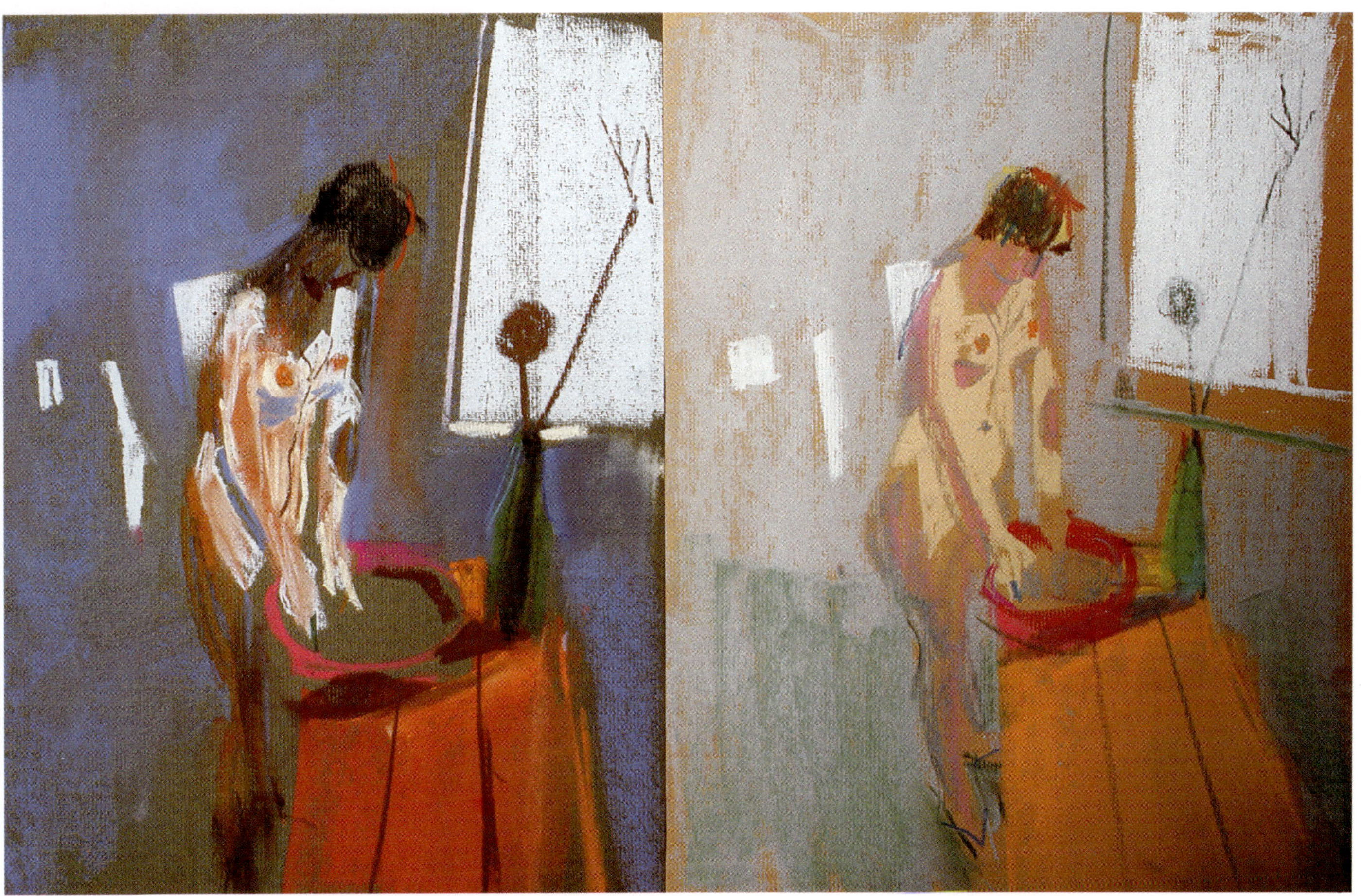

Compare the two finished pictures **(above)**. *Neither drawing is done with a particular colour theme, but each is entirely different in mood and feeling. The heavy, dusky atmosphere of the first picture* **(left)** *is set by the dark paper and rich, deep colours; in the other, the mood is set by the pale paper and light warm colours.*

MATCHES — AN UNUSUAL SUBJECT

For this exercise the artist has taken a small and commonplace object and made it the basis of a painting. The subject is familiar, yet unfamiliar. It is unlikely that you have ever paid more than passing attention to a match. It is useful to try exercises like this every now and then, for the subject, though familiar, is new and fresh and you will be forced to concentrate in order to draw and paint it. It is an excellent way of improving your powers of perception.

A match is very small so there will not be sufficient information for you to become distracted by details. Look for shapes, planes and areas of colour. The painting process will inevitably become a process of abstraction for as the image is enlarged it will begin to break down.

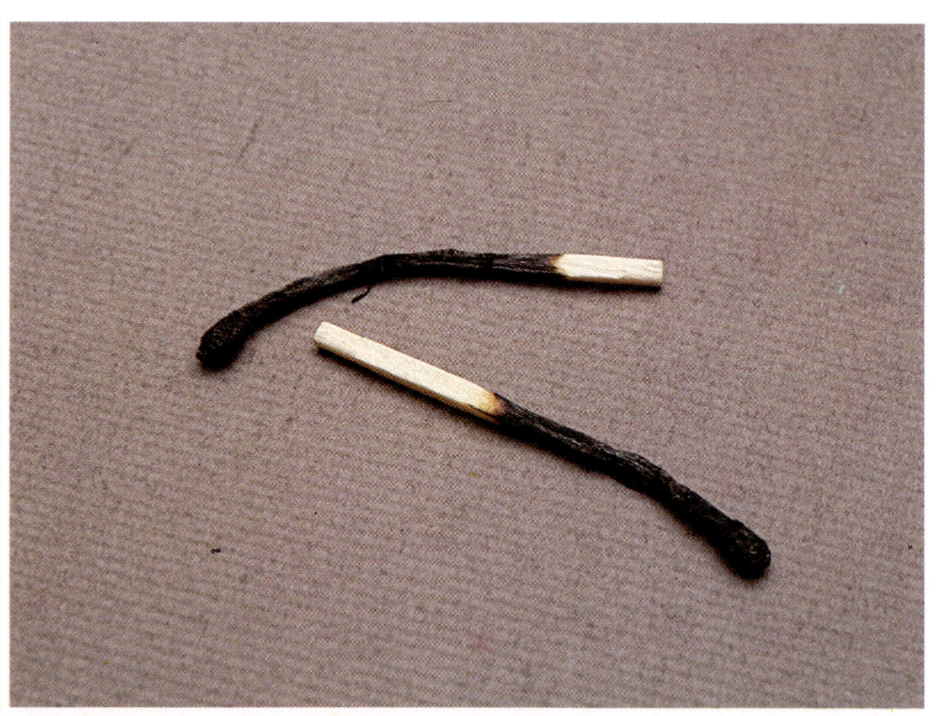

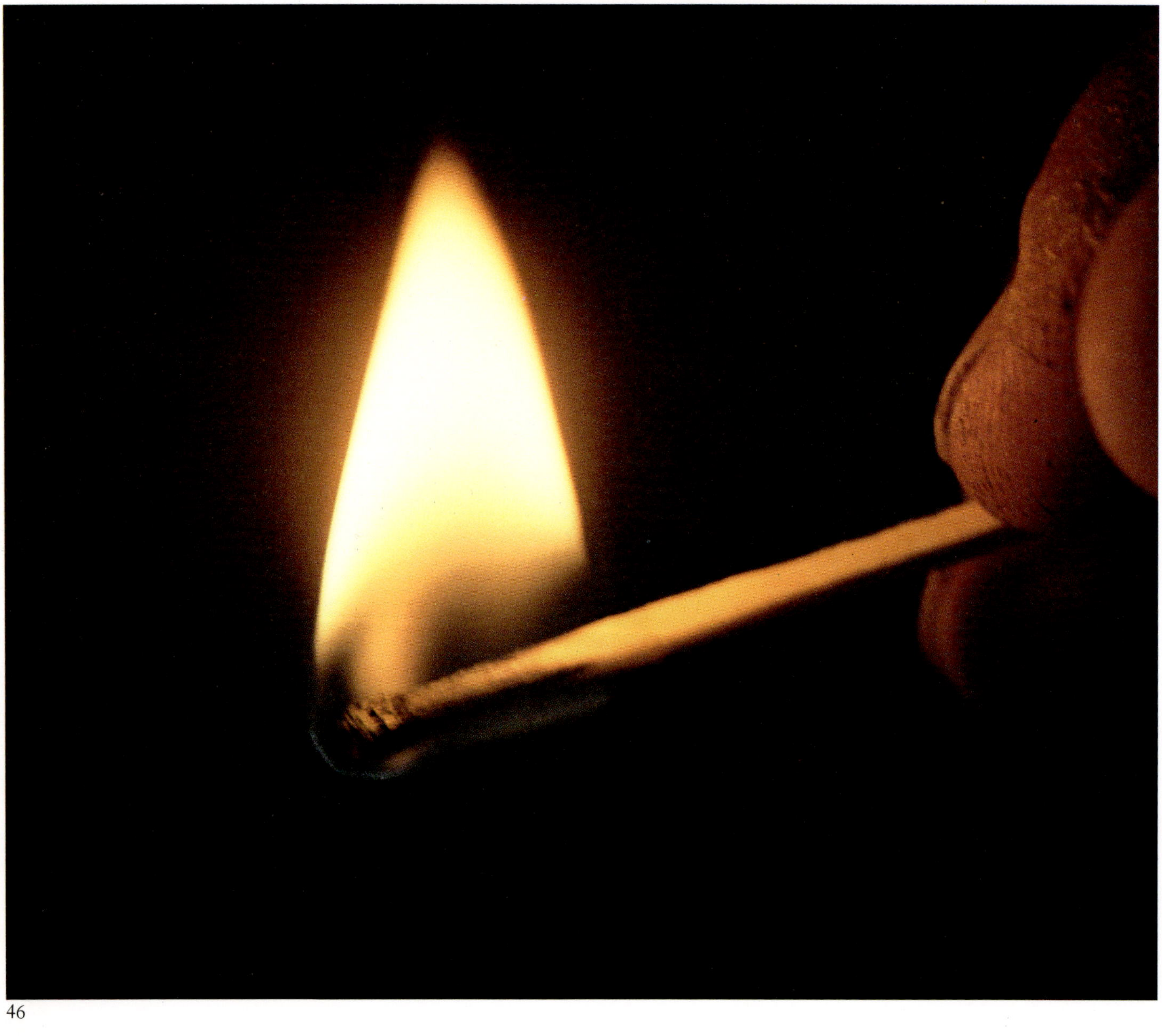

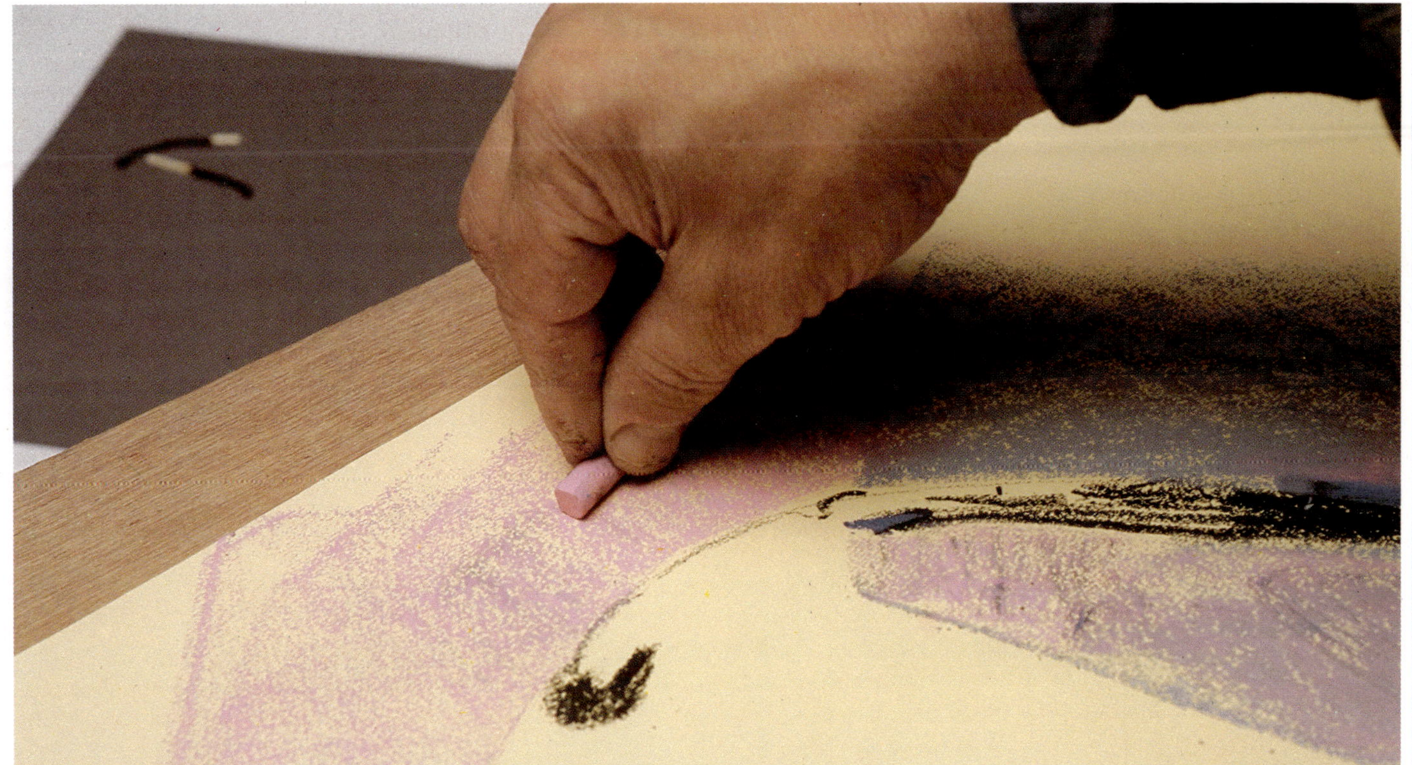

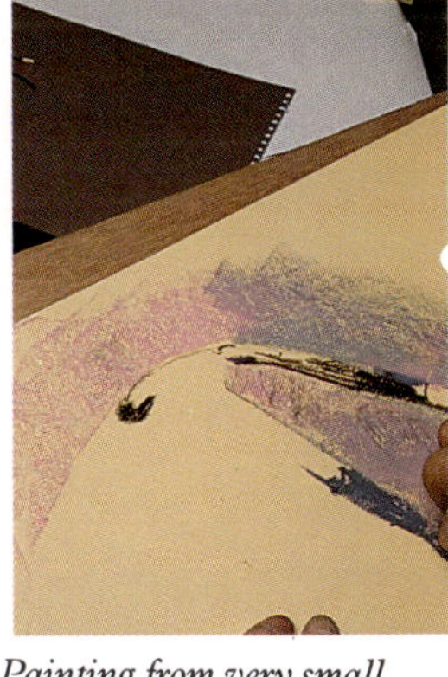

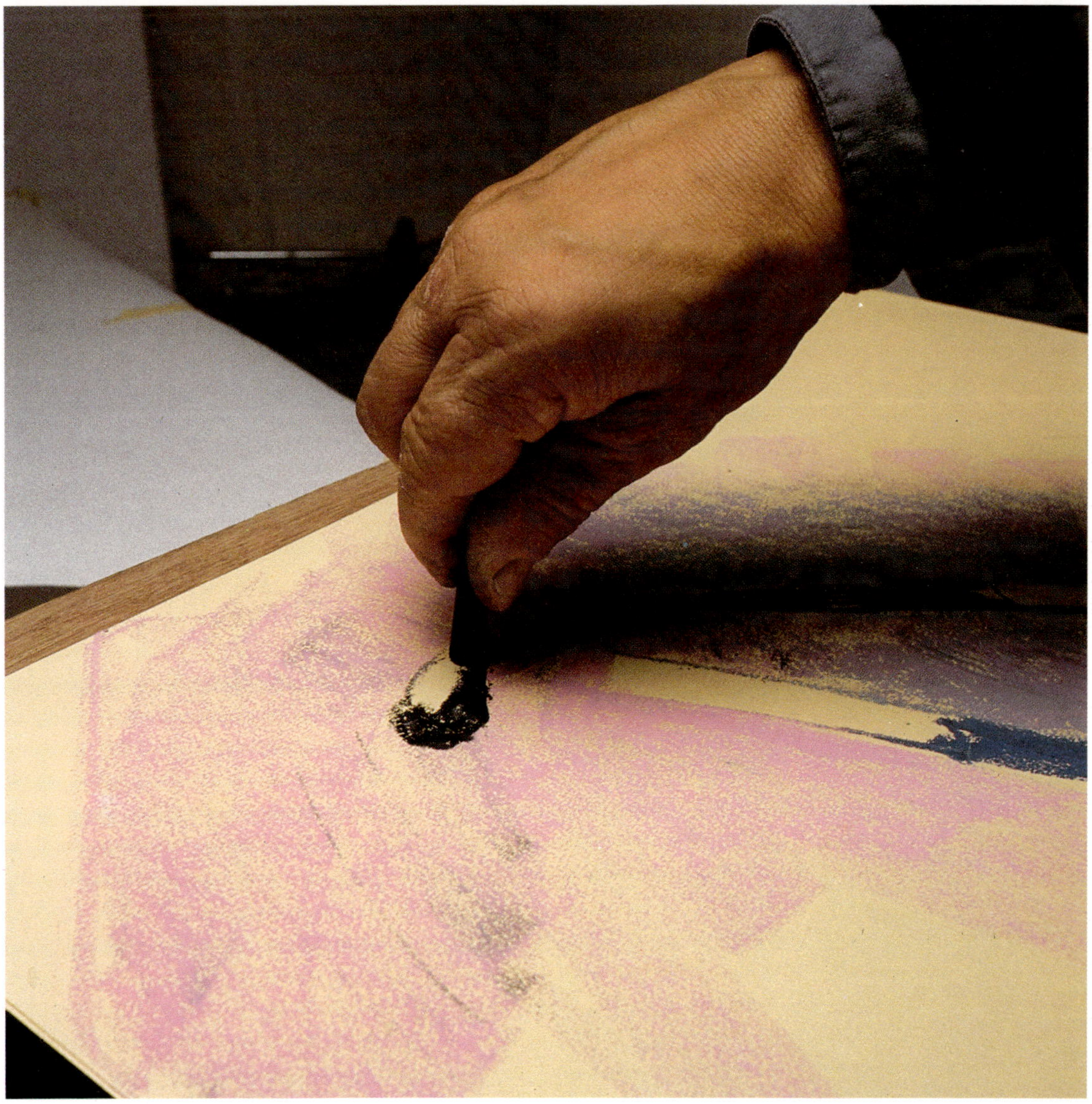

Painting from very small objects entails looking closely at shapes and colours and translating these into a much larger image. The burnt matches **(opposite)** *are a very common 'found object'. The artist put the matches where he could see them easily and sketched them roughly in charcoal. He exaggerated the colours so that they make an impact in the enlarged drawing and uses the background to give him the negative shapes of the subject.*

He uses several closely related colours in the background **(top)**, *blending them to establish an approximate tone to work on* **(above)**. *Keeping the drawing strong and the image clear, he presses hard on the pastels to produce dense, positive colours* **(right)**.

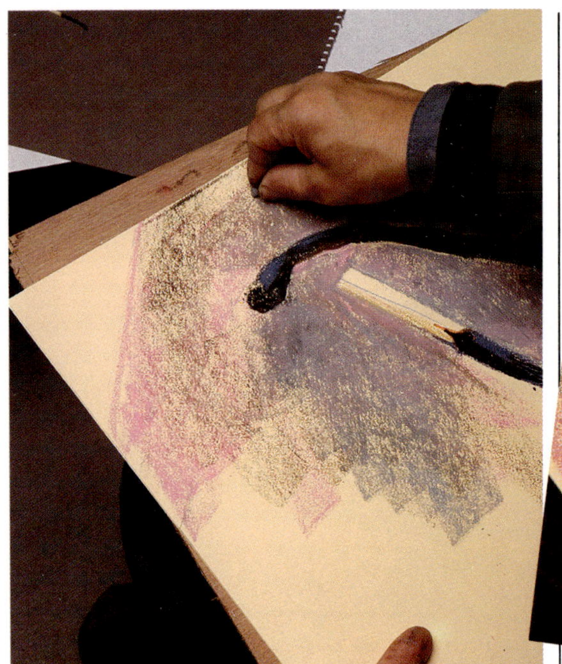

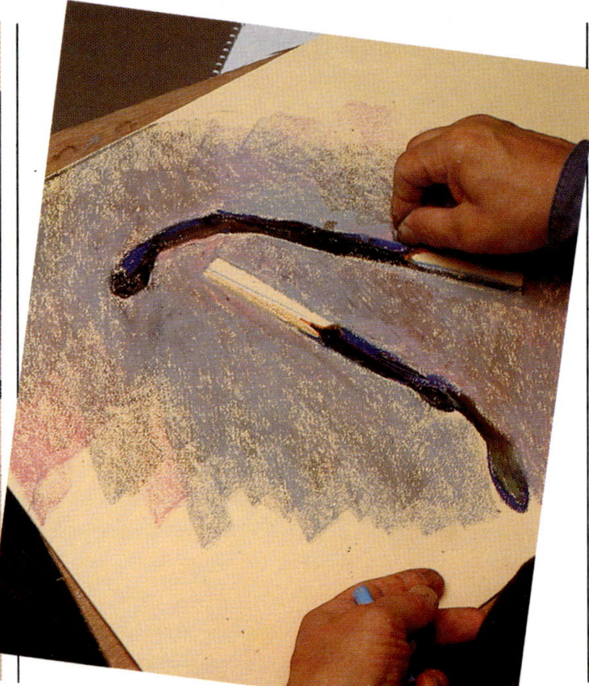

He continues to introduce new colours to increase the richness of the composition. He does not attempt to achieve a realistic effect, but uses the pastels to make a vibrant, interesting picture. He uses a black pastel to intensify the black of the charred part of the match **(bottom left)** *and a brown outline to emphasize the shaded side of the unburnt wood* **(below)**. *The finished picture* **(opposite)** *demonstrates the way in which an everyday object can be used to create an unusual image.*

He continues to build up the colours and tones of the match sticks, using large blocks of colour and bold strokes. He works into the background tones so that they relate to the rest of the picture. He uses the sides of the pastel sticks to cover wide areas **(above)** *working quickly in smooth, broad strokes. Make the background colours denser around the objects to give a feeling of solidity to the arrangement* **(top right)**.

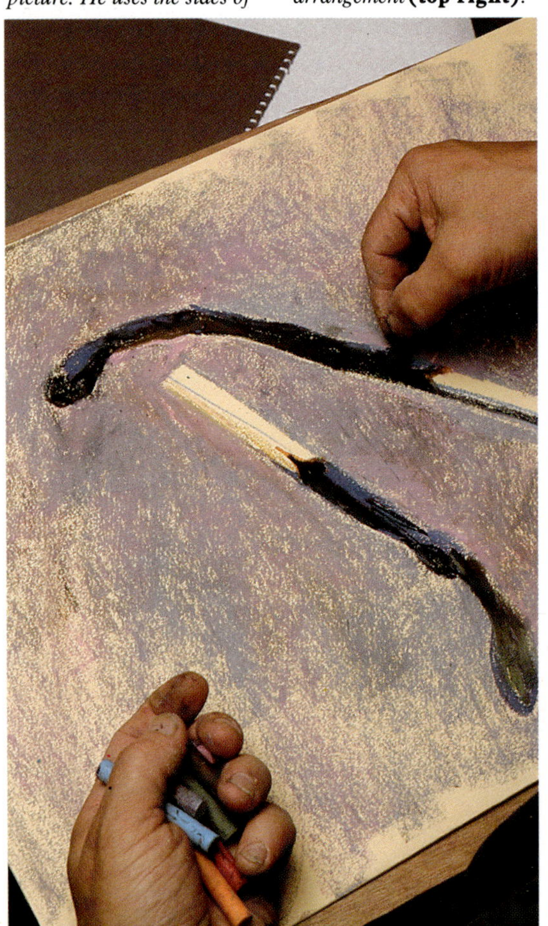

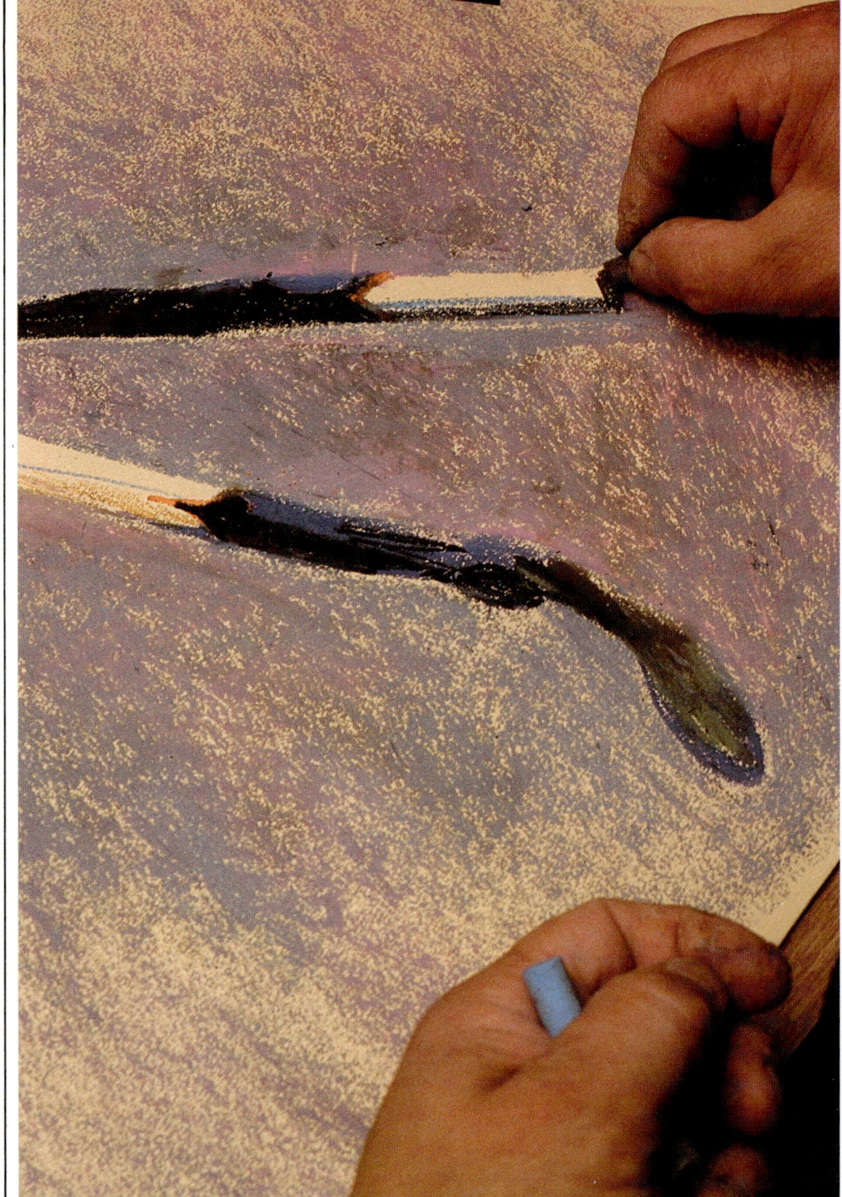

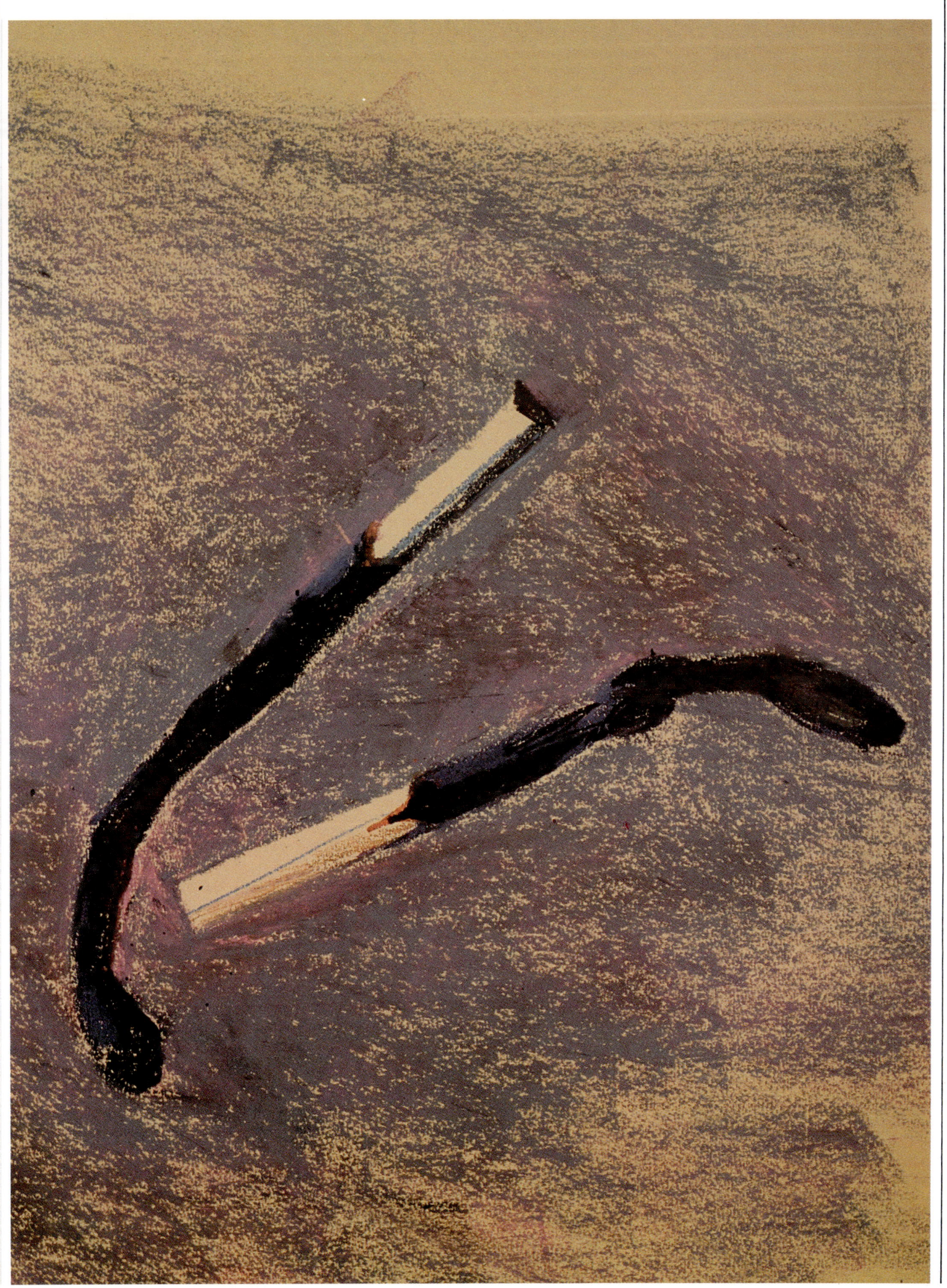

STILL LIFE WITH REFLECTIONS

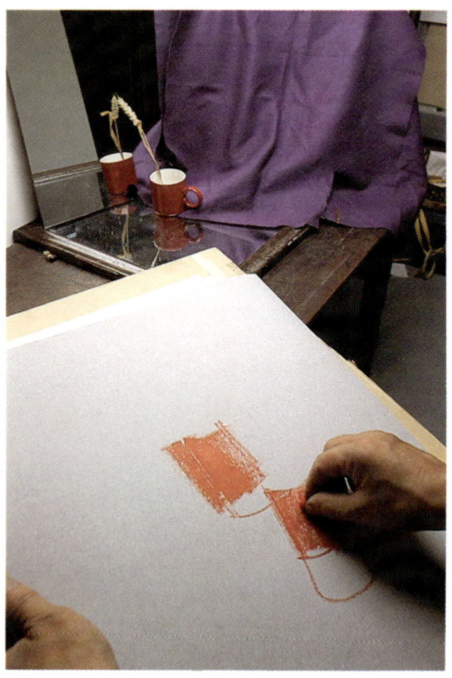

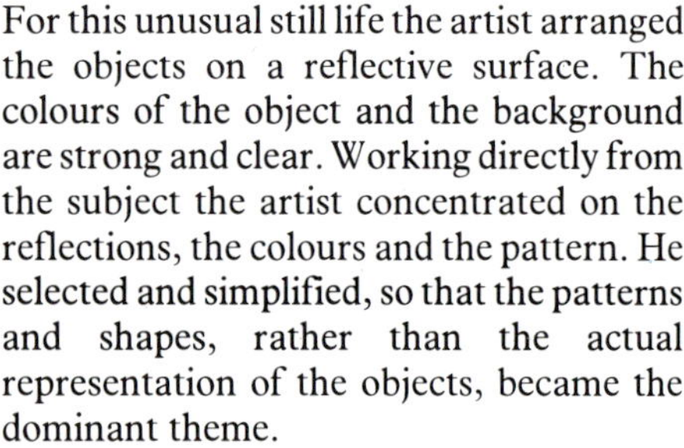

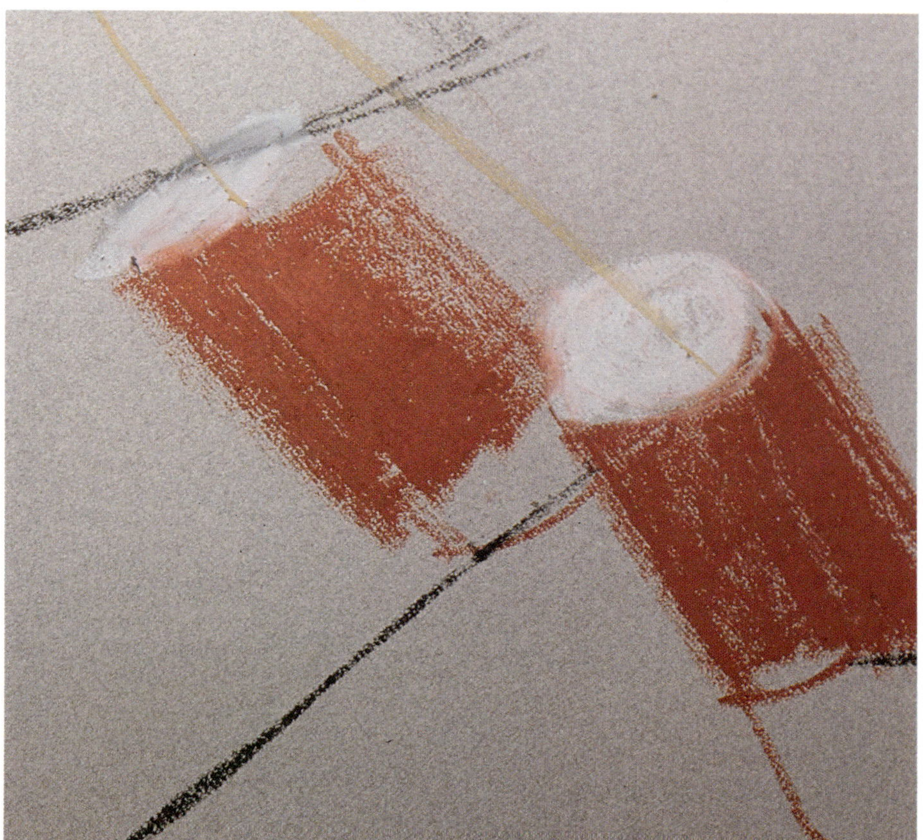

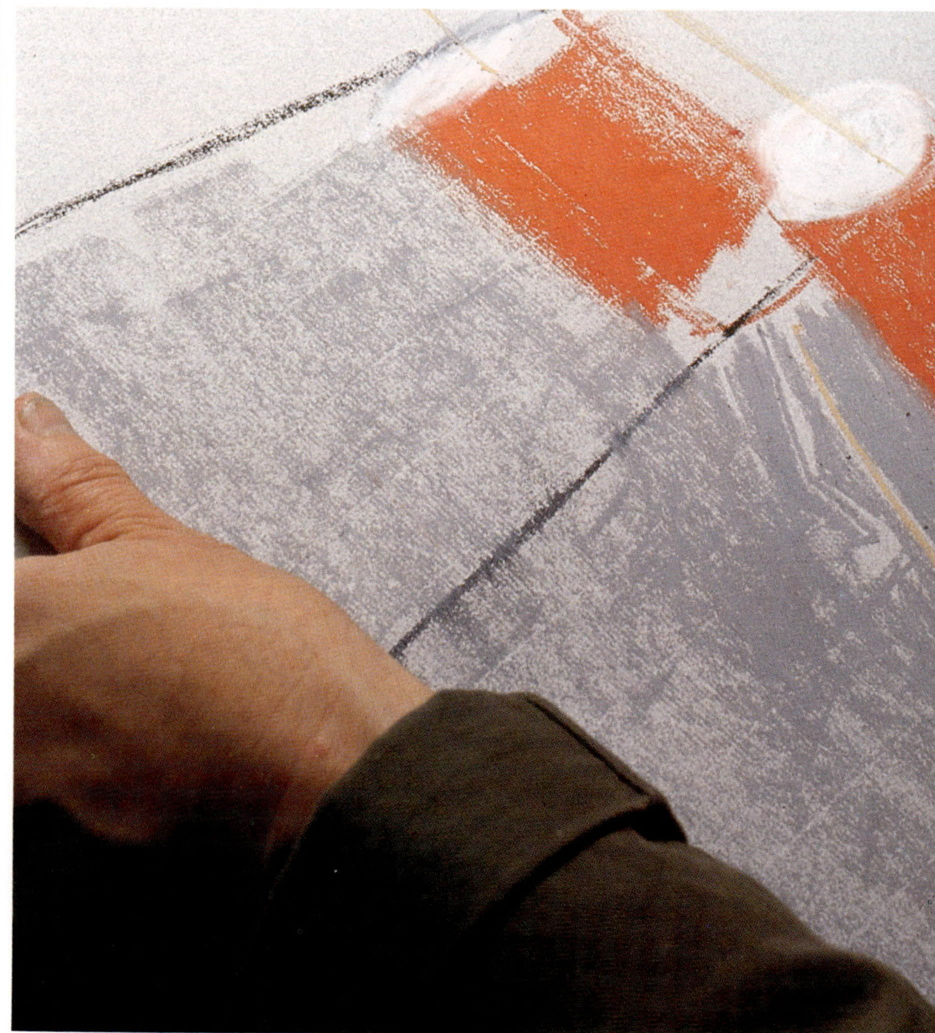

For this unusual still life the artist arranged the objects on a reflective surface. The colours of the object and the background are strong and clear. Working directly from the subject the artist concentrated on the reflections, the colours and the pattern. He selected and simplified, so that the patterns and shapes, rather than the actual representation of the objects, became the dominant theme.

He worked in pastel because it can be used at speed and he wanted to minimize the time between his eye observing the subject and his hands making a mark on the paper. He chose a grey toned paper, which had enough texture to hold the grains of pastel. Using the side of the pastel he covered the paper as broadly and flatly as possible and worked the pigment into the paper texture. Pastel has a tendency to sit on top of the paper unless it is well worked in and fixed. If you want to create a thick impasto fix each layer of pastel before applying the next layer.

The painting is composed of areas of flat colour except in the reflection where white chalk has been worked into the black to create an oily effect. The result is a fresh, brightly coloured image in which the pattern and shapes of the objects dominate — it is a very personal interpretation of the subject.

By introducing a reflective material such as glass or a mirror you can add considerable interest to your still life. The reflection introduces repeated colours and shapes, mirror images and an extra spatial dimension. The artist worked with oil pastels on tinted paper, starting with the outline of the main shapes **(far left)**. *Next he blocked in the background* **(left)** *and surrounding tones* **(below)**.

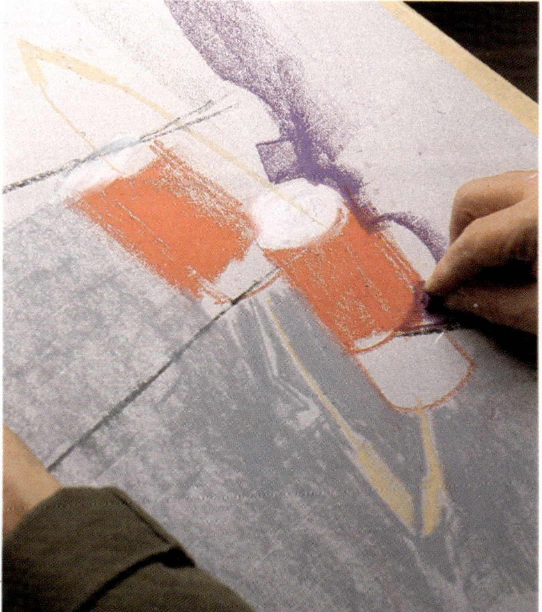

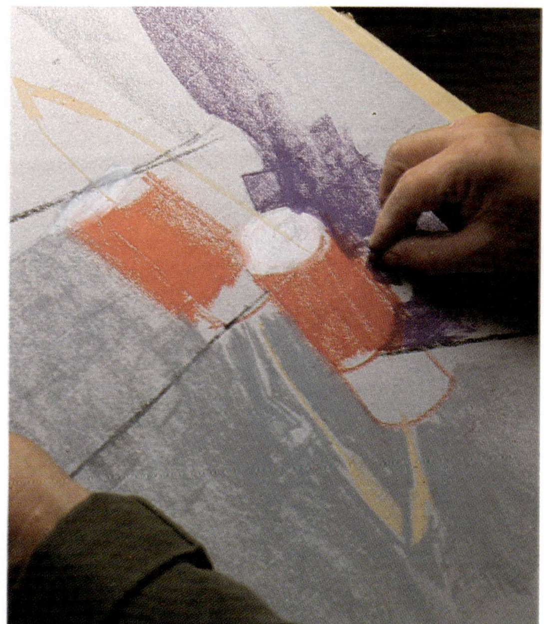

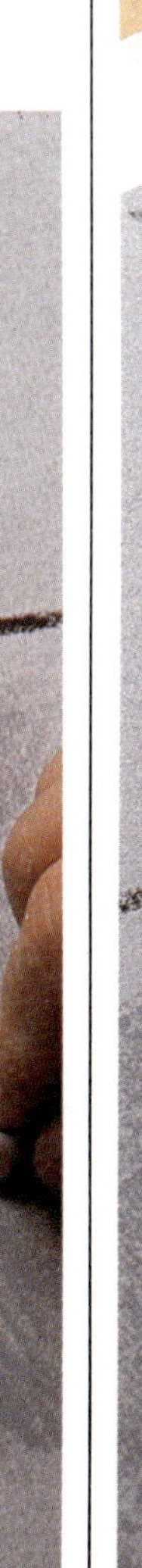

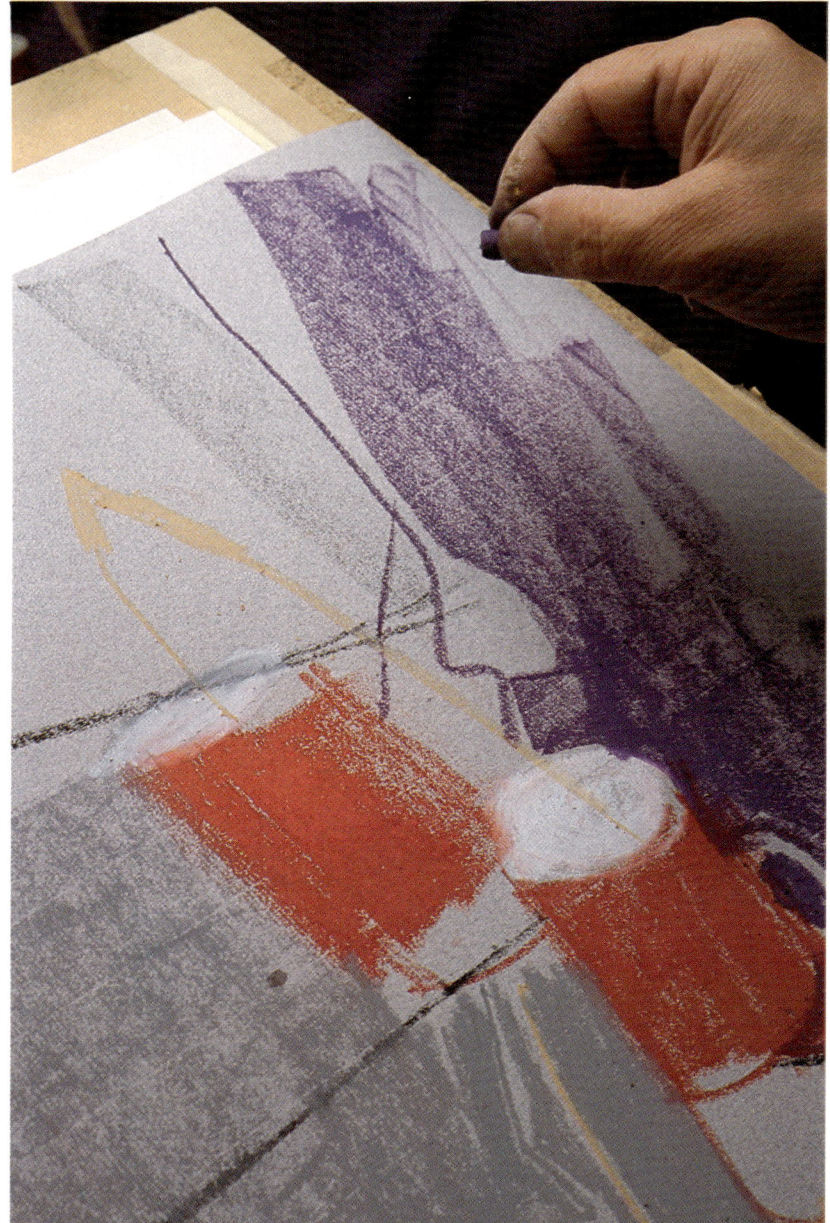

He uses the side of the pastel stick to lay in large areas of colour **(above left)**, *working into this with stronger tones to intensify the colour* **(above)**. *He takes the colour right up to the edge of the paper* **(left)**, *making the negative spaces of background into positive shapes which are important elements in the overall composition.*

1

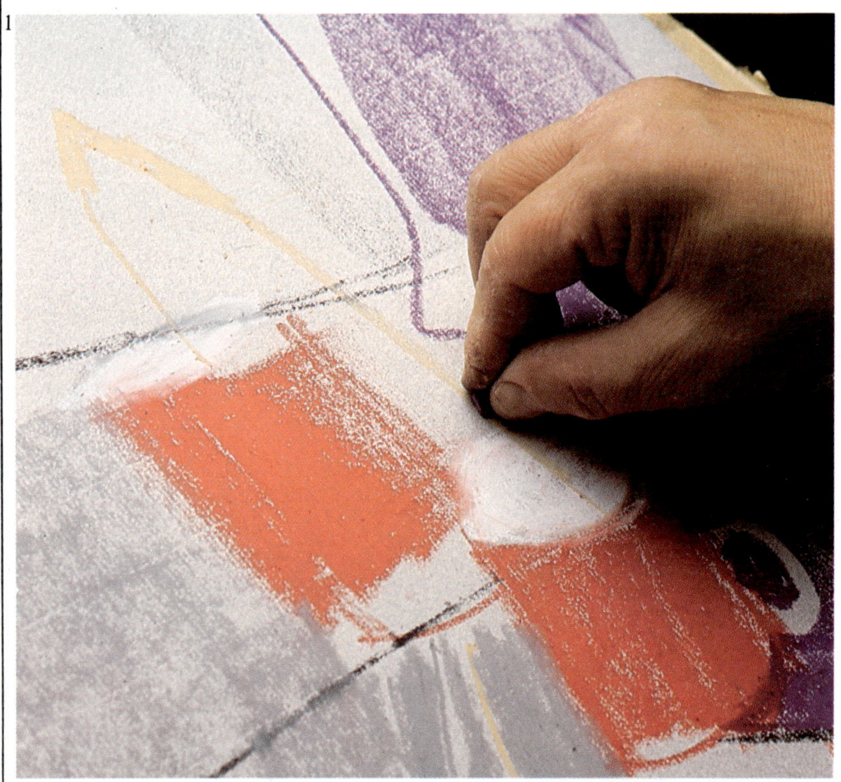

2

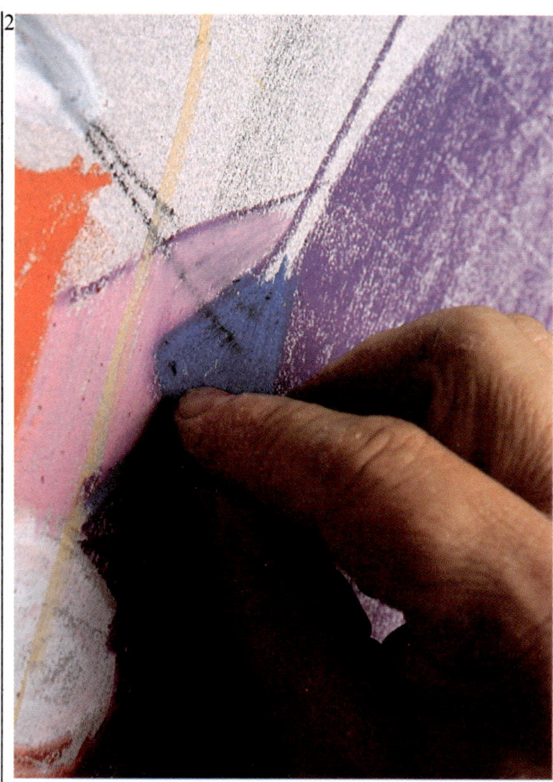

3

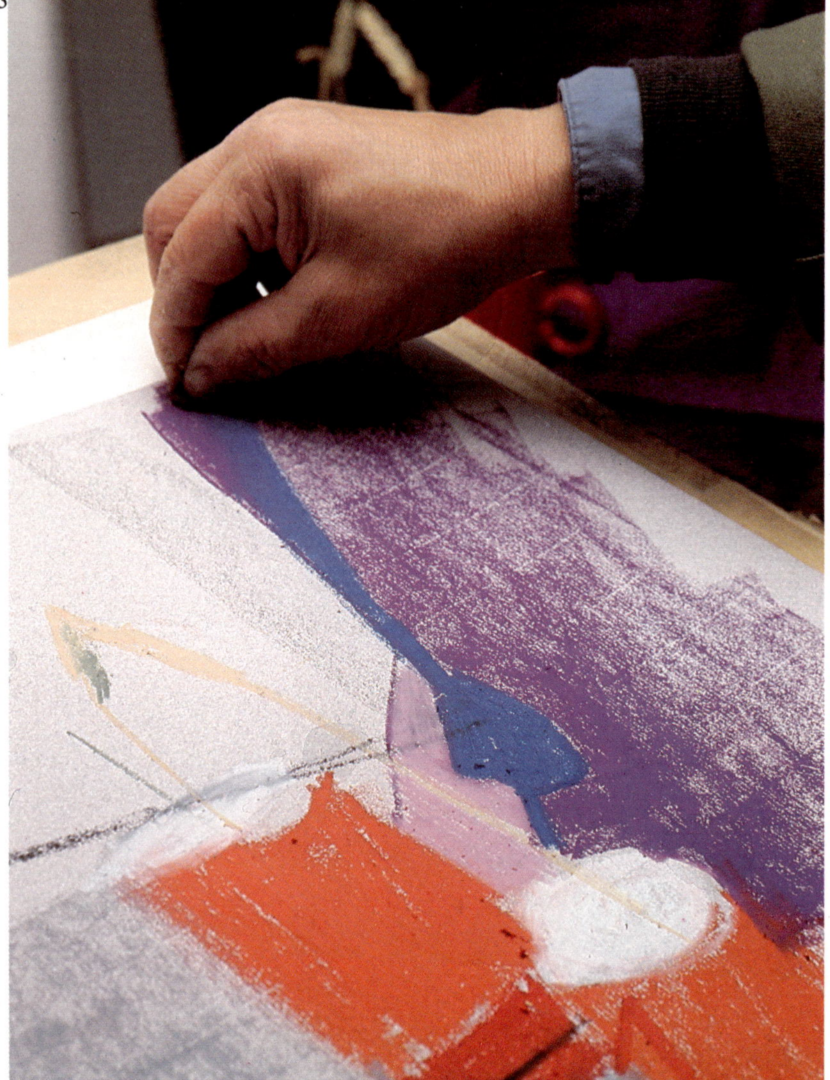

The artist continues to develop the main shapes **(above left)**, *introducing other colours to increase the vibrancy and brilliance of the composition* **(above)**. *He keeps the colours bright and clear, avoiding the mistake of overworking the drawing or clogging the paper with too many layers of pastel. Again he extends the large background shapes to the edge of the composition* **(left)**. *He defines smaller forms and details with a sharpened pastel but does not lose sight of the overall design* **(below)**. *By bringing the background colour right up to the objects he achieves a sharp, clear edge.*

4

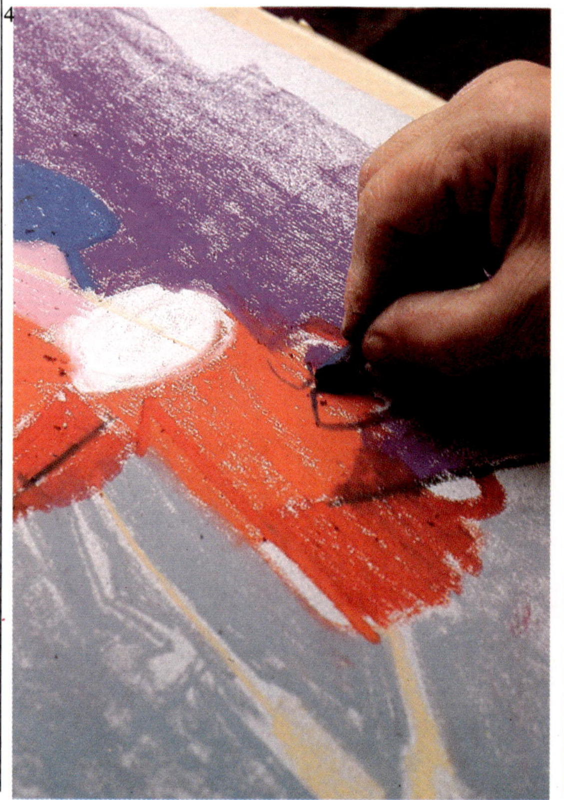

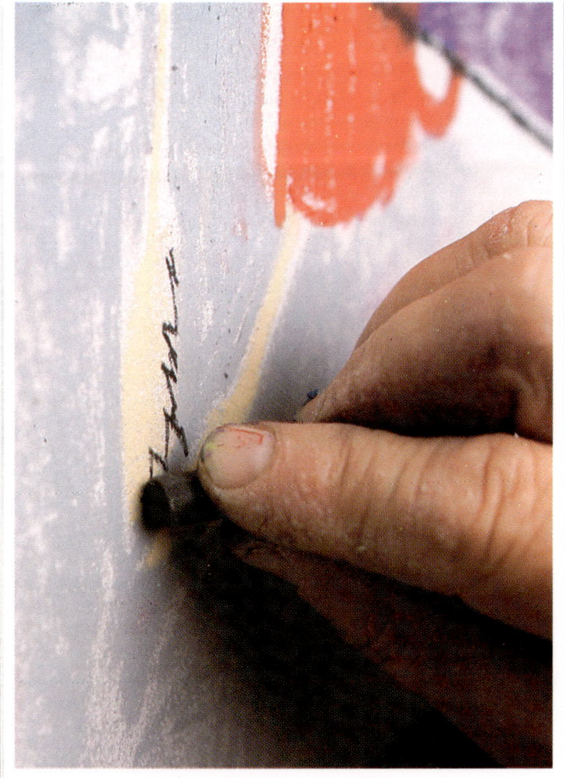

The artist uses black pastel to create darker tones and to define smaller objects and linear details **(left)**. *He then develops the highlight areas using white pastel* **(right)**. *Having increased the tonal contrasts he enriches the areas of local colour by adding black lines, treating the image and its reflection as a single subject* **(below)**.

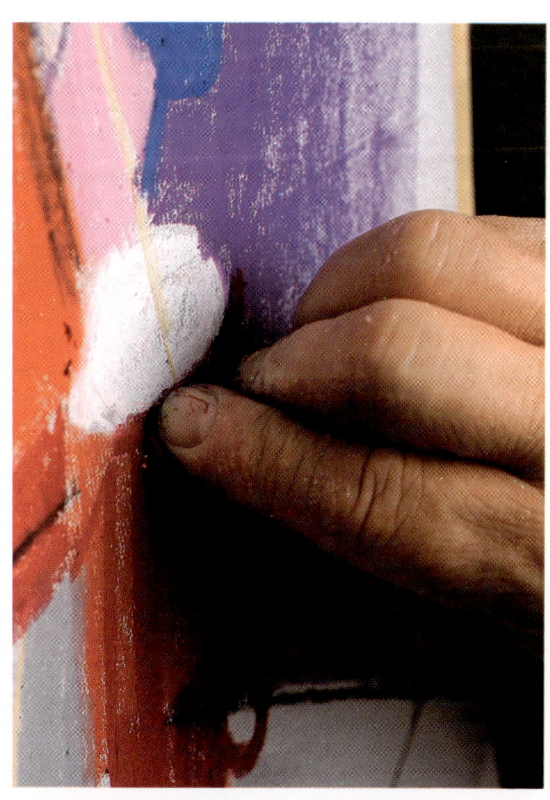

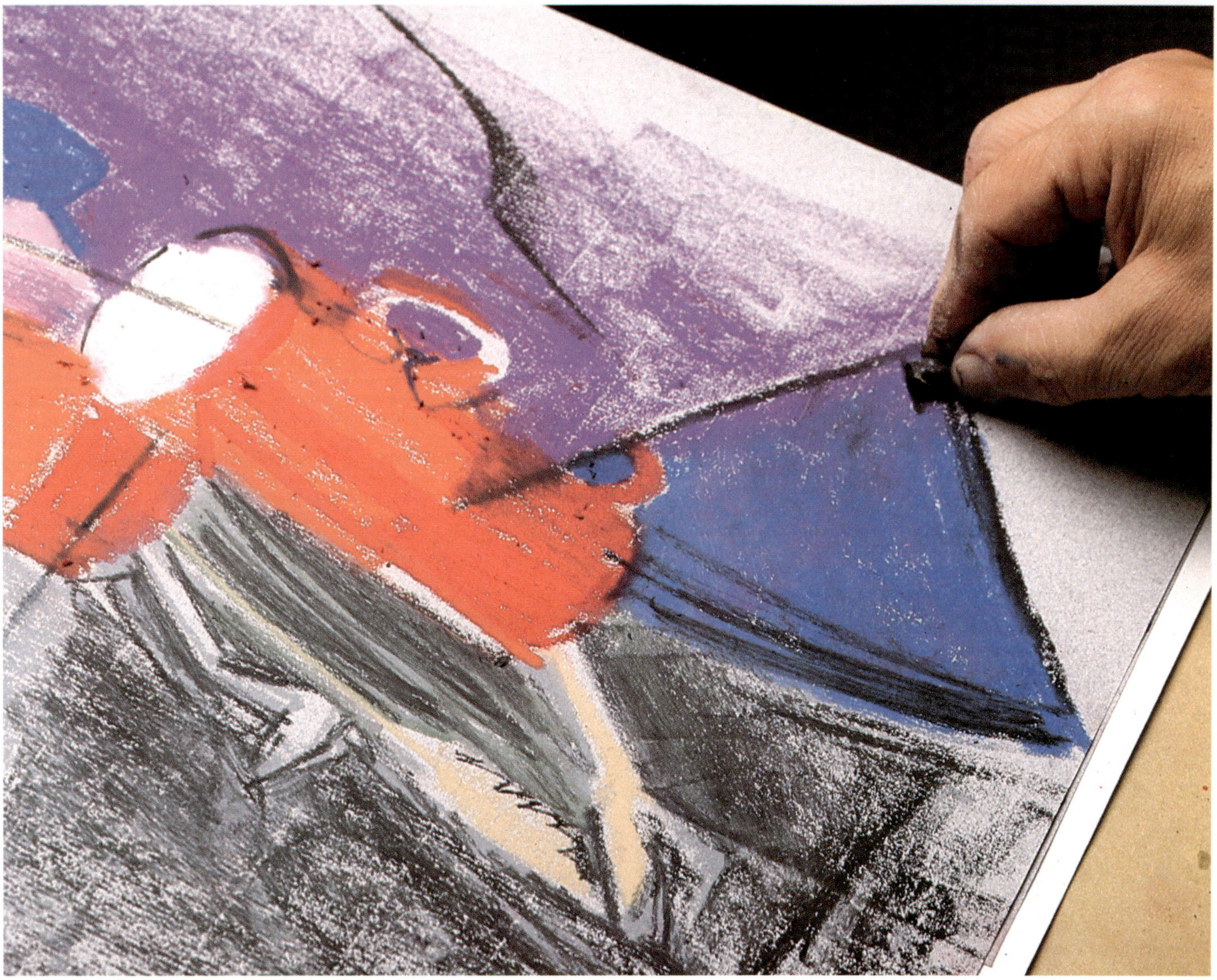

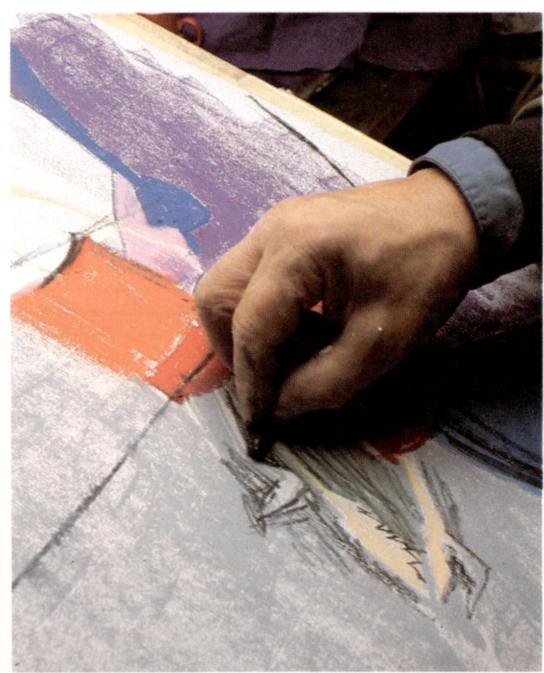

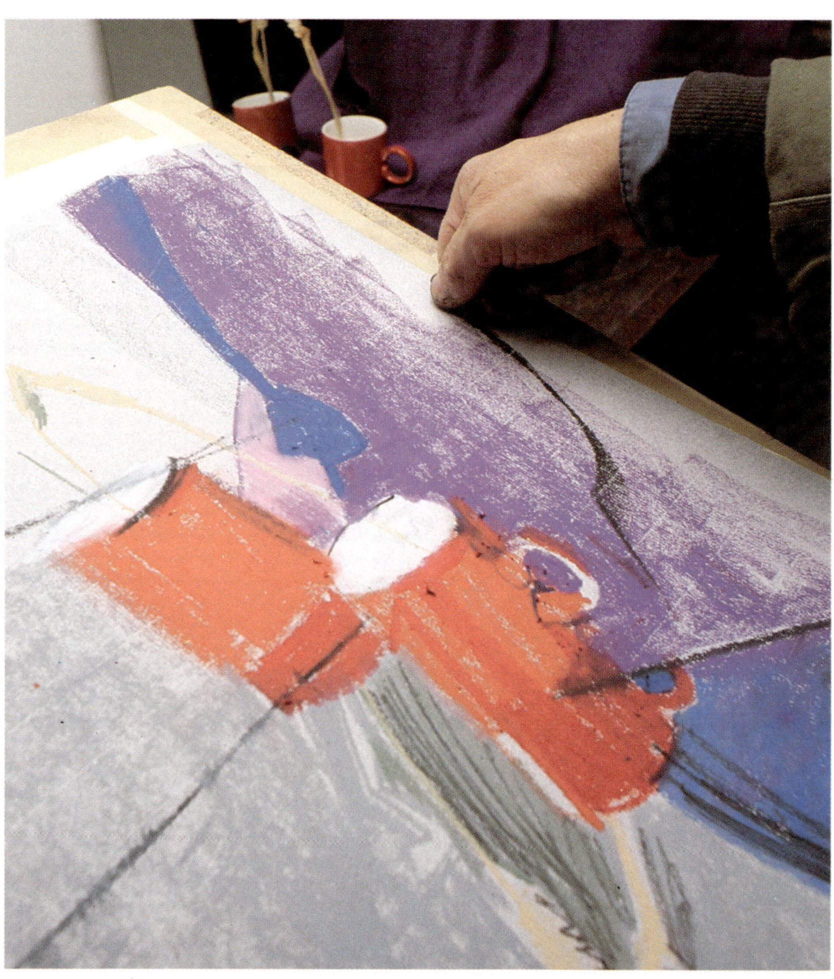

The artist continues to define the shapes and colours, constantly returning to the subject for information **(below and right)**. *The drawing is accurate but by emphasizing the areas of flat colour and the outlines he draws attention to the pattern-making qualities of the composition. He pays equal attention to the reflected images* **(above)** *making them as clear and precise as the objects themselves and creating a three-dimensional but ambiguous space.*

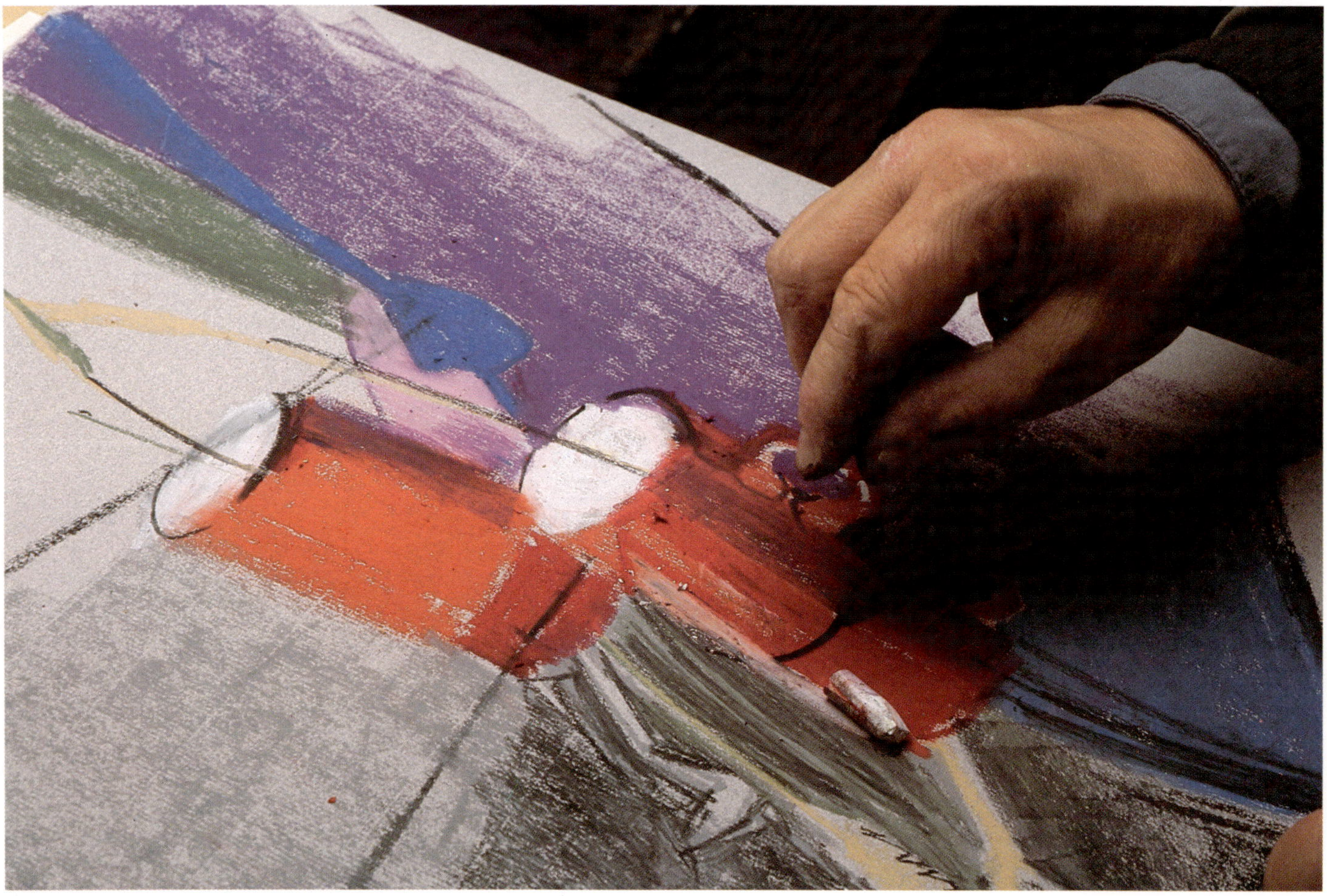

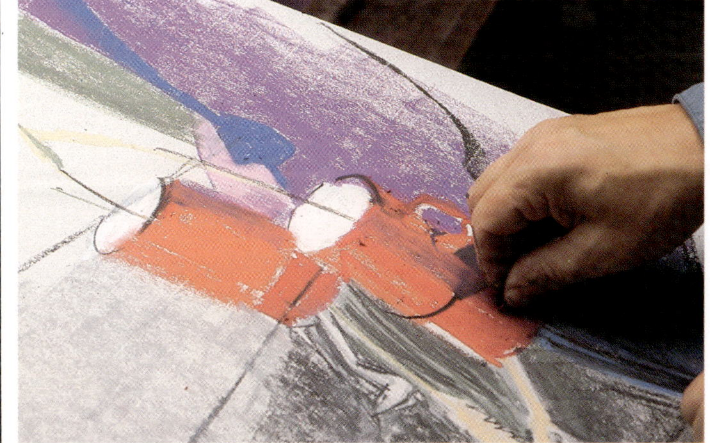

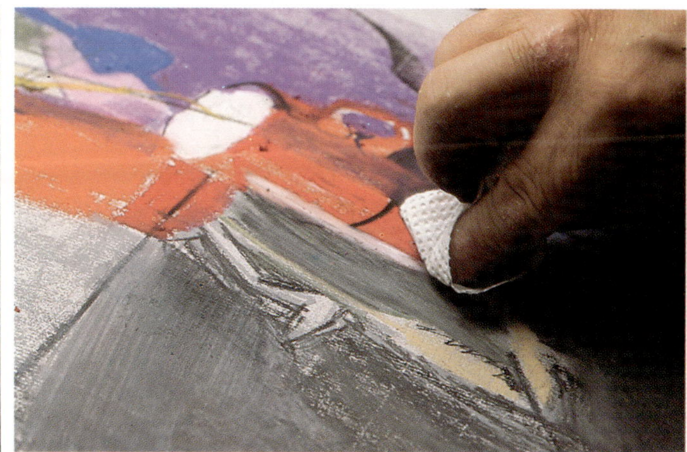

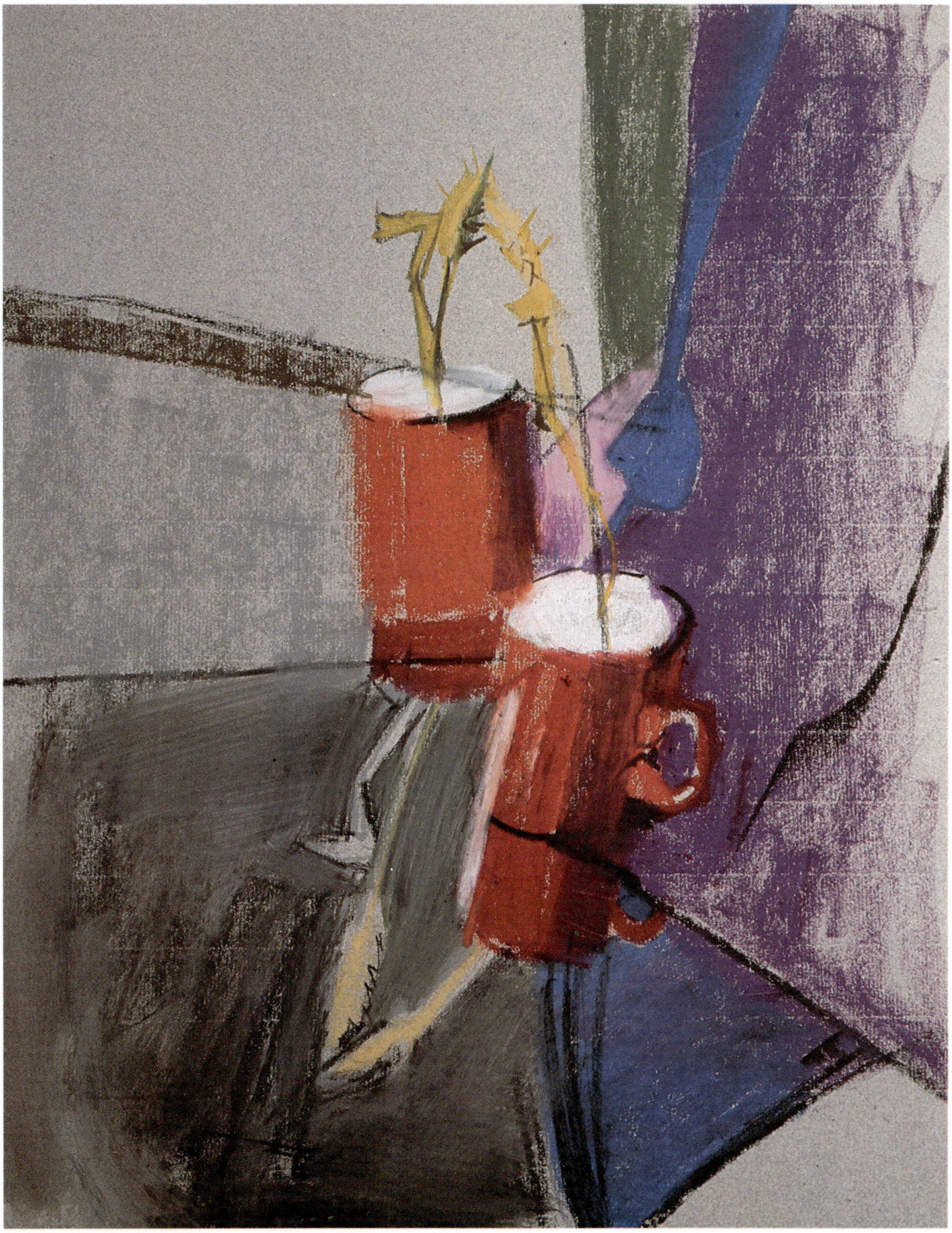

By making the reflected images deeper and richer than the actual objects, the artist implies the surface of the reflective material **(top left)**. *He buffs the picture surface with a piece of tissue, smearing the pastels to create the impression of a shiny, reflective effect* **(top right)**. *He completes the picture by drawing a fine black line of shadow between the objects and their mirror image* **(bottom)**.

TWO PORTRAITS

Pastels are an especially sensitive medium to use for figure and portrait work — with their velvety bloom and softness they suit the delicate textures and tones of flesh. Selecting a suitable range of colours is very much a matter of personal taste. All the major manufacturers sell sets of colours designed specifically for figure work and faced with the daunting task of selecting from the great range of colours and tones you may find this the easy way out of a dilemma.

Pastels have an intimacy and immediacy of presentation which makes many people think that they are somehow dashed off in a very short time. This, as you will soon discover, is an illusion. A letter from the artist la Tour (1704–1788) to the Marquis de Marigny, the brother of Mme de Pompadour, is reassuring, for it lists the same difficulties as anyone working with the medium today will experience.

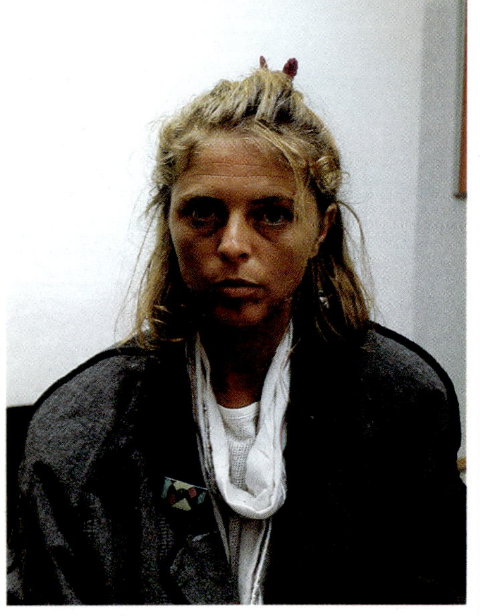

'Pastels, my Lord Marquis, involve a number of further obstacles, such as dust, the weakness of some pigments, the fact that the tone is never correct, that one must blend one's colours on the paper and apply a number of strokes with different crayons instead of one, that there is a risk of spoiling the work done and that one has no expedient if the spirit is lost...'

The problem of having to apply a number of strokes with different crayons instead of one is very real. For this reason it is important to lay the pastels out in a methodical order on corrugated paper rather than in the box, and to replace them in their correct positions. There is nothing more irritating if you are in full spate than to have to stop work to search for the missing colour.

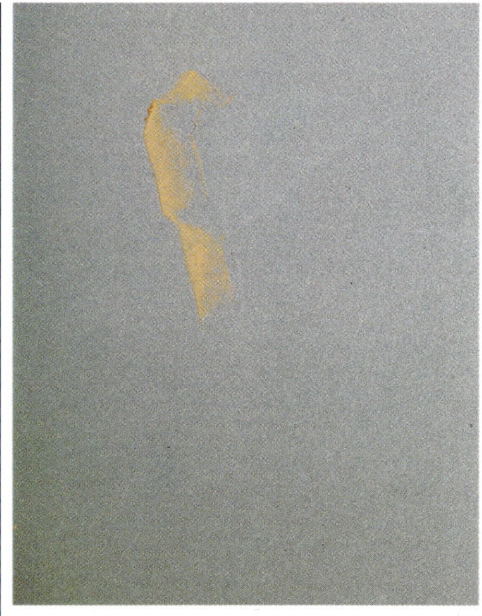

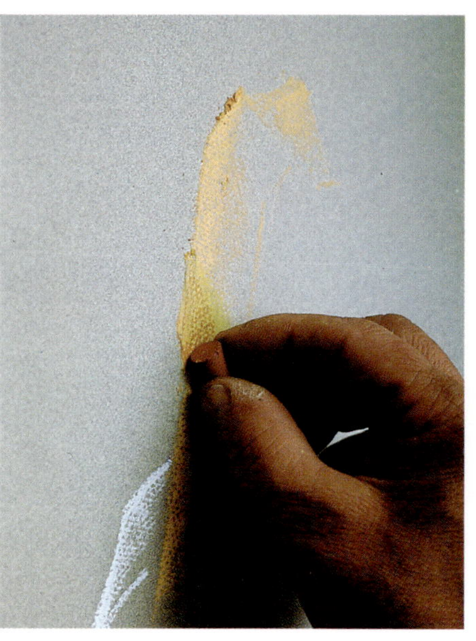

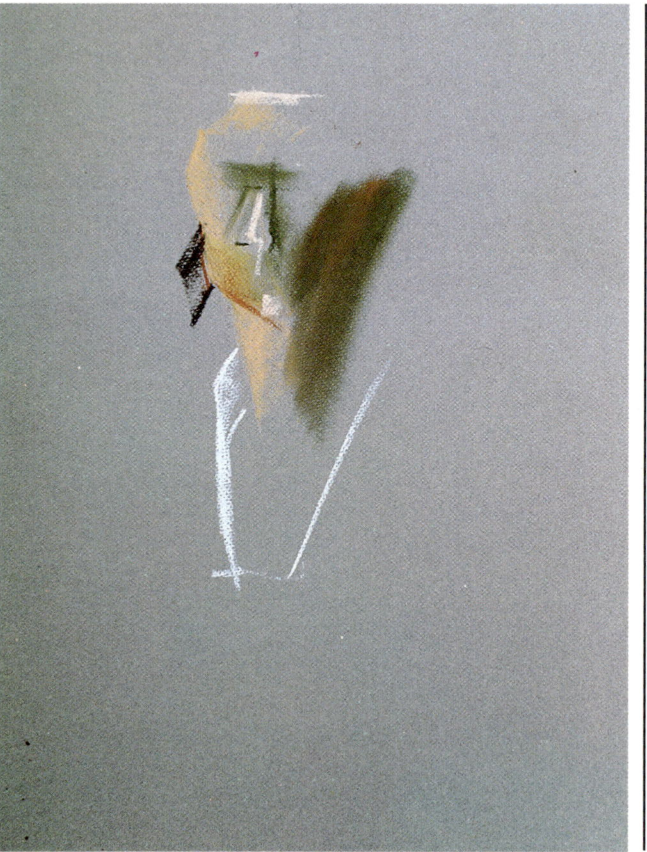

The artist wanted to make a rapid drawing of the model **(far left)** *to be used as the basis of a portrait at a later date. He chose to work with pastel because it is soft and responsive, lines and solid colours building up rapidly to create an effective image. It also provides him with plenty of colour reference.*

He chose a tinted paper because this gives him a useful mid-tone and the opaque pigments show to advantage on a coloured ground. Selecting a flesh tinted pastel he starts to block in the lighter tones of the face **(top left** *and* **right)**.

With white he indicates the position of the main features and the broad outlines of the girl's clothing. At the same time he develops the darkest areas by smudging in greeny-brown pigment **(left)**.

With his finger he uses the same pigment to lay in the shadowy areas of the eye sockets and the side of the nose **(right)**.

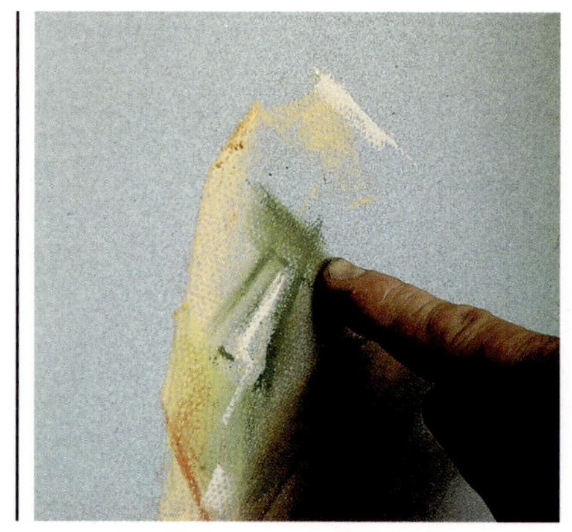

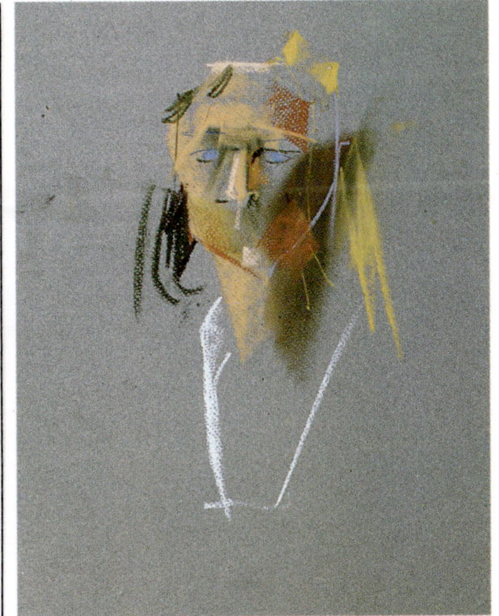

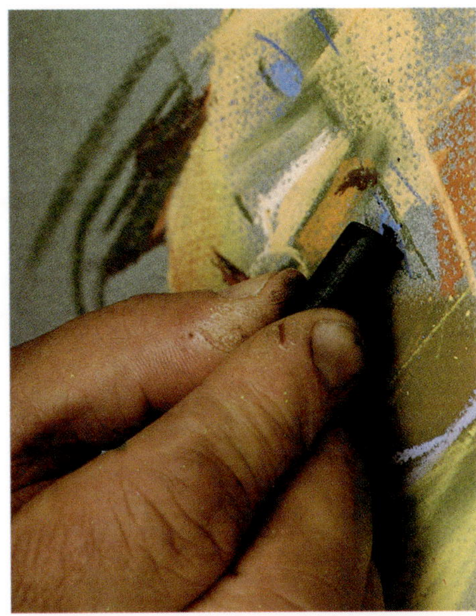

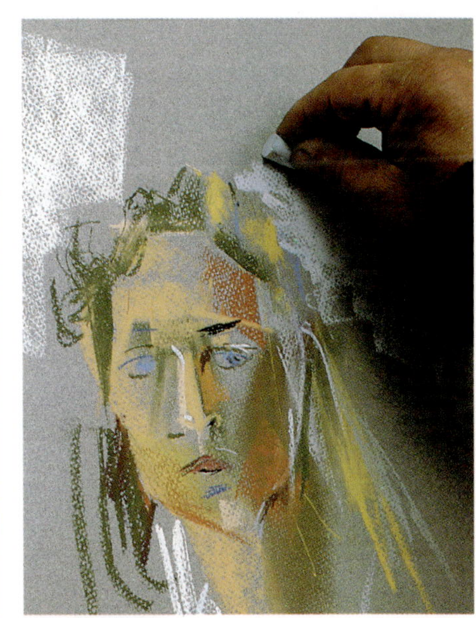

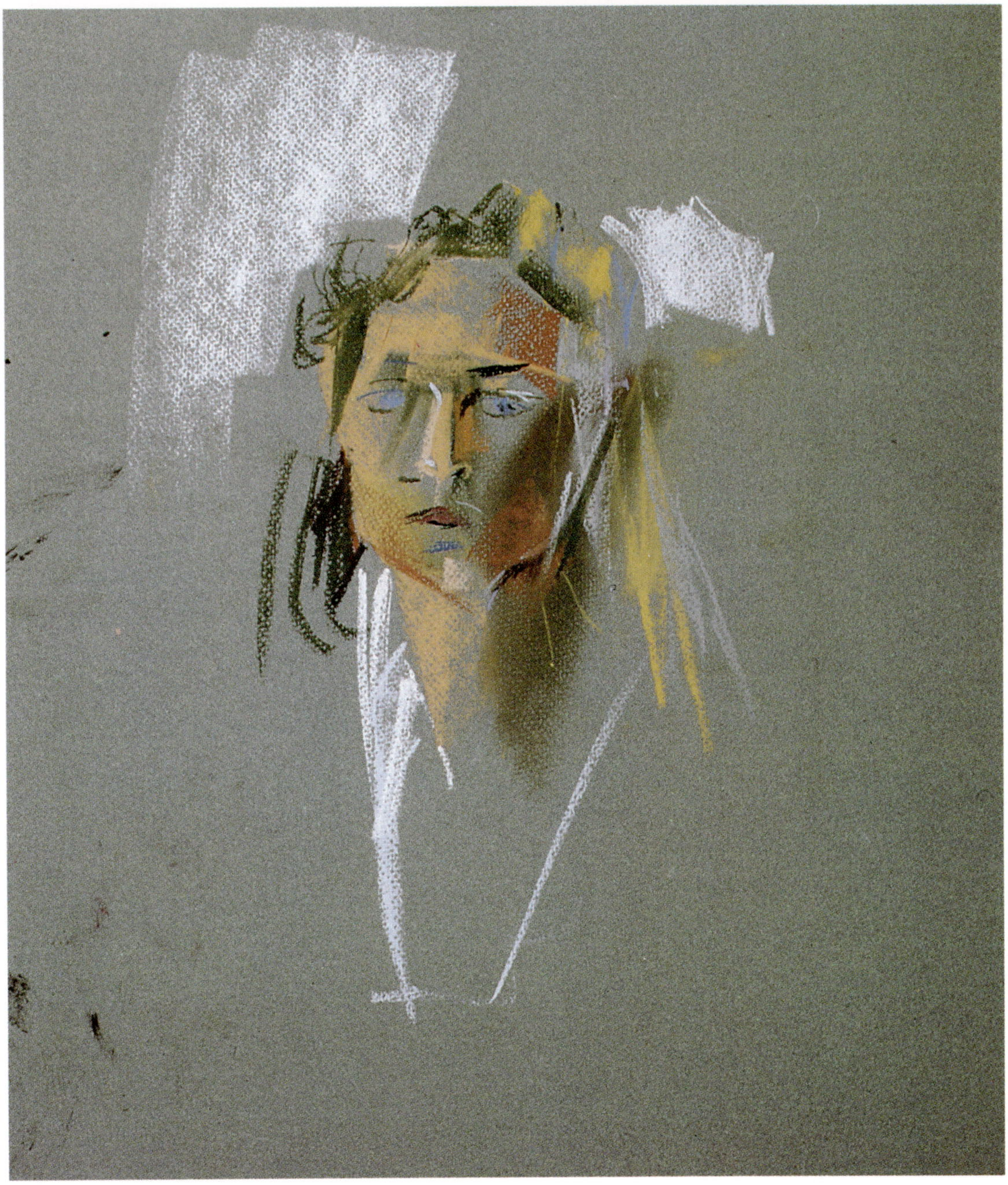

The artist continues to work broadly and quickly, adding broad strokes of warm tones to the head and hair, half-closing his eyes to help him isolate the lights and darks **(top left)**. *With a black pastel he defines some of the features — the eyes, nose and eyebrows* **(above centre)**. *He uses the side of the pastel to lay in broad planes of colour, brick red and flesh tint describing the facets of the forehead. With a white pastel he starts to scumble in the background, the tinted ground modifying the white pigment* **(left)**. *He continues to develop the background using the side of a grey pastel to create patches of solid colour* **(above)**. *He uses a black pastel to strengthen the darker tones, drawing with the sharpened tip of the stick and laying in broader areas of colour with the side of the stick. Finally he blends the background whites and greys by rubbing them lightly with his finger* **(over)**.

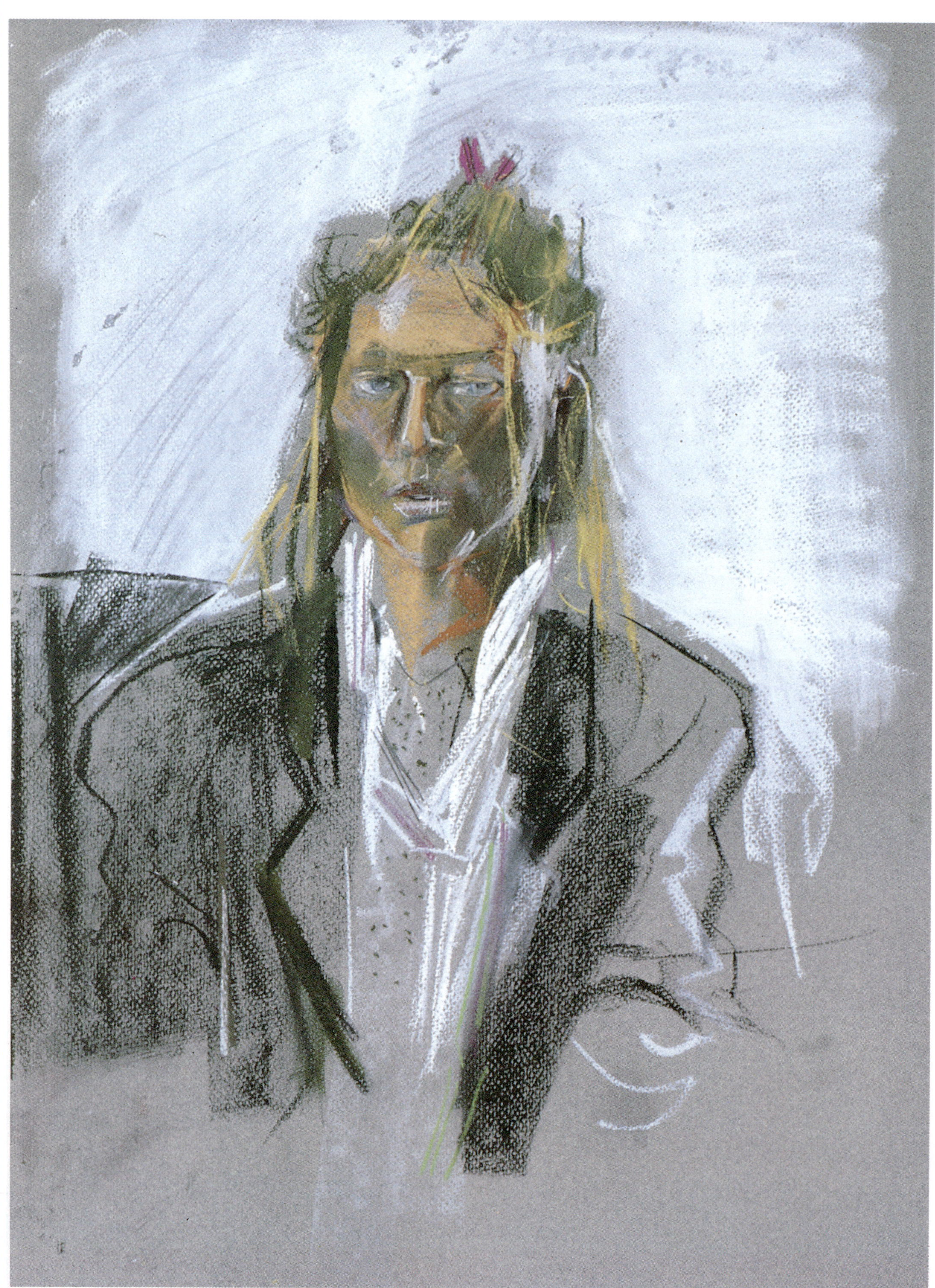

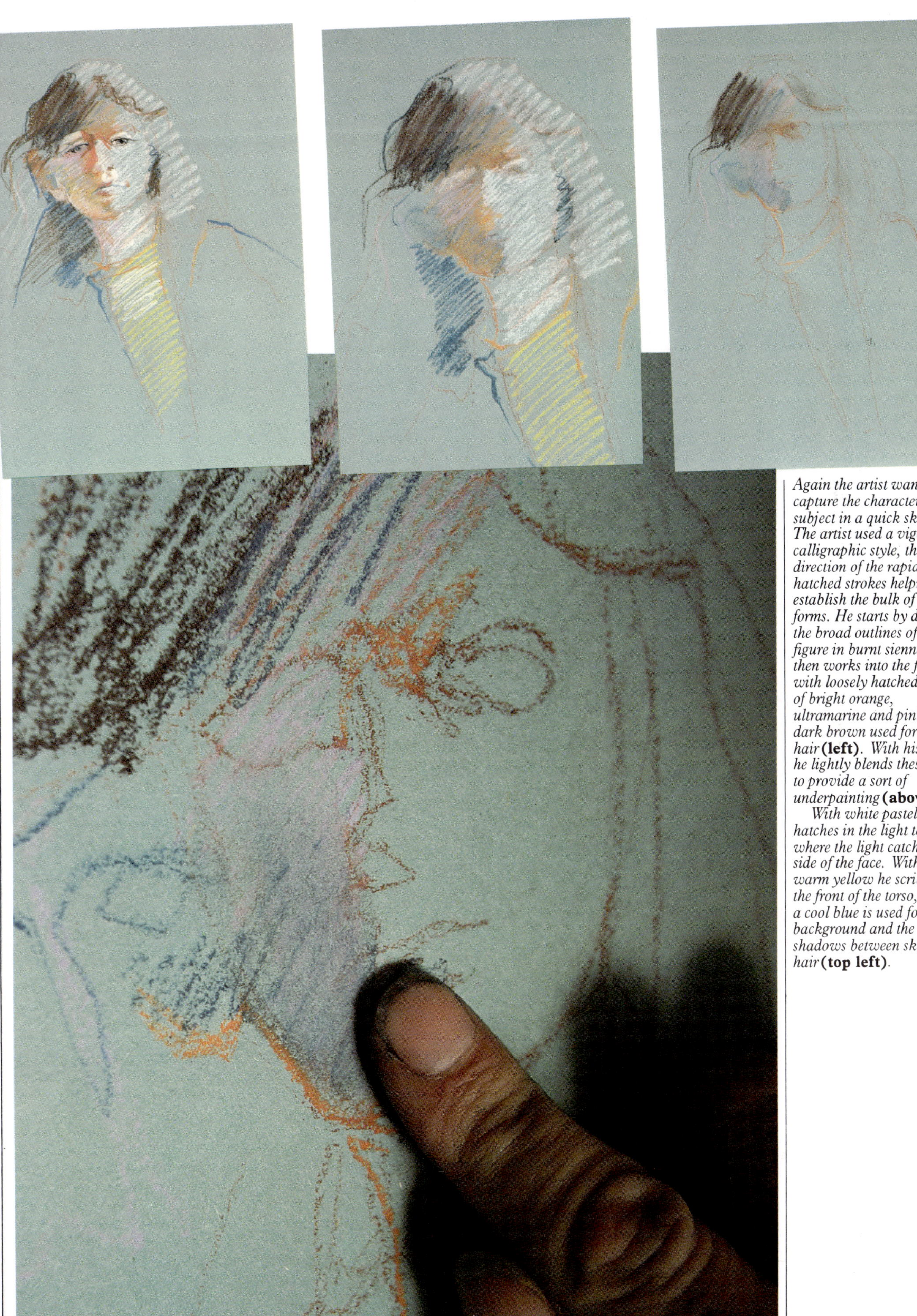

Again the artist wanted to capture the character of the subject in a quick sketch. The artist used a vigorous, calligraphic style, the direction of the rapidly hatched strokes helping to establish the bulk of the forms. He starts by drawing the broad outlines of the figure in burnt sienna. He then works into the face with loosely hatched areas of bright orange, ultramarine and pink, with dark brown used for the hair **(left)**. *With his finger he lightly blends these tones to provide a sort of underpainting* **(above)**.

With white pastel he hatches in the light tones where the light catches the side of the face. With a warm yellow he scribbles in the front of the torso, while a cool blue is used for the background and the shadows between skull and hair **(top left)**.

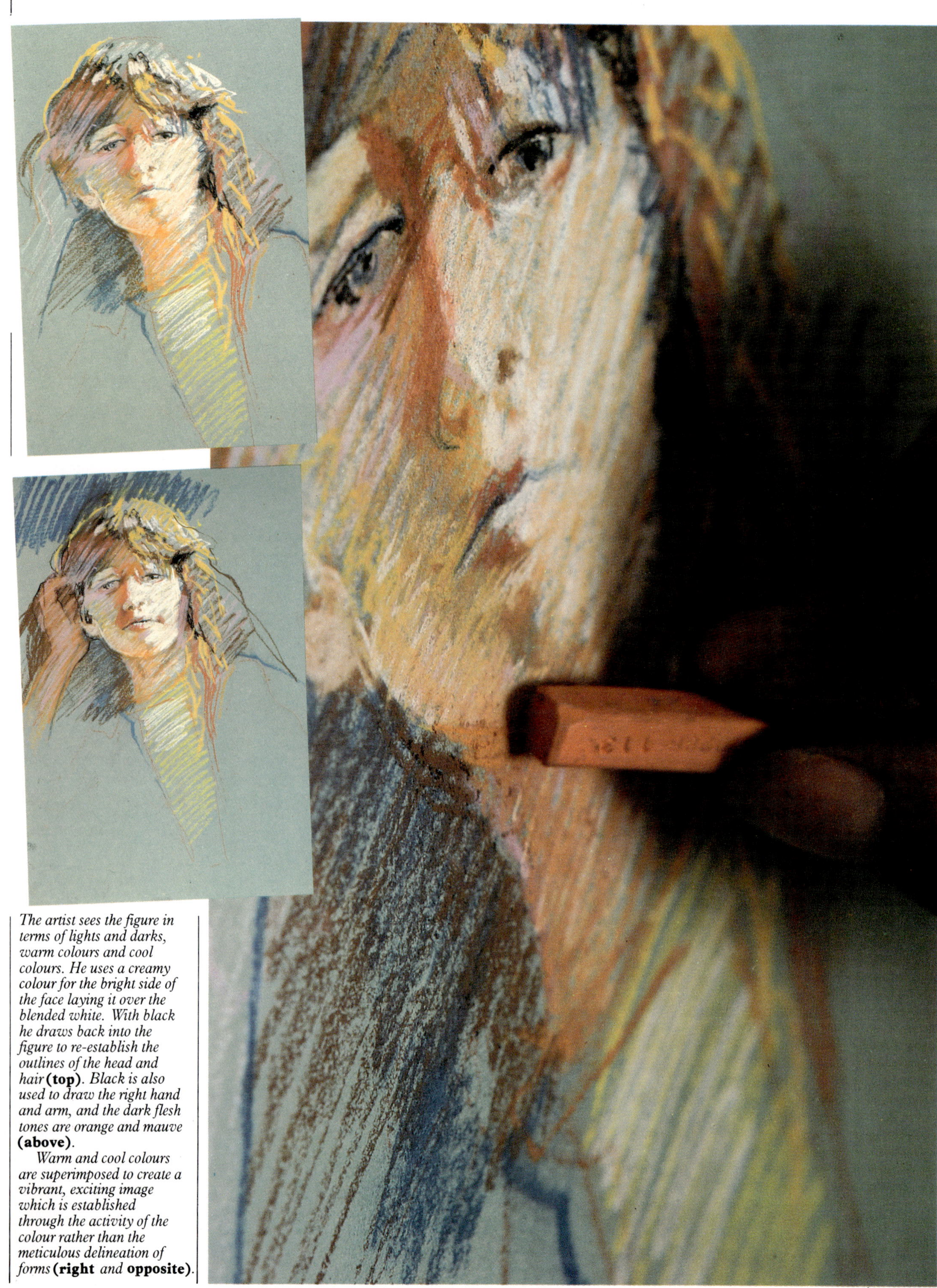

The artist sees the figure in terms of lights and darks, warm colours and cool colours. He uses a creamy colour for the bright side of the face laying it over the blended white. With black he draws back into the figure to re-establish the outlines of the head and hair **(top)**. *Black is also used to draw the right hand and arm, and the dark flesh tones are orange and mauve* **(above)**.

Warm and cool colours are superimposed to create a vibrant, exciting image which is established through the activity of the colour rather than the meticulous delineation of forms **(right** *and* **opposite)**.

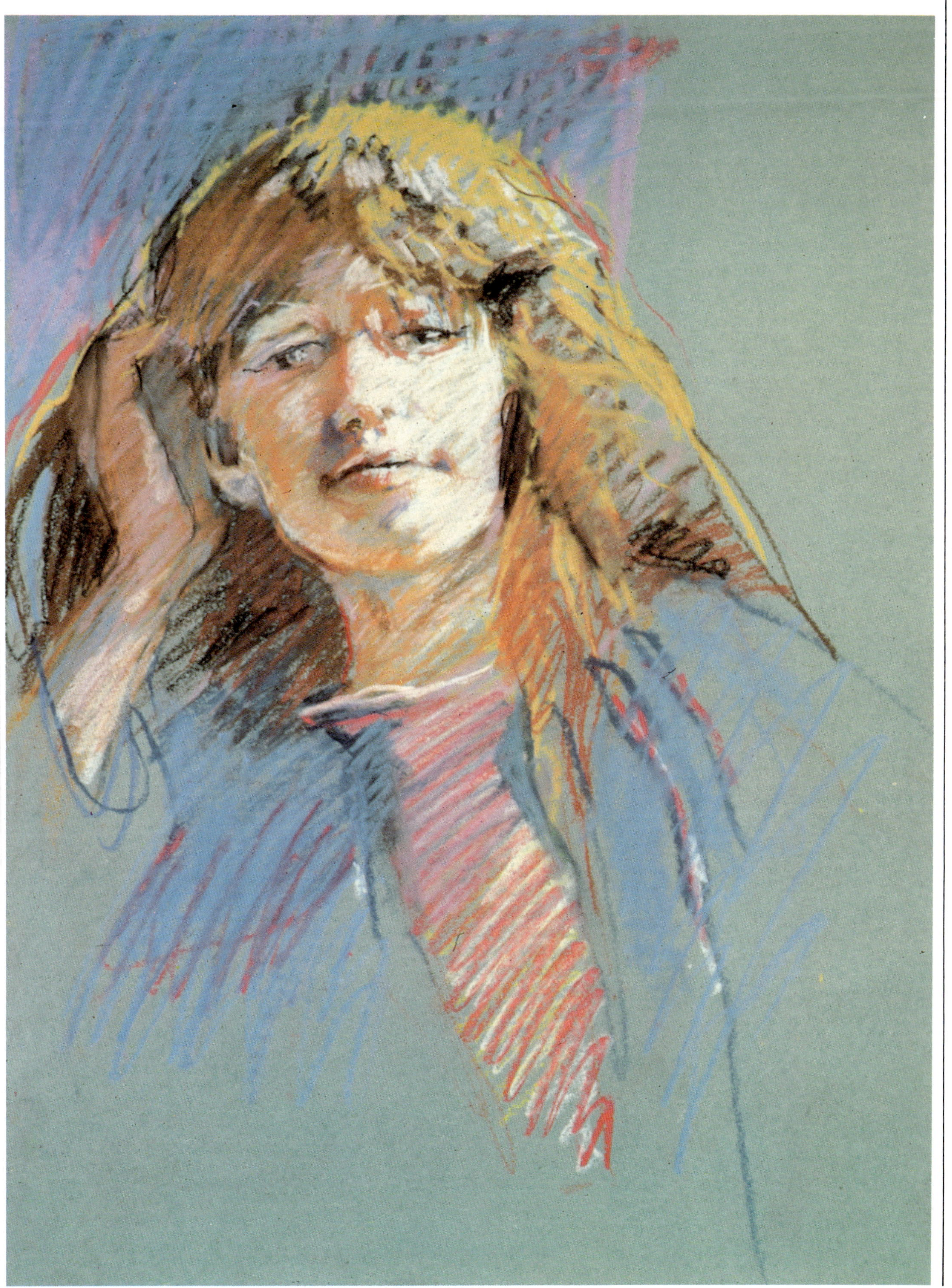

DEVELOPING A COMPOSITION

If you have not used pastel before, you can start with a very small range of colours, four will be quite sufficient; black, white, red and brown. Rectangular black, sanguine and brown Conté crayons are very useful for preliminary drawings and for accenting lines. If you select a larger range choose a light, medium and dark tone of each colour. Note, also, that the tint charts accompanying the boxed sets are printed on white paper, so that for work on darker or coloured paper it is best to make your own tint chart.

The artist made this sketch on tinted paper using a very small range of colours. He was developing material for a large figurative painting. He laid down colour in broad smudgy areas, investigating the main shapes and the way the elements occupied the picture area and related to each other. The colour areas were discrete, softly blended at the margins, rather than overlaid to create new colours. Used in this way the purity of the pigment is shown to great advantage, the freshness of the colour having much in common with pure watercolour. The sketch started as an investigation but the finished drawing is a delightful and satisfying piece in its own right.

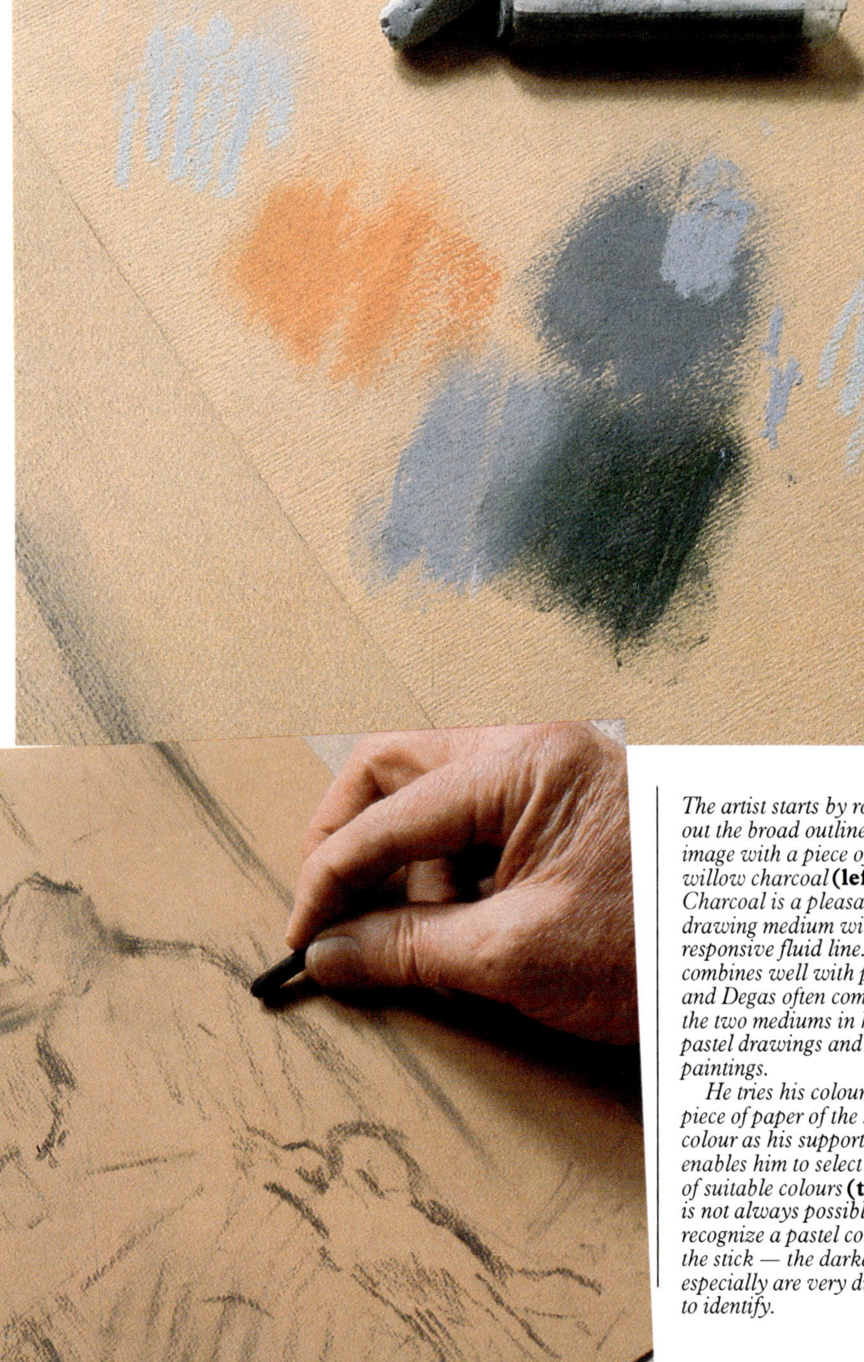

The artist starts by roughing out the broad outlines of the image with a piece of thin willow charcoal **(left)**. *Charcoal is a pleasant drawing medium with a responsive fluid line. It combines well with pastel and Degas often combined the two mediums in his pastel drawings and paintings.*

He tries his colours on a piece of paper of the same colour as his support, this enables him to select a range of suitable colours **(top)**. *It is not always possible to recognize a pastel colour in the stick — the darker tones especially are very difficult to identify.*

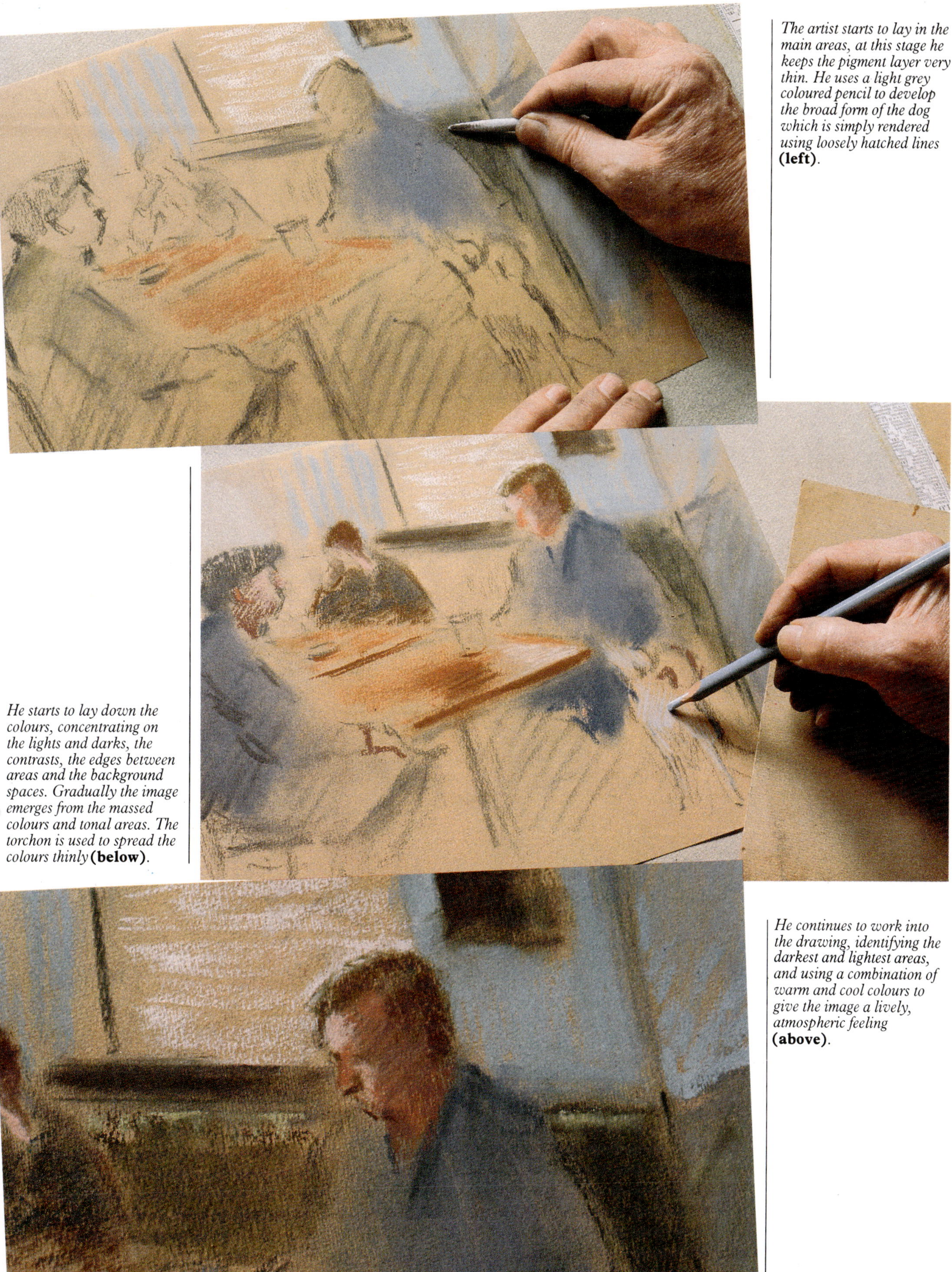

The artist starts to lay in the main areas, at this stage he keeps the pigment layer very thin. He uses a light grey coloured pencil to develop the broad form of the dog which is simply rendered using loosely hatched lines **(left)**.

He starts to lay down the colours, concentrating on the lights and darks, the contrasts, the edges between areas and the background spaces. Gradually the image emerges from the massed colours and tonal areas. The torchon is used to spread the colours thinly **(below)**.

He continues to work into the drawing, identifying the darkest and lightest areas, and using a combination of warm and cool colours to give the image a lively, atmospheric feeling **(above)**.

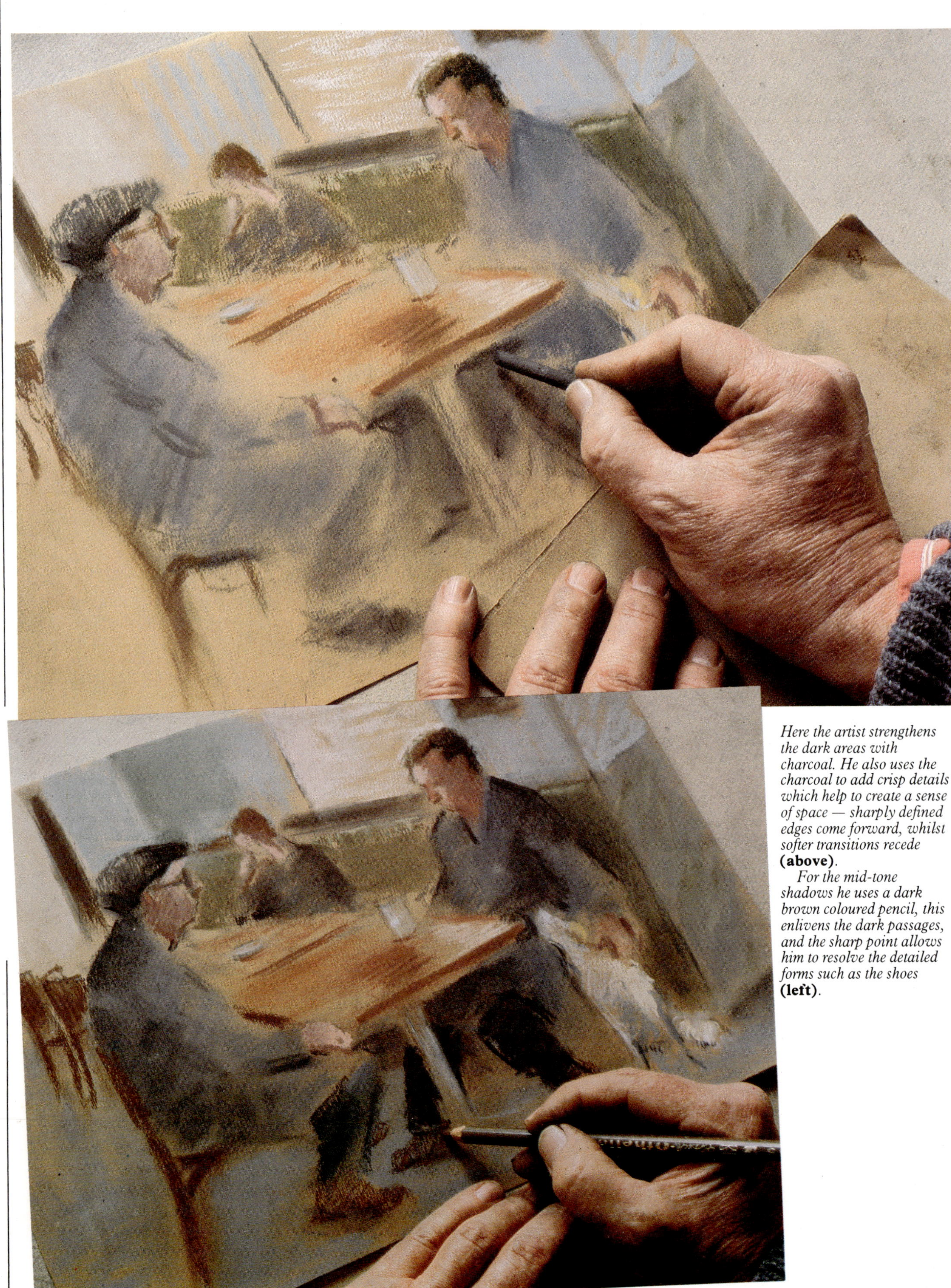

Here the artist strengthens the dark areas with charcoal. He also uses the charcoal to add crisp details which help to create a sense of space — sharply defined edges come forward, whilst softer transitions recede **(above)**.

For the mid-tone shadows he uses a dark brown coloured pencil, this enlivens the dark passages, and the sharp point allows him to resolve the detailed forms such as the shoes **(left)**.